Better Homes and Gardens®

THE BEST OF
WOOD®
BOOK 1

All of us at Meredith® Books are dedicated to giving you the
information and ideas you need to create beautiful and useful
woodworking projects. We guarantee your satisfaction with this book
for as long as you own it. We also welcome your comments and
suggestions. Please write us at Meredith® Books, RW-240,
1716 Locust St., Des Moines, IA 50309-3023.

A WOOD BOOK
Published by Meredith Books

MEREDITH BOOKS
President, Book Group: Joseph J. Ward
Vice President and Editorial Director: Elizabeth P. Rice
Executive Editor: Connie Schrader
Art Director: Ernest Shelton
Prepress Production Manager: Randall Yontz

WOOD MAGAZINE
President, Magazine Group: William T. Kerr
Editor: Larry Clayton

THE BEST OF WOOD BOOK 1
Produced by Roundtable Press, Inc.
Directors: Susan E. Meyer, Marsha Melnick
Senior Editor: Marisa Bulzone
Managing Editor: Ross L. Horowitz
Graphic Designer: Leah Lococo
Design Assistant: Leslie Goldman
Art Assistant: Marianna Canelo Francis
Proofreader: Amy Handy

For Meredith Books
Editorial Project Manager/Associate Art Director: Tom Wegner
Contributing How-To Editor: Marlen Kemmet
Contributing Techniques Editor: Bill Krier
Contributing Tool Editor: Larry Johnston
Contributing Outline Editor: David A. Kirchner

Special thanks to Khristy Benoit

On the front cover: All Aboard the Wood Express, pages 70–75
On the back cover: Simply Stated Shaker Wall Clock, pages 7–11 (left);
    Winter Wonderland, pages 147–149 (top center); A Workhorse of a
    Workbench, pages 94–99 (bottom center); Shelving Showcase,
    pages 118–123 (right)

Meredith Corporation Corporate Officers:
Chairman of the Executive Committee: E. T. Meredith III
Chairman of the Board, President and Chief Executive Officer: Jack D. Rehm
Group Presidents: Joseph J. Ward, Books; William T. Kerr, Magazines;
    Philip A. Jones, Broadcasting; Allen L. Sabbag, Real Estate
Vice Presidents: Leo R. Armatis, Corporate Relations;
    Thomas G. Fisher, General Counsel and Secretary;
    Larry D. Hartsook, Finance; Michael A. Sell, Treasurer;
    Kathleen J. Zehr, Controller and Assistant Secretary

Throughout each year, WOOD® Magazine publishes instructions for building a wonderful array of woodworking projects. These projects are designed to help craftspeople of every skill level create pieces that will be appreciated for years to come. In this special collection, we invite you to look back on some of our best from 1992.

Contents

For the Young at Heart
50

Pride of the Shop
78

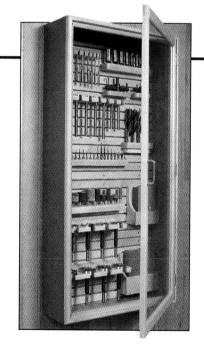

Heirlooms for Home and Hearth

Seasonal Trimmings and Trinkets

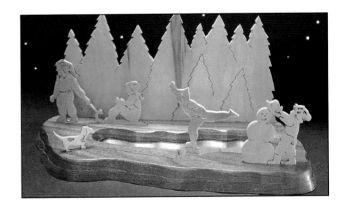

Acknowledgments

Recalling Days Gone By

For centuries, wood has captured artisans' craftsmanship in time. In tribute to their lasting works, we present this collection of projects. Whether it's the simplicity of our Country-Colors Quilt Stand or the simply elegant Shaker-Style Tall Chest, each of these projects can make a bit of time stand still.

Simply Stated Shaker Wall Clock

Like wall clocks built by the Shakers in the early 19th century, our version features clean, unadorned design lines. Although the Shakers frowned upon watches, wall clocks abounded. Today, collectors seek out the originals and pay dearly for them.

START WITH THE CHERRY CLOCK CASE

1 From ¾"-thick cherry, cut the sides (A) and the interior top and bottom (B) to the sizes listed in the Bill of Materials on *page 9*.

2 Cut or rout a ¾" rabbet ¼" deep across the ends and a ¼" rabbet ½" deep along back inside edge of both side pieces where shown
continued

To build your own Shaker-style classic, use a solid panel in the door bottom. Or, for a more modern appearance and a view of the pendulum (something considered showy and therefore an unusual Shaker practice), try a glass insert.

Simply Stated Shaker Wall Clock

continued

on the Exploded View drawing on *page 9*. Then, form a ¼" rabbet ½" deep along the back edge of the top and bottom interior pieces.

3 Glue and clamp the clock assembly (A, B), checking for square. Remove excess glue with a damp cloth.

4 Cut the exterior top and bottom pieces (C) to size.

5 Fit your table-mounted router with an edge-rounding bit (we used a Craftsman 9GT26337) and fence. Raise the bit where shown on the Routing detail accompanying the Exploded View drawing. Using the same detail for reference, position the fence and bit where shown. (We test-cut ¾" scrap stock first to verify that the routed cut was centered along the edge of the stock.)

6 Rout the front and side edges (not the back edge) of the exterior top and bottom pieces (C). When making the last cut (across the grain), use a piece of scrap stock to reduce splintering as shown on the drawing *below*.

7 Mark the ¼x4" notch on the back edge of the top exterior part (C) where shown on the Exploded View drawing. With a bandsaw or scroll-saw, cut the marked notch to shape.

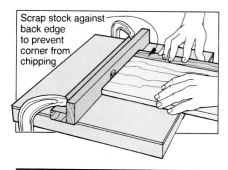

Scrap stock against back edge to prevent corner from chipping

IT'S TIME TO ADD THE CLEATS, CLOCK FACE, SUPPORT, AND BACK

1 Cut the three cleats (D) to size. Glue and clamp them to the

inside of the case where shown on the Exploded View drawing.

2 Cut the bottom cleat (E) and the clock-face panel (F) to size. Glue the bottom cleat to the front bottom edge of the clock-face panel, with the ends and bottom edges flush, where shown on the Exploded View drawing.

3 Place the clock face on the clock-face panel (F). Trace the shaft hole and four screw-mounting holes from the clock-face openings onto the plywood panel. Remove the clock face and drill a ⅜" shaft hole where marked. Then, drill four 1⁄16" screw holes where marked.

4 Measure the opening and cut the back panel (G) to size from ¼" cherry plywood.

5 Transfer the full-sized half-round clock-support (H) outline and the three hole center points to ¾" cherry. Bore a 1" hole where marked. Next, drill and counter-sink a pair of 5⁄32" shank holes where marked.

6 Cut the clock support to shape. Sand the radiused edge smooth to remove the saw marks.

7 Glue the clock support into the notch in the exterior top piece (C). Then, using the previously drilled shank holes in the notch as guides, drill a pair of 7⁄64" pilot holes ¾" deep into the top piece (C). Drill the same-sized mounting hole through the top interior piece (B) and into the support where shown on the Exploded View drawing and accompanying the Clock Support Mounting detail. Drive a trio of #8x1½" wood screws to further secure the clock support to the clock assembly.

Cut a ¼" groove ⅜" deep centered along the door parts. Clamp a feather board securely to your saw table to hold the pieces firmly against the fence.

NOW, FOR THE DOOR

1 Cut the door stiles (I), top and bottom rails (J), and center rail (K) to size.

2 Fit your tablesaw with a ¼" dado set and cut a ¼" groove ⅜" deep centered along *one* edge of parts I and J and *both* edges of the center rail (K) as shown in the photo *above*. (Note that we used a feather board to keep the pieces firmly against the fence. We also test-cut scrap first to verify that the groove was accurately centered along the edge.)

continued

Cutting Diagram

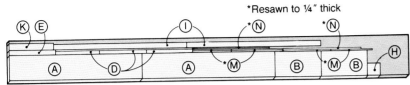

*Resawn to ¼″ thick
K
E
I
*N
*N
H
A
D
A
*M
B
*M
B
¾ × 9¼ × 96″ Cherry
C
C
J
¾ × 7¼ × 48″ Cherry
L
L
½ × 7¼ × 48″ Cherry
F
G
½ × 24 × 48″ Cherry

ROUTING DETAIL
Center bit along edge of board
Fence
Edge-rounding bit
C
Router table
CLOCK SUPPORT MOUNTING DETAIL
7/64″ pilot holes ¾″ deep
H
C
B
G
5/32″ hole, countersunk
H
#8 × 1½″ F.H. wood screws
C
4″
4½″
¾ × 4″ notch
EXPLODED VIEW
¼″ rabbet ½″ deep
B
Screw clock face to F (screws supplied with clock face)
¾″ × #19 brads
¾″ rabbet ¼″ deep
D
Movement and pendulum
1/16″ pilot hole
D
D
⅜″ hole
F
E
G
1¼″
¼″
A
Clock face
Note: Back edge of B and C are flush
1¼″
External-threaded nut
¼″
B
¼″ rabbet ½″ deep
A
¾″ rabbet ¼″ deep
Edge round
13″
C

Bill of Materials

Part	Finished Size* T	W	L	Mat.	Qty.
CLOCK CASE					
A sides	¾"	6"	32"	C	2
B top & bottom	¾"	6"	11½"	C	2
C top & bottom	¾"	7⅞"	13"	C	2
D cleats	¾"	¾"	11"	C	3
E cleat	¾"	1"	11"	C	1
F panel	¼"	11"	11¾"	CP	1
G back panel	¼"	12"	31½"	CP	1
H support	¾"	4"	2¾"	C	1
DOOR					
I stiles	¾"	1¼"	31⅞"	C	2
J rails	¾"	1¼"	10¾"	C	2
K center rail	¾"	1½"	10¾"	C	1
L panel	½"	10⅝"	18 9/16"	EC	1
M stops	¼"	¼"	10¾"	C	4
N stops	¼"	¼"	18⅝"	C	2

Material Key: C—cherry, CP—cherry plywood, EC—edge-joined cherry
Supplies: ½"x#19 brads, ¾"x#19 brads, #8x1½" flathead wood screws, ⅛x10 11/16x10 11/16" glass, clear finish.

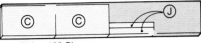

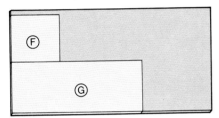

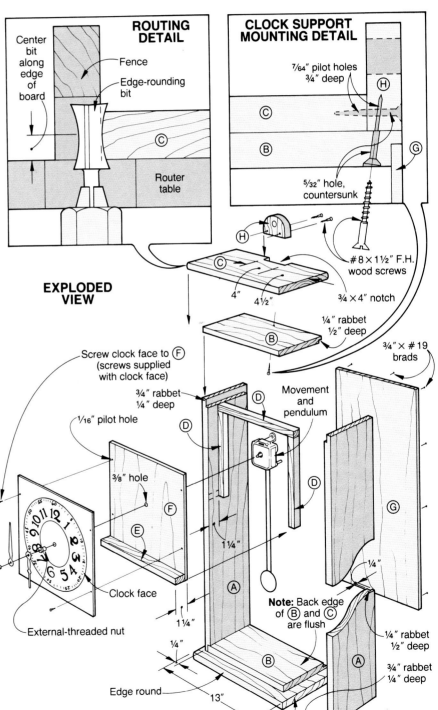

Simply Stated Shaker Wall Clock

continued

Cut a ¼" tenon ⅜" long across the ends of the rails. Clamp a stop to the miter-gauge fence for consistent tenon lengths.

3 As shown in the photo at *left*, cut a ¼" tenon ⅜" long across the ends of the three rails (J, K). See the Tenon detail *below right* for dimensions.

4 If you want to install the solid cherry panel (L) instead of a glass insert, cut two 5½x19" pieces of ½" stock (we planed ¾" stock to ½" thick). Edge-join the ½"-thick pieces, checking that the surfaces and ends are flush. Later, trim both ends and one edge to cut the edge-joined cherry panel to finished size. Sand the panel. Cut or rout a ⅝" rabbet ¼" deep along all front edges of the panel where shown on the Door drawing *below*.

5 Glue and clamp the door pieces, including the door panel if you intend to use it, checking for square. See the Panel detail *below* for reference.

6 Fit your router with a ⅜" rabbeting bit. If you plan to fit both the upper and lower openings with glass, rout along the back inside edge of both openings in the door. See the Glass and Panel details accompanying the Door drawing and the Lower Glass Panel Installation drawing *opposite* for reference.

7 Cut four glass stops (M) to size, miter-cutting the ends for the top opening. Cut the bottom opening glass stops (M, N) if required. Snip the head off a ½"x#19 brad, chuck the brad into your portable electric drill, and use the brad as a bit to drill

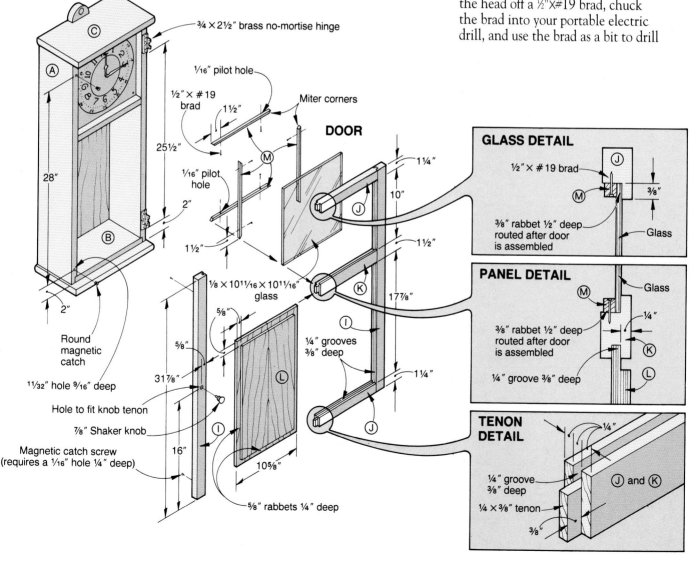

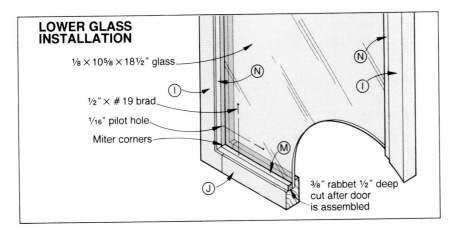

LOWER GLASS INSTALLATION

⅛ × 10⅝ × 18½" glass

½" × # 19 brad

1/16" pilot hole

Miter corners

3/8" rabbet ½" deep cut after door is assembled

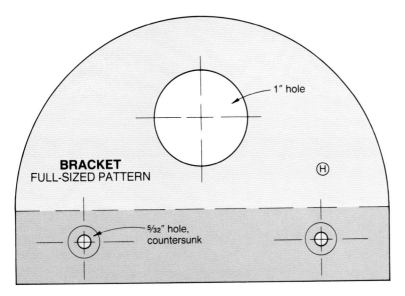

BRACKET FULL-SIZED PATTERN

1" hole

5/32" hole, countersunk

pilot holes through the glass stops 1½" in from the ends where shown on the Door drawing.

8 Drill the holes for the knob and magnetic catches. Glue the knob in place.

ADD THE FINISH, HARDWARE, AND MOVEMENT

1 Stain and/or finish the case, door, back panel, knob, and glass stops as desired. (We left ours unstained and applied three coats of satin polyurethane.)

2 Install the glass and the glass stops. See the Glass detail accompanying the Door drawing for reference. Screw the clock face to the plywood panel (F).

3 Attach the hinges to the front edge of the right-hand side piece (A) where shown on the Door drawing. Then, fasten the hinges to the door stile. When positioning the door for attaching the hinges, allow a 1/16" gap between the clock case and the top and bottom of the door.

4 Insert the magnetic catches into the previously drilled holes, and mark their mating locations on the back face of the door stile. Drill a pair of mounting holes in the back face of the door, and drive the screws, which act as strike plates.

5 Brad the back panel (G) into the rabbet in the clock back.

6 Stick the clock shaft through the hole in the plywood panel,

and fasten the movement (minus the pendulum) to the panel and clock face with the external-threaded nut. Add the hands to the clock shaft. Hang the clock on the wall (or a Shaker peg as shown in the opening photograph). Add the pendulum and battery, and set the time.

BUYING GUIDE

• **Shaker clock kit.** Quartz pendulum movement, Shaker hands and dial, ⅞" Shaker peg, two ¾×2½" brass no-mortise hinges, two 5/16" magnetic catches. Kit No. 6401. For current prices, contact Turncraft Clocks, Inc., P.O. Box 100, Mound, MN 55364-0100, or call 800/544-1711 to order.

WANT TO LEARN MORE ABOUT CRAFTSMANSHIP?

For insight into the austere lives of the Shakers, their craftsmanship aimed at function not fancy, and their furniture, we'd like to recommend *The Book of Shaker Furniture* by John Kassay, The University of Massachusetts Press, Amherst.

PROJECT TOOL LIST
• Tablesaw
• Dado blade or dado set
• Bandsaw or scrollsaw
• Router
• Router table
• Bits: edge-rounding, ¼" rabbeting, ⅜" rabbeting
• Drill
• Bits: 1/16", 7/64", 5/32", 11/32", ⅜", 1"
• Disc or belt sander
• Finishing sander

Note: *We built the project using the tools listed. You may be able to substitute other tools or equipment for listed items you don't have. Additional common hand tools and clamps may be required to complete the project.*

Bandsawed Through-Dovetail Joints

Our innovative jig makes 'em easy to do

From time to time I drop by Design Editor Jim Downing's office and find him hard at work—leaned back in a chair, his feet propped up, his mind deep in thought. At times like these, you can bet he's cooking up a new or better way to perform some woodworking task. On one such occasion recently, Jim seemed especially entranced, so I asked him what he was thinking.

"A jig," he replied in a soft monotone, his eyes still fixed on a distant point. "One for making through-dovetails quick and easy with a bandsaw," he added.

Before the day was out, Jim shared a sketch of his jig idea with me. And within a week, we found ourselves standing shoulder to shoulder in the shop bandsawing clean, accurate, and downright great-looking through-dovetails with a working model of the jig. (See the photo *above*.) Needless to say, I could hardly wait to show you how to use this ingenious device.

—*Bill Krier*
Products and Techniques Editor

WHAT'S A THROUGH-DOVETAIL JOINT?

As you can see in the drawing *opposite top*, the *tails* of through-dovetail joints extend completely through the thickness of the *pins* on

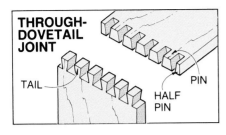

THROUGH-DOVETAIL JOINT

TAIL

PIN

HALF PIN

the adjoining workpiece. In the days before power tools and modern adhesives, skilled craftsmen painstakingly scribed, hand-sawed, and chiseled these joints in the making of furniture, trunks, and all sorts of boxes. The resulting joints proved mechanically strong and aesthetically pleasing.

Today, through-dovetail joints serve primarily as a design element. Several router jigs on today's market will make through-dovetail joints, but these cost upwards of $200. In this article, we'll show you how to cut through-dovetail joints with a jig costing just a few dollars.

UP-FRONT PLANNING POINTERS

Before you get knee-deep into the actual cutting of the workpieces, keep the following in mind:

• Knowing the difference between tails and pins is one of the most important tasks in planning and making through-dovetail joints. Things will work out fine, though, if you just remember this: the face grain of tails looks like a dove's tail (trapezoid), and the face grain of pins is rectangular.

• When working out a dovetail project design, take note that you can change the size and spacing of the tails and pins for a pleasing, custom-made look. On the following pages, we've provided four examples of attractively designed dovetail joinery as a guide. During layout, don't forget to plan for two equally sized half-pins at either end of the joint.

• You'll also have to decide which sides of your project have tails and which sides have pins. If you're building a box such as the Knitter's Companion on *page 21*, the front and back pieces should have tails for appearance's sake. But, if you're building drawers, the sides should have tails for the strength to survive opening and closing.

START BY MAKING OUR HANDY-DANDY JIG

To construct the dovetail jig, turn to *page 18*. After you assemble the jig, we'll see you back here!

Note: This jig helps you make dovetail joints in stock as wide as your bandsaw's throat depth. For example, with a 14" bandsaw, you can make dovetailed boxes or drawers with sides up to 14" wide.

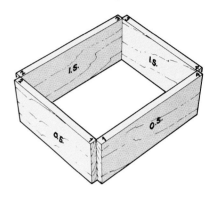

LADIES AND GENTLEMEN, MARK YOUR WORKPIECES

To help keep everything straight, gather the four sides of your project, mark each of the *inside* and *outside* surfaces, and number each corner as shown *above*.

continued

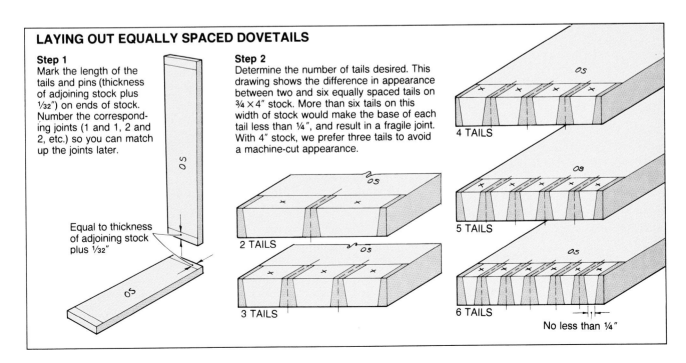

LAYING OUT EQUALLY SPACED DOVETAILS

Step 1
Mark the length of the tails and pins (thickness of adjoining stock plus 1/32") on ends of stock. Number the corresponding joints (1 and 1, 2 and 2, etc.) so you can match up the joints later.

Equal to thickness of adjoining stock plus 1/32"

Step 2
Determine the number of tails desired. This drawing shows the difference in appearance between two and six equally spaced tails on 3/4 × 4" stock. More than six tails on this width of stock would make the base of each tail less than 1/4", and result in a fragile joint. With 4" stock, we prefer three tails to avoid a machine-cut appearance.

2 TAILS
3 TAILS
4 TAILS
5 TAILS
6 TAILS
No less than 1/4"

Bandsawed Through-Dovetail Joints

continued

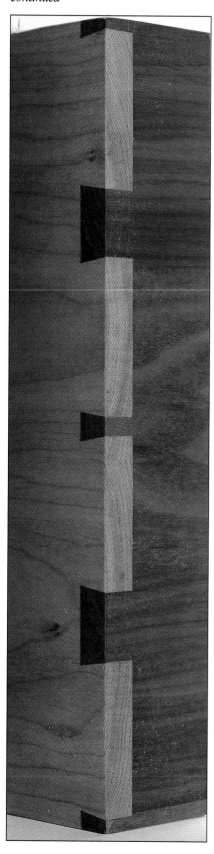

NOW, LAY OUT THE PINS AND HALF-PINS

For each dovetail joint, follow the five-step marking process for equally spaced dovetails on *page 13* and at *right*. Note that to mark the pins, you also need to lay out the tails on the end of the stock. This will give you a good idea of what the assembled joint will look like.

To mark the 8° dovetail angles, rest the body of your sliding T-bevel on the pivoting table of the through-dovetail jig and align its blade with the jig's side as shown in Photo A. This way, you can transfer the exact dovetail angle as determined by the "pitch" of the jig's table (see Photo B).

As shown in Photo C, you can save time and ensure consistent joints by transferring the pin marks to the other workpiece (and in turn, to the opposite end of the originally marked board).

If you're feeling especially adventurous, you can try your hand at laying out unequally spaced dovetails and dovetails of varying widths. (See the examples here and on *pages 12* and *17*.) Just remember to keep your design symmetrical for the most pleasing result.

Tip: For thin, consistent marks that will help you cut better-fitting joints, use a 0.5mm mechanical pencil.

HERE'S HOW TO CUT THE PINS AND HALF-PINS

For the following steps, use a ¼" bandsaw blade. And, make sure your bandsaw's guides are adjusted so the blade doesn't wander during cuts.

Adjust the bandsaw table for a 90° cut, and clamp the base of

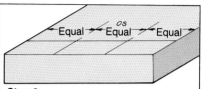

Step 3
Divide stock into equal parts Your marks are centerpoints for the tails.

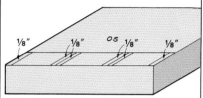

Step 4
Lay out cutting guidelines for the pins ⅛" to either side of the tail centerlines. Lay out half-pin cutting guidelines ⅛" in from the edges of the stock.

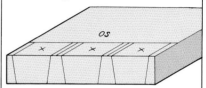

Step 5
Starting with the half-pins, transfer 8° tail lines from all pin guidelines as shown. Mark an X on the waste area between the pin guidelines.

the through-dovetail jig onto the bandsaw table. Set the jig's stop so the blade cuts to within ⅟₁₆" of the full length of the pins as shown in Photo D. Tilt the jig's table to your left, and cut inside the lines on the right side of each waste ("X") area as shown in Photo E. Remember to hold the workpiece firmly against the fence during all cuts.

Tilt the jig's table to the right, and cut the other side of the pins as shown in Photo F. Next, remove all the waste between the two bandsaw kerfs by making multiple cuts as shown in Photo G.

continued

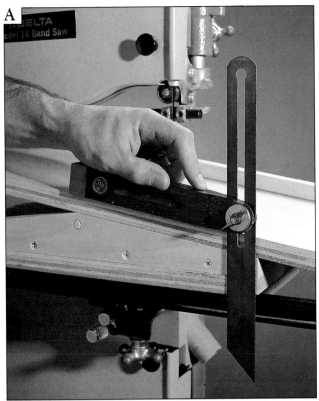

Align the blade of your sliding T-bevel with the side of the jig to set it for the dovetail angle.

Transfer the dovetail angle to your workpiece with the sliding T-bevel.

For consistent pins, transfer the pin marks from one workpiece to another.

Slide the jig and workpiece to within 1/16" of the pin length, and tighten the stop's wing nuts.

Bandsawed Through-Dovetail Joints

continued

E

With the jig tilted to the left, cut inside the lines on the right side of the waste areas.

F

Tilt the jig to the right, then cut inside the lines on the left side of the waste areas.

G

Remove the waste material by making multiple cuts. Be careful not to cut into the pins.

Tilt the jig's table as necessary so you remove *only* the waste material. Do not cut into the pins.

Now, adjust the jig's stop so the bandsaw blade cuts up to the marked line. Remove the remaining material by slowly sliding the stock across the bandsaw-blade teeth as shown *below*. Remember to tilt the jig's table while nearing the end of each cut.

NEXT, MARK THE TAILS

After cutting all the pins and half-pins, reassemble your workpieces so the numbered corners match up. It's important to keep these pieces organized because you will custom-cut the tails to fit each set of pins and half-pins.

For a cutting guide, you need to trace the outline of the pins and half-pins onto the adjoining piece of stock. First, place the workpiece that you'll cut tails into on the bench, inside surface up. Position an L-shaped bracket made from ¾" plywood on this workpiece as shown *opposite, top*. Clamp the workpiece and bracket onto your bench.

Now, place the already-cut workpiece against the bracket, with the outside surface facing away from the bracket, and clamp it into place

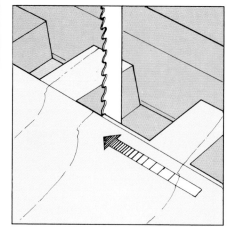

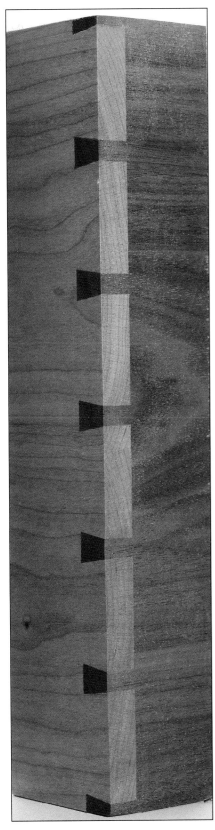

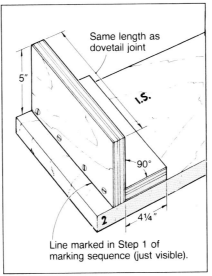

Line marked in Step 1 of marking sequence (just visible).

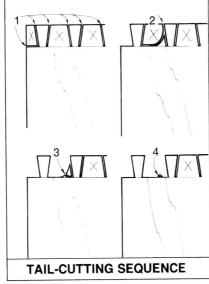

TAIL-CUTTING SEQUENCE

as shown in the photo *below left.* Be sure to align the edges of the boards flush with each other. With a sharp pencil, trace the outline of the pins and half-pins. Remove the clamps, and mark X's on the material between the tails.

IT'S TIME TO CUT THE TAILS

To remove the material between the tails, follow the four-step sequence shown *below left.* (You don't need the jig because these cuts are 90° to the surface of the workpiece.) Be careful to cut along the pencil marks without completely removing them. Removing too much material will result in a sloppy fit.

ASSEMBLE THE JOINTS

Before gluing, test-fit all four joints and bandsaw away any high spots that prevent the joints from coming together. Then, with a small brush, apply a light coat of white woodworker's glue to all mating surfaces. The white glue sets up slower than yellow glue, so you have time to check the box or drawer for square.

After the glue dries, belt-sand the protruding tails flush with surrounding surfaces.

Tilting-Table Dovetail Jig

Cutting dovetails just got a whole lot simpler

3 Glue and screw the fence to the table with the bottom edges flush.

4 Mark diagonals on both ends of the support block. Next, drill a ⅜" hole ¾" deep centered in each end of the block. (To ensure straight holes, we clamped the support in a hand-screw clamp, squared it with the drill-press table, and then drilled the holes.)

5 Mark a pair of center points on the top of the table (A)

where shown on the Exploded View drawing. Drill and countersink a pair of ⁵⁄₃₂" holes where marked.

6 Glue and clamp the support block (C) to the bottom of the table, centered from side to side and ¾" from the back edge of the table. Then, using the previously drilled holes in the table as guides, drill a pair of ⁷⁄₆₄" pilot holes in the support block. Secure the support block to the table with a pair of wood screws.

I've often admired the good looks of through-dovetails. But the hassle of setting up, adjusting, and using most jigs has kept me at bay. So, when Jim Downing, our Design Editor, came up with this jig, my first thought was, "not another complicated jig."

Boy, was I in for a surprise. My very first joints cut on this jig fit tight and looked professional.

Take a look at the knitting carrier on *page 21* for proof of how easy it is to do quality work with this jig.

—*Marlen Kemmet*
How-To Editor

Note: We built our dovetail jig to fit a Delta 14" bandsaw. If the throat depth on your bandsaw is less than 14", you'll have to shorten the overall length of the table fence assembly.

START WITH THE PIVOTING-TABLE ASSEMBLY

1 Cut the table (A), fence (B), and support block (C) to the sizes listed in the Bill of Materials.

2 Mark the location, and cut a ³⁄₁₆" dust-relief groove ³⁄₁₆" deep along one face of the fence (B) where shown on the Exploded View drawing at *right*.

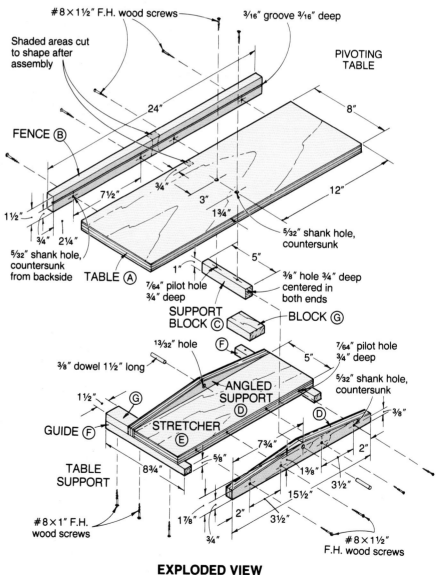

EXPLODED VIEW

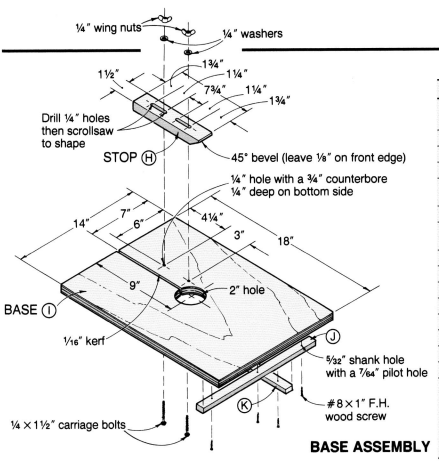

¼" wing nuts

¼" washers

1½" 1¾" 1¼"
7¾" 1¼"
1¾"

Drill ¼" holes
then scrollsaw
to shape

STOP Ⓗ

45° bevel (leave ⅛" on front edge)

¼" hole with a ¾" counterbore
¼" deep on bottom side

14" 7" 6" 4¼" 3" 18"

9" 2" hole

BASE Ⓘ

1/16" kerf

Ⓙ

5/32" shank hole
with a 7/64" pilot hole

Ⓚ

¼ × 1½" carriage bolts

#8 × 1" F.H.
wood screw

BASE ASSEMBLY

Bill of Materials

Part	Finished Size			Mat.	Qty.
	T	W	L		
PIVOTING TABLE					
A table	¾"	8"	24"	BP	1
B fence	¾"	1½"	24"	B	1
C support block	¾"	1"	5"	B	1
TABLE SUPPORT					
D angled supports	¾"	1⅞"	15½"	B	2
E stretcher	¾"	5"	15½"	BP	1
F guides	⅝"	¾"	8¾"	B	2
G blocks	¾"	1½"	2¼"	B	2
BASE					
H stop	¾"	1½"	7¾"	B	1
I base	¾"	14"	18"	BP	1
J guide	⅜"	¾"	14"	B	1
K guide	⅜"	¾"	17¼"	B	1

Material Key: BP—birch plywood, B—birch
Supplies: #8x1" flathead wood screws,
#8x1½" flathead wood screws, double-faced
tape, ⅜" dowel stock, 2—¼x1½" carriage bolts,
¼" wing nuts, ¼" flat washers, paraffin, clear
finish.

AND NOW FOR THE TABLE SUPPORT

1 Cut the angled supports (D) to the size listed in the Bill of Materials. Using double-faced tape, stick the pieces together face-to-face, with the edges and ends flush. Mark the layout lines and hole center points where dimensioned on the Exploded View drawing.

2 Cut the angled supports to shape (we used a bandsaw). Sand the angled top edges smooth. Drill a 13/32" hole through both pieces. Drill and countersink four 5/32" holes through the taped-together pieces where marked. Separate the pieces, and remove the tape.

3 Cut the table-support stretcher (E), guides (F), and blocks (G) to size. With the ends and bottom edges flush, glue and clamp the angled supports (D) to the stretcher (E). Using the previously drilled holes in the angled supports (D) as guides, drill 7/64" pilot holes into the stretcher, and drive #8x1½" wood screws to further strengthen the joints.

4 Glue and screw the blocks (G) to the guides (F). Glue and screw the guide/block assemblies to the stretcher assembly, flush with the ends of the stretcher and parallel to each other.

CONSTRUCT THE BASE ASSEMBLY

1 Cut the stop (H), base (I), and alignment guides (J, K) to size. The base must fit between the guides (F) with no free play. Angle-cut one end of the stop where shown on the Base Assembly drawing above.

2 To form the ¼"-wide slots in the stop (H), mark the hole center-points, drill the holes, and then cut between the holes with a scrollsaw. You also could drill overlapping holes, and clean the waste with a sharp chisel.

3 Mark the center points on the top face of the base for a pair of carriage bolts. Drill the ¼" holes, and then drill a ¾" counterbore ¼" deep on the bottom side.

4 Mark the kerf and 2" hole center point on the base (I). Bandsaw the kerf. (We cut the hole in our base the same size as the hole in our bandsaw table.)

5 Glue and screw the alignment guides to the bottom side of the base as described on the Top View portion of the drawing titled Locating the Guides. (See the Cutaway and Back View drawings on *page 20* for further reference.)

FINISHING UP YOUR JIG

1 Sand the assemblies smooth.

2 Cut two ⅜" dowels to 1½" long. Put a drop of glue in each ⅜" hole in the support block (C). Position the pivoting table on the table support, and drive the ⅜" dowels through the holes in the angled supports (D) and into the holes in the support block.

continued

Tilting-Table Dovetail Jig

continued

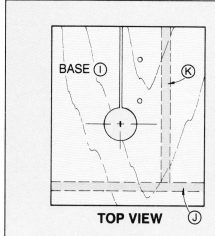

BASE ⓘ

Ⓚ

TOP VIEW   Ⓙ

Step 1: Install a ¼" blade in your bandsaw. Adjust the blade guides, and square the bandsaw table to blade.

Step 2: Align the front edge of your bandsaw blade with the center of the 2" hole.

Step 3: Glue the guides (J, K) to the bottom side of base. After the glue dries, drill mounting holes, and install screws to further secure the guides to the jig's base.

3 For a smooth sliding action of the table support to the base, apply paraffin to the bottom sides of the stretcher (E) and the inside edges of the guides (F).

4 If desired, add a coat of clear finish to all but the waxed areas. Although a finish helps keep the jig clean, it is not necessary.

5 Insert the carriage bolts through the base. Using the guides as guides, clamp the base assembly to the bandsaw table. Position the front edge of the stop (H) ¾" ahead of the front edge of the bandsaw blade where shown on the Cutaway drawing. Tighten the stop to the base.

6 As shown on the Back View drawing, tilt the table to one side and cut into the table (¾") until the table support comes in contact with the stop. Tilt the table in the opposite direction and make a second cut. Now, using successive cuts and tilting the table back and forth, remove all of the waste material from between the first two bandsaw cuts.

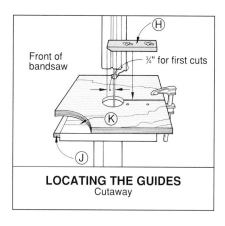

Ⓗ

Front of bandsaw

¾" for first cuts

Ⓚ

Ⓙ

LOCATING THE GUIDES
Cutaway

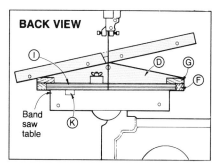

BACK VIEW

ⓘ   Ⓓ   Ⓖ

Ⓕ

Band saw table   Ⓚ

7 Refer to the preceding techniques article for instructions on using the jig, and then proceed to the following article to build a beautiful knitting carrier.

Knitter's Companion

Featuring fine dovetail joinery

Bill of Materials

Part	Finished Size			Mat.	Qty.
	T	W	L		
A*sides	½"	10½"	18"	EJC	2
B ends	½"	10½"	12"	EJW	2
C*divider	½"	11⅞"	17½"	EJW	1
D shelves	½"	5⅛"	17"	EJC	2
E cleats	½"	¾"	5⅛"	W	4

*Initially cut parts marked with an * oversized. Then, trim each to finished size according to the how-to instructions.

Material Key: EJC—edge-joined cherry, EJW—edge-joined walnut, W—walnut
Supplies: masking tape, #8 x ¾" flathead wood screws, clear finish.

Don't let the dovetails we used for this fancy walnut and cherry knitting carrier scare you off. Armed with our dovetail jig *(page 18)* and our tips on how to use it with a bandsaw *(page 12)*, you can complete this project successfully in an evening or two, no problem. And who knows, maybe someone will knit you a new scarf or sweater for your efforts.

Note: *To keep the project lightweight, we used ½" stock. You can either resaw or plane thicker stock, and then edge-join the ½"-thick boards. The drawing How to Resaw on page 22 shows the method we used to resaw thicker stock.*

EDGE-JOIN NARROW STOCK TO FORM THE WIDE PIECES

1 Cut enough ½"-thick walnut and cherry strips to form panels for the sides (A), ends (B), and divider (C). (We edge-joined two boards for each A and B panel, and three boards for the C panel.) Cut the pieces so the edge-joined panels measure about ¼" wider and 1" longer than the finished size listed in the Bill of Materials.

2 Glue and clamp the pieces for each panel edge-to-edge, with the surfaces flush. Later, remove the clamps and sand smooth.

3 Rip and crosscut the panels (A, B, C) to the sizes listed in the Bill of Materials.

CUT THE DOVETAILS, AND ASSEMBLE THE PARTS

1 To make the dovetail markings easier to see, apply masking tape to the surfaces to be marked. (Pencil lines on walnut are hard to see.) Mark the dovetails as described in the article Bandsawed Through-Dovetail Joints *(page 12)*.

2 Cut matching dovetails in the ends of the side and end panels.

3 Cut or rout a ½" dado ¼" deep centered on the inside face of the end panels (B).

4 Assemble, but don't glue, the pieces (A, B, C) to check the fit.

5 Transfer the full-sized Half Handle pattern on *page 22,* including the hole center points, to the top of the divider (C) where located on the Exploded View drawing. Drill a pair of 1" holes inside the marked handle opening. Then, use a scrollsaw or coping saw to cut the opening and handle to shape.

6 Rout ¼" round-overs in the handle opening and along the top edge of the divider where shown on the Exploded View drawing.

continued

Knitter's Companion

continued

7 Mark the cutout along the bottom edge of each side and end panel where dimensioned on the drawing. Cut to shape.

8 Cut the shelves (D) and cleats (E) to size. Sand all the pieces.

9 Mark the locations on the inside of the end panels, drill mounting holes, and fasten the cleats.

10 Then, glue and clamp the pieces together, checking for square. Using a damp cloth, wipe off any excess glue immediately.

11 Finish-sand, glue the shelves in place, and apply the finish.

PROJECT TOOL LIST
- Tablesaw
- Dado blade or dado set
- Bandsaw
- Scrollsaw
- Drill
- Bits: $\frac{7}{64}$", $\frac{5}{32}$", 1"
- Jointer
- Router
- Bits: $\frac{1}{4}$" round-over bit
- Finishing sander

Note: *We built the project using the tools listed. You may be able to substitute other tools or equipment for listed items you don't have. Additional common hand tools and clamps may be required to complete the project.*

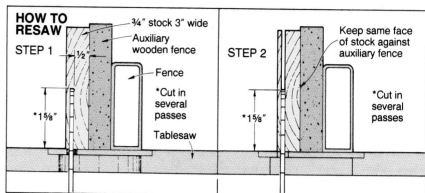

HOW TO RESAW

STEP 1 — $\frac{3}{4}$" stock 3" wide — Auxiliary wooden fence — Fence — *Cut in several passes — Tablesaw — $\frac{1}{2}$" — *$1\frac{5}{8}$"

STEP 2 — Keep same face of stock against auxiliary fence — *Cut in several passes — *$1\frac{5}{8}$"

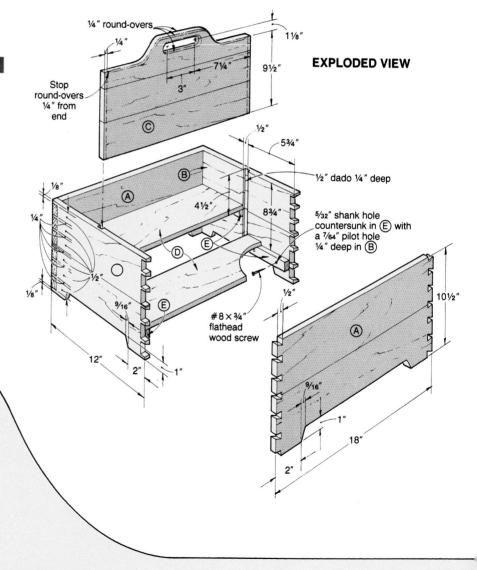

EXPLODED VIEW

$\frac{1}{4}$" round-overs — Stop round-overs $\frac{1}{4}$" from end — $\frac{1}{4}$" — $7\frac{1}{4}$" — 3" — $1\frac{1}{8}$" — $9\frac{1}{2}$" — C — $\frac{1}{2}$" — $5\frac{3}{4}$" — $\frac{1}{2}$" dado $\frac{1}{4}$" deep — $\frac{5}{32}$" shank hole countersunk in E with a $\frac{7}{64}$" pilot hole $\frac{1}{4}$" deep in B — B — $\frac{1}{8}$" — A — $4\frac{1}{2}$" — $8\frac{3}{4}$" — $\frac{1}{4}$" — D — E — $\frac{1}{2}$" — $\frac{1}{8}$" — E — $\frac{9}{16}$" — 12" — 2" — 1" — #8 × $\frac{3}{4}$" flathead wood screw — $\frac{1}{2}$" — A — $10\frac{1}{2}$" — $\frac{9}{16}$" — 1" — 18" — 2"

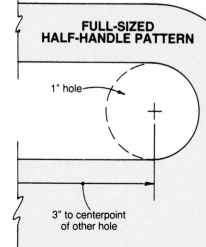

FULL-SIZED HALF-HANDLE PATTERN

1" hole

3" to centerpoint of other hole

Country-Colors Quilt Stand

A great way to show off your best work

With this template, mark the profile on one end of each 36"-long board for the uprights (A). See the Exploded View drawing for reference.

2 Lay out the stretcher (B) on the 24"-long piece, and the legs (C) on the 18"-long pieces, following the dimensions on the radiused drawings on *page 24*. Now, bandsaw the stretcher, legs, and upright tops. With your tablesaw, crosscut the uprights to 33".

3 Tilt your drill-press table to 30°, and with a brad-point bit, drill ½" holes 1½" deep centered on the edges of the uprights where shown. With the table at 0°, bore ¾" holes ⅝" deep at the screw-hole locations on the outer face of the uprights and the underside of the legs. Then, with a ⁹⁄₃₂" brad-point bit, drill the screw holes through the uprights and legs.

4 Now, clamp each leg to its upright. Chuck the ⁹⁄₃₂" brad-point bit into a portable electric drill. Bore a center point on the upright at each hole, and then remove the legs from the uprights.

R = ¾"   3"

R = 2"

¼"

R = ½"

1½"   2"

LEG ENDS

Whenever spring turns to summer, you may wonder where to store those winter quilts or colorful blankets. They're often too beautiful to hide in a drawer. Our quilt stand provides the perfect answer. Designed to hold one quilt or a couple, it's handsome and easy to build.

Note: You'll need two 1¹⁄₁₆"x4x36" hardwood boards, two more at 1¹⁄₁₆x3x18", and one at 1¹⁄₁₆x4½x24" to build the stand. (We used maple.) Make the quilt rods from two 1x28½" dowels and four 2" hardwood balls.

1 Trace the full-sized pattern, on *page 24*, onto cardboard and cut it out.

5 Clamp the stretcher to the uprights, and mark as *above*. Drill a ³⁄₁₆" hole at each mark, 1½" deep into the uprights and 2½" deep into the stretcher.

6 Assemble the legs, uprights, and stretcher with woodworker's glue and ¼x3" lag screws with washers. Install ¾"-diameter wooden buttons to cover the screw heads in the uprights.

continued

Country Colors Quilt Stand

continued

7 Cut twelve 4" lengths of ½" dowel. Chuck each into the drill press about 1" deep, and then round-over the end using 80-grit sandpaper on a sanding block. Finish-sand with 120-grit. Glue the dowels, rounded ends out, into the angled holes on the uprights.

8 To make the quilt rods, cut two 1" dowels to 28½". Bore a 1" hole ¾" deep in a 2"-diameter wooden ball for each end of each rod. To do so, clamp a piece of scrap wood about 2x4x6" to the drill-press table, and bore a 1½" hole about 1" deep in the center of one side. Then, without moving the block, change to a 1" bit. Place the wooden ball into the hole, and grip it with a hand-screw clamp while boring the hole.

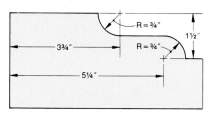

STRETCHER ENDS

9 Sand, and apply a clear finish. (We sprayed on three coats of clear lacquer, rubbing with 00 steel wool between coats.)

PROJECT TOOL LIST
- Tablesaw
- Bandsaw
- Drill
- Drill press
- Bits: ³⁄₁₆", ⁹⁄₃₂", ½", ¾", 1", 1½"
- Finishing sander

Note: *We built the project using the tools listed. You may be able to substitute other tools or equipment for listed items you don't have. Additional common hand tools and clamps may be required to complete the project.*

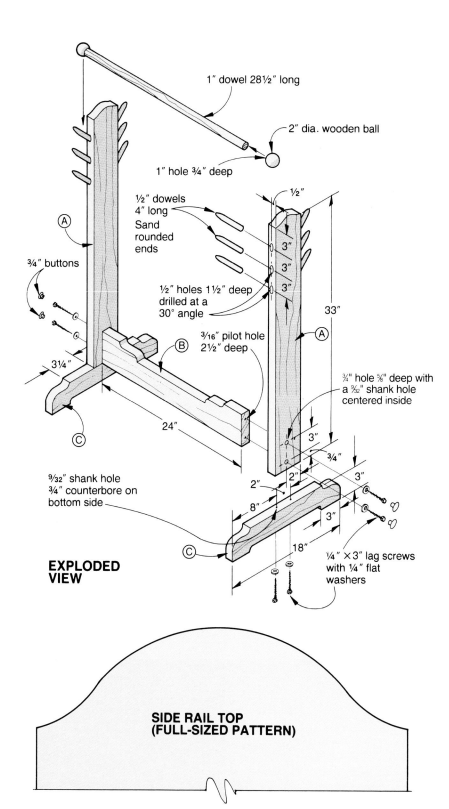

1" dowel 28½" long

2" dia. wooden ball

1" hole ¾" deep

½" dowels 4" long
Sand rounded ends

½" holes 1½" deep drilled at a 30° angle

³⁄₁₆" pilot hole 2½" deep

¾" buttons

¾" hole ⅝" deep with a ⁹⁄₃₂" shank hole centered inside

33"

3"
3"
3"

½"

3¼"

24"

⁹⁄₃₂" shank hole ¾" counterbore on bottom side

3"

¾"

2"   2"   3"

8"

18"

¼" × 3" lag screws with ¼" flat washers

EXPLODED VIEW

SIDE RAIL TOP (FULL-SIZED PATTERN)

R = ¾"
R = ¾"
1½"
3¾"
5¼"

Tin Punching

For some "holesome" fun, try tin punching

Looking for a way to lend an authentic appearance and distinctive flair to your country-style woodworking projects? Then, welcome aboard! Tin-punched panels will make most any project look as though it hails from the 1800s.

Before the turn of the century, punched-tin panels not only were decorative, they were downright practical. In pie safes, the panels allowed air to circulate around the food while keeping flies out. Lanterns also were fashioned from punched-tin panels that allowed light to pass while blocking the wind and preventing it from blowing out the candle.

The simple technology and tools for punching tin have hardly changed since those days. But as we discovered while punching tin in the *WOOD®* magazine shop, there are plenty of little tricks you can use to guarantee a high-quality end product.

YOU'LL NEED THESE TOOLS AND SUPPLIES

To get started, you may need to run out to your local grocery or hardware store for several items not found in most workshops:

• **White cotton gloves** for handling the tin panels. The gloves keep the tin's lead plating off your hands and your skin oil off the tin.

• **Pushpins** (like those in the photo *below*) for holding the tin in place atop a scrap of ¾" plywood.

• **Distilled white vinegar.** The acid in vinegar dulls and darkens the lead in the tin plating to give the panels an aged look. One quart goes a long way.

• **A 2"-or-wider foam brush** for applying the vinegar.

• **Semigloss or satin spray lacquer or polyurethane** for sealing in the lead and protecting the completed panel.

• **Tin panels.** It's difficult to find tin locally these days, but you can order tin panels from Country Accents, a mail-order supplier of tin-punching materials. See the Buying Guide on *page 29.* When ordering, be sure to specify "old-look tin," a thin sheet of steel with a plating of 80 percent lead and 20 percent tin.

We suggest you avoid so-called "black-tin" panels: a heavier-gauge steel sheet without any plating. These panels are harder to punch, rust readily, and do not age as nicely as old-look tin. Likewise, you can purchase other sheet metals, such as galvanized steel and aluminum flashing, locally at a relatively low price, but these products will not give an authentic punched-tin look.

• **Punches.** You can make your own punch for round holes by grinding a ¹⁄₁₆" nail set according to the before-and-after illustration *below.* With just this one tool, you can punch many patterns, but some designs require more varied tool tips such as those shown on *page 26.* Grinding these shapes yourself can be difficult, if not impossible, so you're probably better off ordering them.

continued

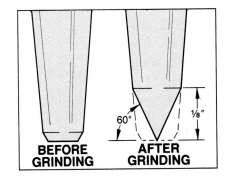

BEFORE GRINDING **AFTER GRINDING** 60° ¹⁄₈"

Tin Punching

continued

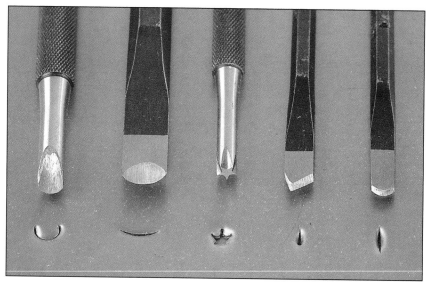

A sampling of specialty punches and the holes they make. From *left:* C chisel, curved chisel, star punch, willow punch, and lampmaker's chisel.

FIVE GREAT DESIGNS FOR YOUR TIN-PUNCHING PLEASURE

We thought you would like some design options for the 10x10" panels in the pie safe on *page 30*, or some other project you have in mind. So, we had the five original patterns *opposite* drawn up. You can order full-sized patterns from Country Accents at the address on *page 29*.

START BY PREPARING THE TIN PANELS

After your tin panels arrive, you'll notice that they have a light protective coating. Clean this away from both sides of the panel, using a rag dampened with mineral spirits or lacquer thinner as shown on *page 28*.

Then, lightly and evenly scuff both surfaces with 0000 steel wool. Be careful not to press too hard with the steel wool. Otherwise, you might put some scratches in the panel. Because the steel wool contains oil, you need to wash both sides of the panel with dishwashing soap after scuffing. Rinse away all traces of the soap with water.

From here on, you must be careful not to get any fingerprints, oils, or dirty smudges on either side of the panel. These contaminants may cause a splotchy appearance during the aging process, so remember to wear white cotton gloves whenever you handle the panel.

NOW, AGE THE PANELS FOR THAT AUTHENTIC LOOK

At this point, the tin panels look too shiny, so you need a way to dull and darken the surface. Here's a simple method.

After spreading some newspapers over your work surface, pour some vinegar into a clean, shallow container (a tuna or cat-food can works well). Saturate a foam brush with vinegar, and apply the vinegar to the panel in straight, overlapping strokes as shown *below*. Do not rebrush the vinegar once you have applied it. Work quickly and pause no longer than a second or two between strokes. Otherwise, the vinegar will react unevenly with the metal plating to create a streaked appearance. Leave the vinegar undisturbed for five minutes, then rinse the panel with running water and dry it with a clean, soft rag.

Repeat this procedure on the other side of the panel, being careful not to get any vinegar or contaminants on the side you just completed.

For an evenly aged panel, generously apply the vinegar in quick, overlapping strokes. Be careful not to allow vinegar to leak onto the opposite side of the panel.

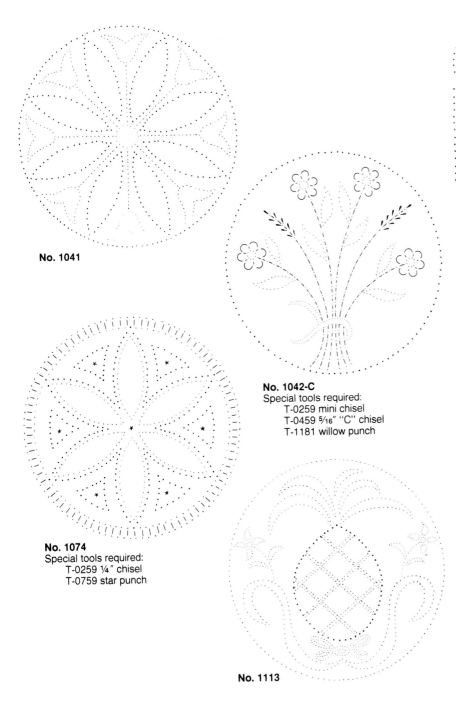

No. 1041

No. 1074
Special tools required:
T-0259 ¼″ chisel
T-0759 star punch

No. 1042-C
Special tools required:
T-0259 mini chisel
T-0459 5/16″ "C" chisel
T-1181 willow punch

No. 1113

No. 1017-A
Special tool required:
T-0259 7/16″ chisel

All patterns require a sharpened ⅟₁₆" nail set. Three of the patterns require special tools other than a sharpened nail set. To order, see the Buying Guide on *page 29.*

Try to avoid low-quality plywoods with lots of voids beneath the surface. If you punch into one of these voids, the punch tip will go deeper than intended and create a hole that's too large.

Secure the tin panel to the base with at least six pushpins positioned to hold the panel flat (see photo on *page 25*). Now, center the pattern on the panel and adhere it with masking tape.

WOODWORKERS, START YOUR PUNCHES!

You can start punching at any place on the pattern; just keep track of what holes you punch so you don't accidentally punch the same ones twice. Most patterns have both large and small round holes, but you can make both hole sizes with the same punch. Just strike the punch harder for the larger holes. Remember to punch all the holes of one size before punching all of the holes of another
continued

NEXT, PREPARE THE TIN PANEL FOR PUNCHING

Before you start punching, you need to position the panel and pattern on a sturdy base of plywood that's larger than the panel by at least 1" all around. Because tin panels are cut from large rolls, they tend to have a slight bow. Place the panel, with the peak of its bow up, onto the base. The punching tends to counteract the panel's bow, and may actually cause it to bow the other way. After punching each panel, you'll need to punch the next panel over a new portion of the base.

Tin Punching

continued

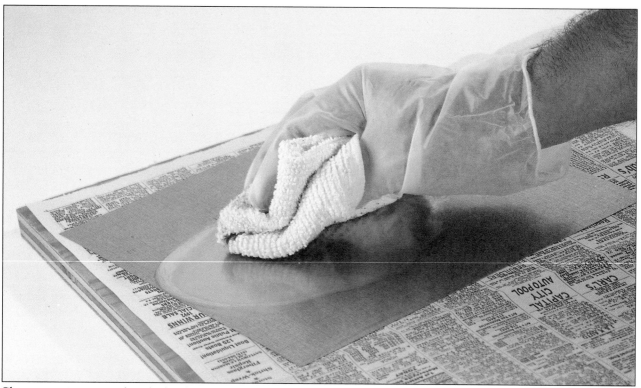

Clean protective coating from both sides of panel, using a rag dampened with mineral spirits or lacquer thinner.

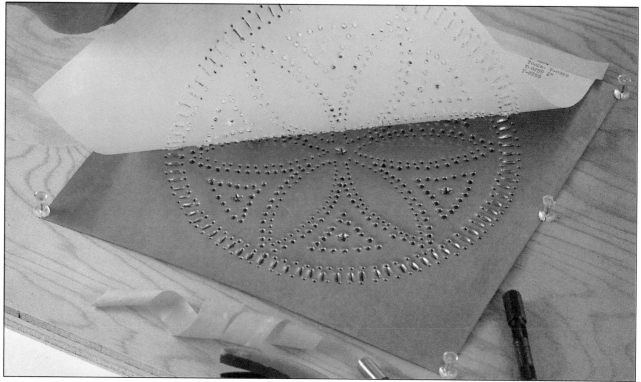

Before completely removing the pattern, check for missed holes.

size. This will help you punch consistently sized holes. We had good success with a 16-oz. hammer.

As you punch away, concentrate on cleanly striking the punch. If the hammer deflects off the punch, it will either strike your hand (ouch!) or put a dent in the panel (drat!). You also can lessen the chances of hammer deflection by grinding the head of the punch flat when it starts to mushroom from repeated blows.

Even a simple panel can take 20 minutes or so to punch, and your eyes and arms can become quite fatigued. We found that the longer we worked, the more mistakes we made, so for best results we suggest you take good, long breaks between panels.

After you've finished the punching, remove all but one of the pieces of masking tape holding the pattern in place. Lift the pattern up, and inspect for any missed holes as shown *opposite*.

THE FINISHING TOUCHES

Before removing the panel from its base, punch a small hole into its corner, no more than 1/16" from

both edges. Remove the push-pins and pass a wire through the corner hole. Use this wire to suspend the panel for spray finishing as shown *below*. Apply two coats of a clear finish (we like semigloss or satin finishes for country projects) to both the front and back of the panel.

See *page 32* of the pie-safe project for a typical means of installing a punched-tin panel.

BUYING GUIDE
• **Tin, brass, and copper panels, punching tools, and punched-tin patterns.** For current prices, contact Country Accents, Box 437, Montoursville, PA 17754, or call 717/478-4127 to order.

Punched-Tin Pie Safe

Just like grandma used to have

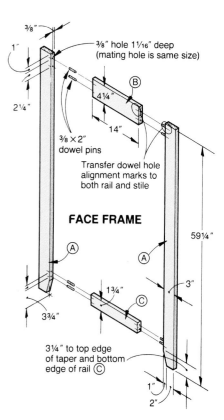

Note: *Unless you already know how to punch tin, see the preceding technique article for our step-by-step instructions. Also, take a look at the Buying Guide on page 34 for our source of blank and pre-punched tin panels.Or, if you want to save a few dollars (and obtain a little different look), use wood panels in the side frames, where shown in the inset photo at left.*

BEGIN WITH THE FACE FRAME

1 From ¾"-thick kiln-dried pine (we used #2 common), cut the two stiles (A), top rail (B), and bottom rail (C) to the sizes listed in the Bill of Materials on *page 32*.

2 Taper-cut the bottom inside edge of each stile (A) where shown on the Face Frame drawing *below*.

3 Lightly dry-clamp (don't glue) the rails between stiles where shown on the drawing *below*. Then,

FACE FRAME

3/8"

1"

2¼"

3/8" hole 1 1/16" deep (mating hole is same size)

Ⓑ

4¼"

14"

3/8 × 2" dowel pins

Transfer dowel hole alignment marks to both rail and stile

Ⓐ

Ⓐ

59¼"

3"

1¾"

Ⓒ

3¾"

3¼" to top edge of taper and bottom edge of rail Ⓒ

1"

2"

Long before iceboxes became a common household item, frugal homemakers everywhere stored their breads and pastries in a pie safe. The pie safe's decorative punched-tin panels allowed ventilation that retarded molding, and protected baked goods from flies and rodents at the same time. It also added a little spice to the kitchen's decor.

Our 14×20×59¼" pine replica does the same thing, but as you can see, it holds a lot more than pies and pastries.

CUTTING DIAGRAM

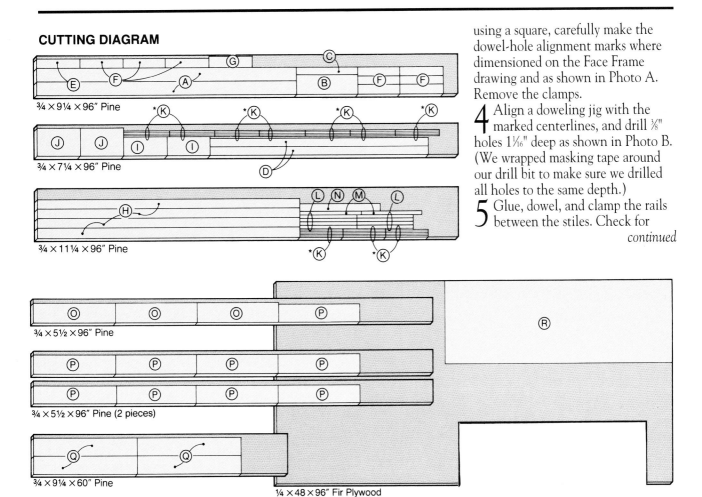

¾ × 9¼ × 96″ Pine

¾ × 7¼ × 96″ Pine

¾ × 11¼ × 96″ Pine

¾ × 5½ × 96″ Pine

¾ × 5½ × 96″ Pine (2 pieces)

¾ × 9¼ × 60″ Pine

¼ × 48 × 96″ Fir Plywood

using a square, carefully make the dowel-hole alignment marks where dimensioned on the Face Frame drawing and as shown in Photo A. Remove the clamps.

4 Align a doweling jig with the marked centerlines, and drill ⅜″ holes 1¹⁄₁₆″ deep as shown in Photo B. (We wrapped masking tape around our drill bit to make sure we drilled all holes to the same depth.)

5 Glue, dowel, and clamp the rails between the stiles. Check for
continued

Dry-clamp the frame pieces, and use a square to make the dowel-hole alignment marks on both mating pieces.

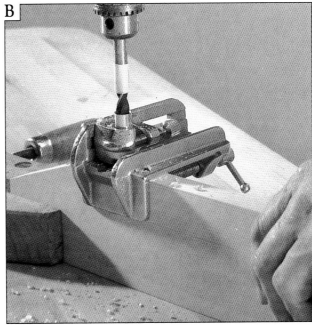

Using a doweling jig for proper alignment, drill ⅜″ dowel holes 1¹⁄₁₆″ deep in the face frame pieces where marked.

Punched-Tin Pie Safe

continued

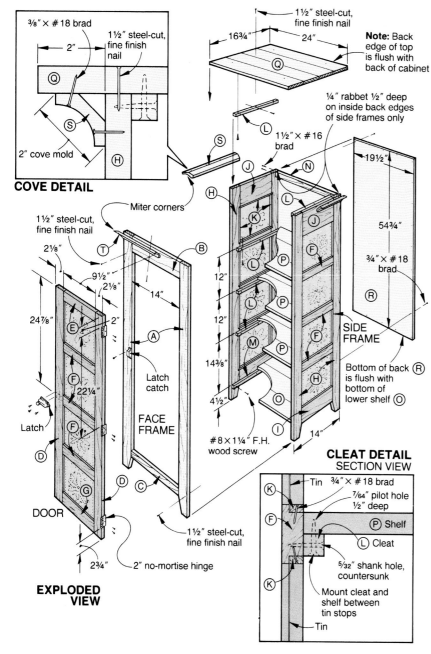

COVE DETAIL

EXPLODED VIEW

DOOR

FACE FRAME

SIDE FRAME

CLEAT DETAIL
SECTION VIEW

Bill of Materials					
Part	**Finished Size***			**Mat.**	**Qty.**
	T	**W**	**L**		
FACE FRAME					
A stiles	¾"	3"	59¼"	P	2
B rail	¾"	4¼"	14"	P	1
C rail	¾"	1¾"	14"	P	1
DOOR AND SIDE FRAMES					
D stiles	¾"	2⅛"	49¾"	P	2
E rail	¾"	2⅛"	9½"	P	1
F rails	¾"	2¼"	9½"	P	9
G rail	¾"	2⅞"	9½"	P	1
H stiles	¾"	2¼"	59¼"	P	4
I rails	¾"	4¾"	9½"	P	2
J rails	¾"	6½"	9½"	P	2
K*stops	¼"	½"	10"	P	48
CLEATS					
L shelf	¾"	¾"	12¾"	P	8
M bottom	¾"	¾"	13¾"	P	2
N back	¾"	1½"	18½"	P	1
EDGE-JOINED PARTS					
O* bottom	¾"	13¾"	18½"	EJP	1
P* shelves	¾"	12¾"	18½"	EJP	3
Q* top	¾"	16¾"	24"	EJP	1
BACK					
R back	¼"	19½"	54¾"	FPLY	1
MOLDING AND OPTIONAL PANELS					
S sides	¾"	2"	16¼"	PCM	2
T front	¾"	2"	23"	PCM	1
U panels (optional)	¼"	10"	10"	EJP	8

*Initially cut parts marked with an * oversized. Then, trim each to finished size according to the how-to instructions.

Material Key: P—pine, EJP—edge-joined pine, FPLY—fir plywood, PCM—pine cove molding

Supplies: ⅜x2" dowel pins, #8x1¼" flathead wood screws, ¾"x#18 brads, 1½"x#16 brads, stain, finish.

square, and make sure that the assembly lies flat. Wipe off the excess glue with a damp cloth.

Next, make the door and side frames

1 Cut the door stiles (D) and rails (E, F, G) to size. Note in the Bill of Materials that you need to cut nine F's. Set aside six of them for building the side frames later.

2 Using the method just described, make the dowel-hole alignment marks, drill the holes, and then glue, dowel, and clamp the door frame together. Check for square, and make sure the assembly clamps flat.

3 Cut the side-frame stiles (H) and rails (I, J) to size. Mark and taper-cut the bottom inside edge of each stile. Make the dowel-hole align-

ment marks, drill the holes, and then glue, dowel, and clamp each side frame. Again, check for square, and make sure that the assembly clamps flat.

4 Cut or rout a ¼" rabbet ½" deep along the back inside edge of the side frames to accept the plywood back (R) later.

5 Fit your router with a ¼" rabbeting bit. Rout a ¼" rabbet ½" deep along the back inside edge of the door-frame openings to accept the punched-tin panels later. Repeat the process along the back inside edge of all panel openings in the side frames to accept the punched-tin or wood panels later.

6 Use a sharp chisel to square the round routed corners in the door- and side-frame openings.

7 Rip and then miter-cut the stops (K) for all the punched-tin panels. (We planed ¾"-thick pine to ½" thickness, and then ripped ¼"-wide strips from the edges for the ¼ × ½" stops.) If you plan to use the solid-wood panels, cut stops to ¼" square and to the same length as those used for the punched-tin panels.

8 Snip the head off a 1½ × #16 brad, and chuck the headless brad into your portable drill. Sharpen the point, and use the brad as a bit to drill angled pilot

holes through the stops (K) where shown on the Panel Assembly drawing and accompanying Side View detail *below*.

IT'S TIME TO ADD THE CABINET'S TOP, BOTTOM, AND SHELVES

1 Cut the shelf cleats (L), bottom cleats (M), and upper back cleat (N) to size.

2 Drill mounting holes (in both directions), and screw (but don't glue) the cleats to the inside of the side frames where shown on the Exploded View drawing and accompanying Cleat detail.

3 Edge-join enough stock for the bottom (O), shelves (P), and top (Q). Cut the individual pieces oversized so each edge-joined panel measures an extra 1" in length and ½" in width. Glue and clamp each panel.

continued

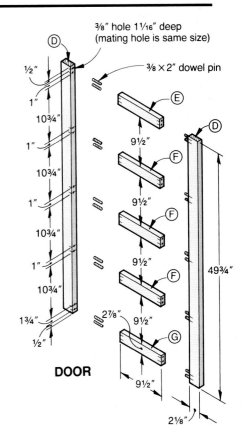

DOOR

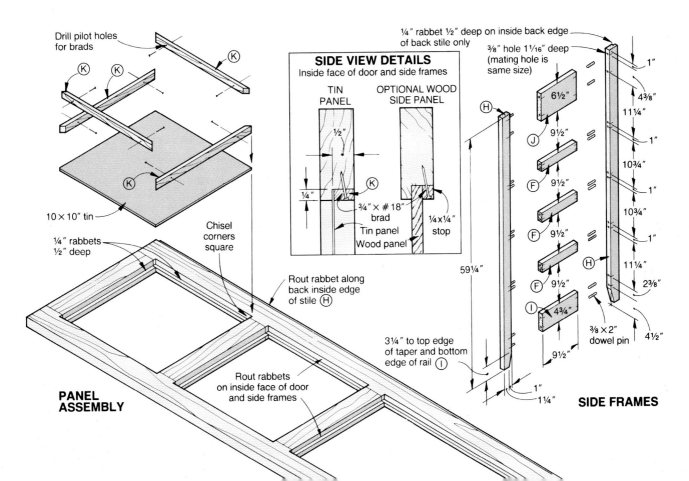

PANEL ASSEMBLY

SIDE VIEW DETAILS
Inside face of door and side frames

SIDE FRAMES

Punched-Tin Pie Safe

continued

4 Later, remove the clamps, trim the bottom (O) to its finished size, and sand it smooth.

5 With the edges of the face frame flush with the outside surface of the sides, glue and nail the face frame to the side frames. (For an authentic look, we used old-fashioned steel-cut nails, commonly called square nails. See the Buying Guide for our source. When you use these, be sure to align the rectangular head of each nail with the grain to lessen the chances of splitting the wood.)

6 Screw the bottom (O) in place to help hold the assembly square while the glue dries. Check for square. Nail the upper back cleat (N) in place.

7 Measure the openings, and cut the shelves (P) to finished size. Trim the top (Q) to size. You want the top to overlap the front face frame and side panels by 2". Sand the parts smooth.

8 Center the top (Q) from side to side on top of the assembly, and align its back edge flush with the back edge of the cabinet. Nail it in place (without glue), using the 1½" steel-cut nails. Then, working from the inside of the cabinet, drive screws through the two top cleats (L) into the bottom surface of the top panel (Q).

9 Measure the routed opening, and cut the back (R) to size from ¼" fir plywood.

AND LASTLY, ADD THE MOLDING, AND FINISH YOUR PIE SAFE

1 As shown in the drawing *above right*, miter-cut the side cove molding pieces (S) and front cove molding piece (T) to the length listed in the Bill of Materials. (We purchased 2" pine cove molding at a local home center for these pieces. Then, as shown in the drawing, we angled the mitersaw 45° from center, supported the flat areas of the molding against the mitersaw table and fence, and miter-cut the pieces to length.)

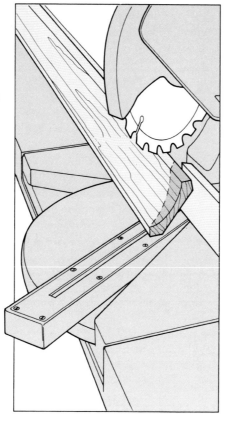

2 Using the Cove detail accompanying the Exploded View drawing for reference, nail the cove moldings (S, T) to the cabinet and to the top (Q).

3 Finish-sand the pie safe cabinet, door, stops, shelves, and wooden side-panel inserts if you're using them. Remove the sawdust from the cabinet and the other parts (we used our shop vacuum and a tack cloth). Finish the pieces as desired. (We chose a distressed antique look. For more on this process, see the information on the *next page* on How to Make Your Pie Safe Look Like an Antique.

4 If you've decided on wood panels for the side frames, edge-join enough ¼" pine stock (we planed thicker stock) for eight panels (U) for the side frames. (Because we wanted ¼" panels with two good faces, we shied away from using ¼" plywood.)

5 Punch the tin panels, using the technique and pattern shown in the previous article. Install the tin panels, and then nail the stops (K) in place.

6 Install the shelves (P) and screw them in place. Attach the hinges and fasten the latch to the door where shown on the Exploded View drawing. Nail the back (R) in place. Finally, bake a few pies, and head to the store for some ice cream while they cool slowly in your new pie safe.

BUYING GUIDE

• **Old-look tin panels.** 10×10" blank panels (unpunched), in sets of 4 or 12. Or, if you prefer to buy prepunched panels, order 4—10×10" RP-1041 panels, or 12 panels. For current prices, contact Country Accents, P.O. Box 437, Montoursville, PA 17754, or call 717/478-4127 to order.
• **Hardware.** Two pairs of ¾×2" antique-finish no-mortise hinges, and one cast-iron latch with catch. Kit No. 71161. For current prices, contact Geneva Specialties, P.O. Box 636, Lake Geneva, WI 53147, or call 800/556-2548 to order.
• **Old-fashioned steel-cut nails.** 4d, fine-finish nails, 1½" long. 1 pound box (approx. 322 nails). For current prices, contact Tremont Nail Co., P.O. Box 111, Wareham, MA 02571, or call 508/295-0038 to order.

PROJECT TOOL LIST
• Tablesaw
• Mitersaw
• Portable drill
• Doweling jig
• Bits: ⅟₆₄", ⁵⁄₃₂", ⅜"
• Router
• ¼" rabbeting bit
• Finishing sander

Note: *We built the project using the tools listed. You may be able to substitute other tools or equipment for listed items you don't have. Additional common hand tools and clamps may be required to complete the project.*

How to make your pie safe look like an antique

To make a natural wood surface look old, as we did with the pie safe on *page 30*, follow these steps:

1 Distress the piece by scratching and denting parts of the cabinet where the original piece would have received the greatest wear through the years. For the pie safe, this would have been near the feet, edges and top, and around the latch. We used a ball peen hammer to make dents, a screwdriver for scratches, and a rasp to scuff areas of heavy use. As shown in Photo A, round-over the edges and corners with 80-grit sandpaper wrapped around a 1" dowel. For a natural "worn" look, remember to sand the edges unevenly from spot to spot.

2 Apply a dark stain to areas such as the base of the legs, around the latch, and other places along edges where dirt would likely accumulate over time as shown in Photo B. Add the same stain to scratches and nicks to accentuate these blemishes. For greater application control, we preferred using gel stains.

3 Apply a lighter stain to the remaining areas, and blend the stains where they meet. Let both stains sit for a few minutes, then wipe away the excess.

4 Lighten heavily worn areas with paint thinner *before* the stain dries, as shown in Photo C. The thinner partially removes stain to simulate wear the pie safe would have incurred over time.

5 Add a bit more character by spattering the surface. To achieve this accent (called "fly specks" by some), first mix two parts gel stain with one part mineral spirits in a shallow container. Then, dab an old toothbrush, or a paintbrush with the bristles trimmed to ½" long, into the mix. Practice your spattering technique on a piece of paper before trying it on the pie safe. Place the brush about 6" away from the paper, and run your finger through the bristles as shown in Photo D. Don't overdo it. A little spattering goes a long way. Later, apply a clear finish.

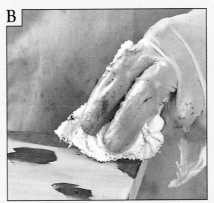

Apply a gel stain to areas prone to dirt and grime buildup.

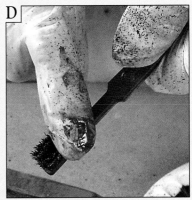

Using a toothbrush, give the project a uniform coat of fine spattering.

For an edge-rounding tool, wrap 80-grit sandpaper around a 1" dowel.

Before the stain dries, lighten any high-wear areas with paint thinner. Don't forget to wear the protective gloves.

Making and Installing Dovetailed Drawers

If you're searching for a straightforward way to make and install sturdy, smooth-sliding drawers that look great, stay tuned. We'll show you how to build dovetailed drawers steered by a simple and inexpensive wooden guide system.

As we sat down to plan this article, we carefully considered the nearly endless options for building a drawer. Eventually, we decided on strong, traditional, ½" half-blind dovetails for joining the sides of the drawer to the front. Any number of commercially available jigs help you make these joints with your router, and we'll share some tips for using them.

To make carcass construction and drawer installation as straightforward as possible, we chose to rest the drawers on ¾" plywood panels. The panels simplify guide installation and make great dust barriers between the drawers.

LET'S TAKE AN INSIDE LOOK AT A BASIC DRAWER SYSTEM

The traditional dovetailed drawer and its cabinet support system must truly be made for each other for effortless operation and a long life. Note, for instance, the key components shown *opposite*.

The drawer has two ½" sides joined to the ½" or ¾" front with half-blind dovetails (so named because you can't see the joint from the front of the drawer). Rabbet-and-dado joints hold a ½" back to the sides, and a ¼"

plywood drawer bottom slips into a groove cut into both sides and the front. Note that the sides extend beyond the back to prevent the drawer from dropping to the floor when fully opened.

Fastened to the underside of the drawer bottom are two ¼" slides that contact both sides of a ¼" guide attached to a ¾" panel beneath each drawer. Together, these parts make up a guide system that channels the drawer straight in and out when pushed and pulled. The guide also serves as a stop that prevents the drawer from striking the back of the carcass when you close the drawer. A kicker prevents the drawer from tipping down as you pull it open. You may not need a kicker if the drawer has a ¾" panel just above it.

BASIC DRAWER SYSTEM ANATOMY

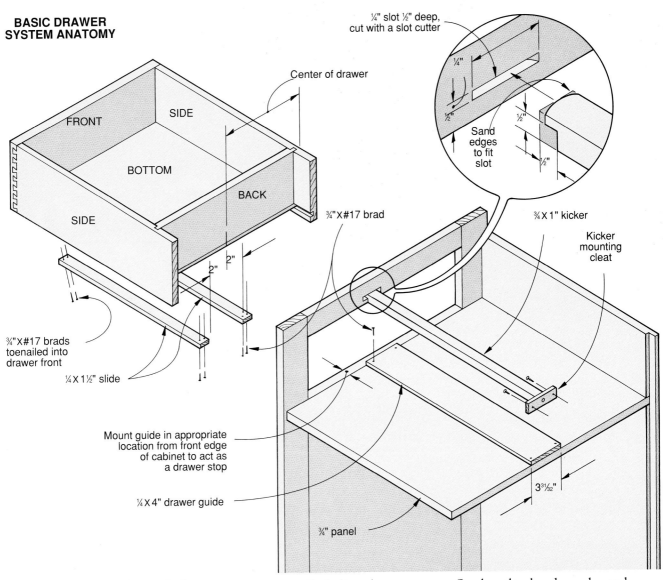

¼" slot ½" deep, cut with a slot cutter

Sand edges to fit slot

¾ X 1" kicker

Kicker mounting cleat

Center of drawer

FRONT   SIDE

BOTTOM

BACK

SIDE

¾" X #17 brad

2"

2"

¾" X #17 brads toenailed into drawer front

¼ X 1½" slide

Mount guide in appropriate location from front edge of cabinet to act as a drawer stop

¼ X 4" drawer guide

¾" panel

3³¹⁄₃₂"

Note: Use a moderately priced, close-grained hardwood such as beech, birch, soft maple, or poplar for the drawer sides, back, slides, guides, and kicker; hardwood plywood for the bottom; and drawer fronts that match the cabinet.

HOW TO SIZE YOUR DRAWERS
Note: With this type of drawer construction, you need to determine the drawer height when you're planning the cabinet.

Before you cut the parts for your drawer, you need to decide which of three drawer-front styles to use for

your project—flush, lipped, or overlap. Though your decision is mainly one of aesthetics, each style functions slightly differently and also affects the dimensions of some parts. The drawings on *page 38* show and tell how to determine the dimensions of the various drawer parts.

Here we'll construct a drawer with a flush front that does not protrude from its surrounding carcass. These fronts make for easy drawer construction, but do require you to carefully fit them and accurately position the drawer guide.

On the other hand, overlay and lipped fronts overlap adjacent edges of the face frame, so you can position the drawers to cover the face frame partially or completely. With these, the overlapping edge acts as a drawer stop.

Since you make a lipped front from a single piece of wood, you must put extra time into cutting the rabbets and setting up your dovetail jig. These extra steps aren't necessary with an overlay front because with this style, you simply screw the front (sometimes called a false front) onto the dovetailed drawer front.

continued

Dovetailed Drawers

continued

Tips on Machining the Drawer Parts

After cutting the drawer parts to size, use a router and a ½" dovetail jig to cut the half-blind dovetails. Most of these jigs work about the same, and all of the models we've tried have adequate instructions for basic use. Here are a few tips that will help ensure success:

- For your comfort, work with the dovetail jig at elbow height. Most workbenches don't reach this high, so you may want to build a simple stand like the one shown *opposite*, using ¾" stock.
- To prevent mix-ups, number the mating edges of the drawer fronts and sides.
- Take your time in adjusting the jig and setting the depth of the router bit. Your patience will result in tight-fitting joints.
- If you properly cut your dovetailed parts, you need only tap them together gently with a rubber mallet. If they fit with any play, they won't hold up in the long run. If they're too tight, you could break them when forcing them together.
- To reduce the chances of grain tearout, make a skimming cut across the inside face of the drawer side (vertical workpiece) by running the router from right to left across the template as shown *opposite, bottom left*. Then, cut the dovetails to their full depth by moving the router from left to right, following the notches in the template. Check to make sure you've cut the dovetails completely.

After cutting the dovetails, round over the top edges of the sides and back with a ¼" roundover bit. Then, turning to your tablesaw and dado blade adjusted for a ¼"-wide kerf, cut a ¼X¼" groove (to hold the bottom) into the front and sides. Without changing the height of your dado blade, cut a dado (for the back) into the sides as shown in the photo *opposite, bottom right*.

SIZING A DRAWER
(Flush-front style shown)

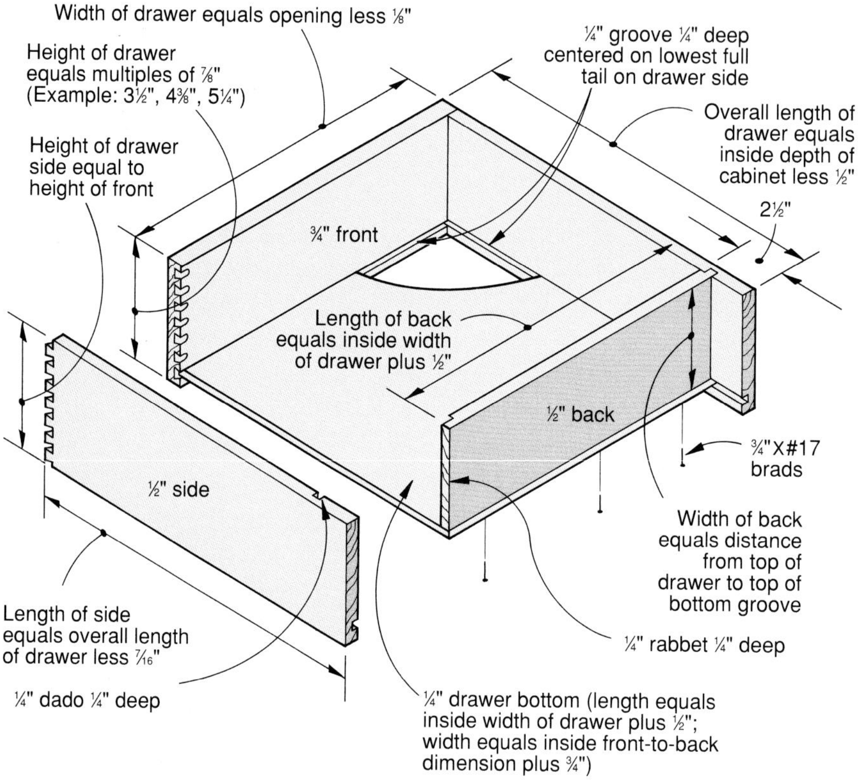
Width of drawer equals opening less ⅛"
Height of drawer equals multiples of ⅞" (Example: 3½", 4⅜", 5¼")
Height of drawer side equal to height of front
¼" groove ¼" deep centered on lowest full tail on drawer side
Overall length of drawer equals inside depth of cabinet less ½"
2½"
¾" front
Length of back equals inside width of drawer plus ½"
½" back
¾"X#17 brads
½" side
Width of back equals distance from top of drawer to top of bottom groove
Length of side equals overall length of drawer less 7/16"
¼" rabbet ¼" deep
¼" dado ¼" deep
¼" drawer bottom (length equals inside width of drawer plus ½"; width equals inside front-to-back dimension plus ¾")

OVERLAY DRAWER FRONT

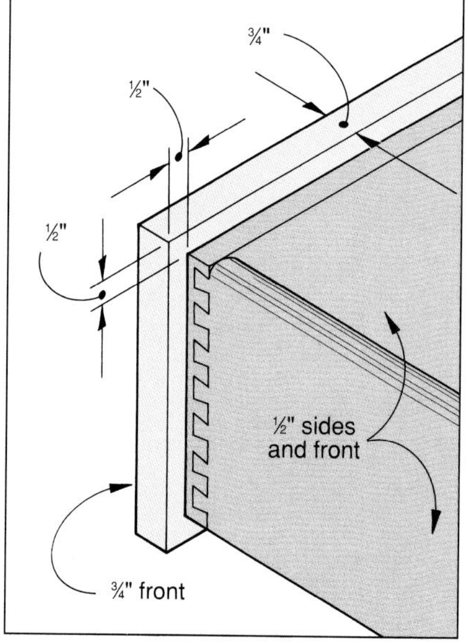
¾"
½"
½"
½" sides and front
¾" front

LIPPED DRAWER FRONT

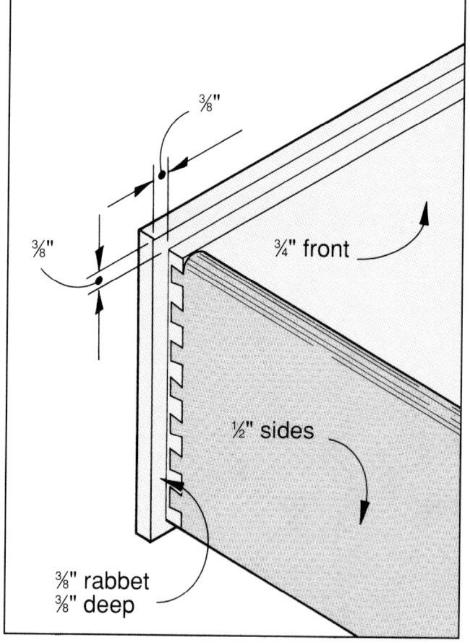
⅜"
⅜"
¾" front
½" sides
⅜" rabbet ⅜" deep

Safety note: *Since we're not cutting completely through the workpiece in the photo we can safely butt the workpiece against the fence. Do not attempt this*

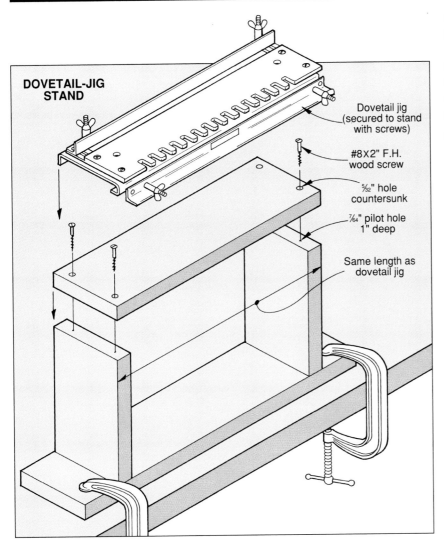

DOVETAIL-JIG STAND

Dovetail jig (secured to stand with screws)

#8X2" F.H. wood screw

5/32" hole countersunk

7/64" pilot hole 1" deep

Same length as dovetail jig

when cutting all the way through narrow pieces.

Now, slide the tablesaw fence up to the dado blade and cut the rabbets on the ends of the back. To prevent damage to your fence, clamp or screw a wooden auxiliary fence to it.

LET'S ASSEMBLE THE DRAWER

Before applying glue to the parts, dry-clamp the drawer together to check for fit and squareness. Then, apply woodworker's glue to both surfaces of the dovetail joints (a ½"-wide brush works well), and to the rabbet-and-dado joints. Attach one side to the front and back, and then attach the other side. Clamp this assembly together as shown on *page 40, bottom left*. Check the drawer for square by measuring across both diagonally opposing corners. If one diagonal measures longer than the other, adjust your clamps until the diagonal measurements equal each other. Make certain that the drawer back does not block the groove that holds the drawer bottom.

After the glue dries, slide the bottom into place and secure it to the back with three ¾" brads. Turn the drawer bottom side up and place *continued*

Before cutting the dovetails, make a skimming cut to help prevent grain tearout. Make light cuts, but hold the router firmly to maintain control.

Use your tablesaw's fence as a stop when cutting dadoes into the drawer sides for holding the drawer back.

Dovetailed Drawers

continued

some weight (such as two one-gallon containers of fluid) onto the center of the bottom. Apply three 1"-long beads of hot-melt glue to the joints between the bottom and sides and bottom and front as shown *below right*. Leave the weight in place until the glue hardens. This prevents the bottom from rattling, and eliminates gaps between the bottom and sides on the inside of the drawer.

HOW TO INSTALL THE DRAWER

Since few of us can build a perfectly square, exactly sized drawer, or a perfect opening to place it into, you'll need to make some slight adjustments for a nice fit. First, place the drawer into its opening, and then follow the three-step process right for creating uniform clearance all around the drawer.

With the back removed from your project's carcass, install the drawer guide system according to the drawing *opposite* titled Installing the Drawer Guide System. In Step 1, take care to butt the slides tightly against the guide before nailing

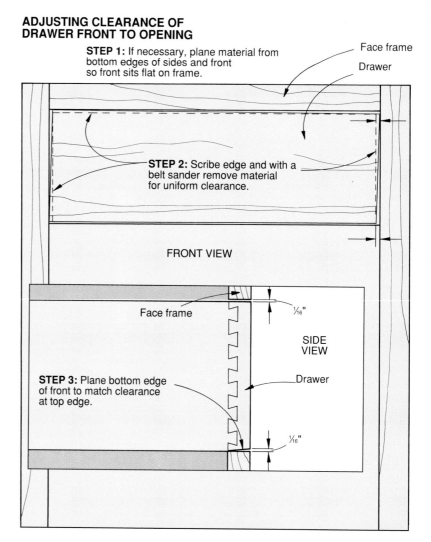

ADJUSTING CLEARANCE OF DRAWER FRONT TO OPENING

STEP 1: If necessary, plane material from bottom edges of sides and front so front sits flat on frame.

Face frame

Drawer

STEP 2: Scribe edge and with a belt sander remove material for uniform clearance.

FRONT VIEW

Face frame

SIDE VIEW

Drawer

STEP 3: Plane bottom edge of front to match clearance at top edge.

1/16"

1/16"

Reposition your clamps slightly to make the drawer square.

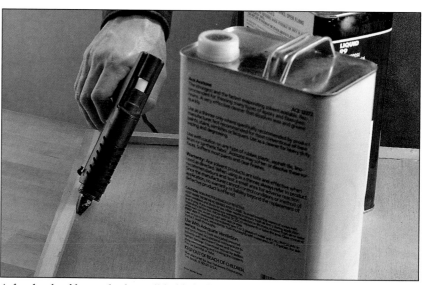

A few beads of hot-melt glue will hold the bottom in place and prevent it from rattling around in its groove.

INSTALLING THE DRAWER GUIDE SYSTEM

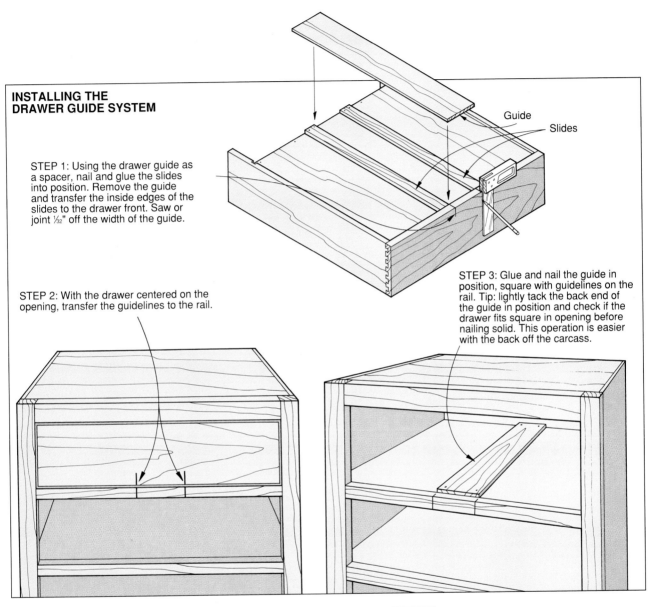

STEP 1: Using the drawer guide as a spacer, nail and glue the slides into position. Remove the guide and transfer the inside edges of the slides to the drawer front. Saw or joint ⅟₃₂" off the width of the guide.

Guide

Slides

STEP 2: With the drawer centered on the opening, transfer the guidelines to the rail.

STEP 3: Glue and nail the guide in position, square with guidelines on the rail. Tip: lightly tack the back end of the guide in position and check if the drawer fits square in opening before nailing solid. This operation is easier with the back off the carcass.

them into position. By sawing or jointing ⅟₃₂" off the width of the guide before installing it, you allow the drawer to slide over the guide without excessive play. If the drawer does not have a panel directly above it, then position and secure a kicker according to the drawing and notes on *page 37*.

THE FINAL TOUCHES

Before applying finish to the drawer, drill any holes necessary for attaching the pull. Then, apply equal amounts of finish to all surfaces of the drawer. This will help prevent the drawer parts from shrinking or expanding at different rates, which could throw the drawer out of square. Finally, rub paraffin wax onto the bottom surface of the kicker, the bottom edges of the drawer sides, the inside edges of the slides, and the outside edges of the guide for smooth operation.

Shaker-Style Tall Chest

Bedroom storage never looked so good

Elegantly simple in design and straightforward in construction, this handsome project reflects a much simpler time when craftsmanship and practicality reigned supreme.

The adaptation you see here has its roots in a classic Shaker project, the upright cupboard. Loaded with drawers and a convenient cabinet for storing shirts and sweaters, this tall chest replaces the more common form of Shaker bedroom storage drawers built into the walls.

SOLID CONSTRUCTION STARTS WITH THE CARCASS

1 Rip and crosscut the dresser sides (A), fixed shelves (B, C), divider (D), top (E), and adjustable shelves (F) to the sizes listed in the Bill of Materials on *page 45* from ¾" cherry plywood. For ease in laying out and cutting, see the Cutting Diagram on *page 45* for our layout.

2 Cut or rout all the rabbets and dadoes in pieces A, D, and E where dimensioned on the Exploded View and Divider drawings on *page 44* and *opposite*. (We applied pieces of masking tape to each piece, marking the good face, top, bottom, and back edges where necessary. This helped prevent us from dadoing or rabbeting the wrong face and proved helpful later when assembling the cabinet.)

3 Dry-clamp the pieces (except for the adjustable shelves) to check the fit. The interior parts (B, C, D, E) set ⅜" back from the front edges of the side pieces (A). The back edges of B, C, and D should be flush with the shoulder of the rabbet along the back edges of parts A and E. Trim if necessary. Now, glue and clamp the pieces, checking to make sure they are square.

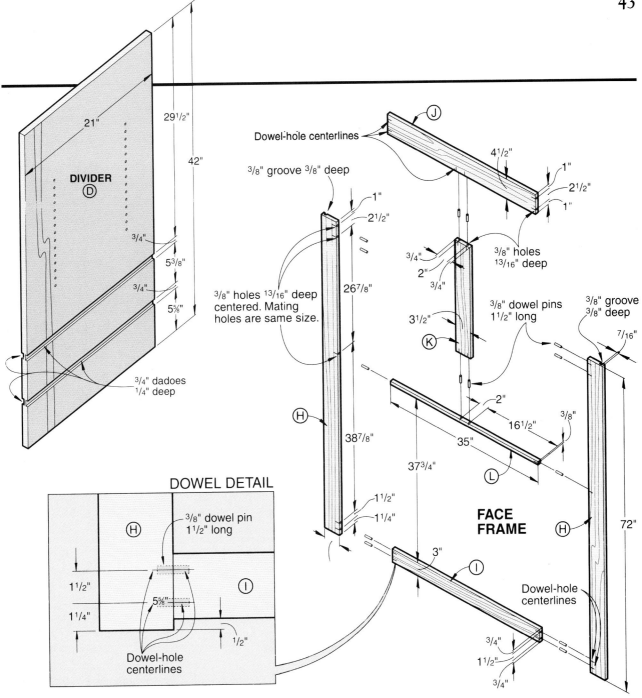

21"

29 1/2"

42"

DIVIDER
Ⓓ

3/4"

5 3/8"

3/4"

5 5/8"

3/4" dadoes
1/4" deep

Dowel-hole centerlines

Ⓙ

4 1/2"

1"

2 1/2"

1"

3/8" groove 3/8" deep

1"

2 1/2"

3/4"

2"

3/4"

3/8" holes
13/16" deep

3/8" holes 13/16" deep
centered. Mating
holes are same size.

26 7/8"

3 1/2"

Ⓚ

3/8" dowel pins
1 1/2" long

3/8" groove
3/8" deep

7/16"

Ⓗ

38 7/8"

2"

16 1/2"

3/8"

37 3/4"

35"

Ⓛ

**FACE
FRAME**

Ⓗ

72"

1 1/2"

1 1/4"

Dowel-hole
centerlines

DOWEL DETAIL

Ⓗ

3/8" dowel pin
1 1/2" long

Ⓘ

1 1/2"

5 5/8"

1 1/4"

1/2"

Dowel-hole
centerlines

3"

Ⓘ

3/4"

1 1/2"

3/4"

4 Measure the opening, and cut the back (G) to size. Set it aside for now.

ADD THE SOLID-CHERRY FACE FRAME

1 From solid ¾" cherry stock, cut the face frame stiles (H) to the sizes listed in the Bill of Materials plus 1/16" extra in width. (We cut them extra wide so we could rout them flush with the sides of the carcass later.) Cut or

rout a ⅜" groove ⅜" deep along the back side of each stile where shown on the Face Frame drawing *above* and Rabbet detail accompanying the Exploded View drawing on *page 44*.

2 Now, cut the bottom rail (I), top rail (J), mullion (K), and middle rail (L) to size.

3 Dry-clamp (no glue) the face frame together. With a helper, set the cabinet carcass on its back. Then, position the clamped-up face frame

on the front of the cabinet to verify the tongue on the front edge of the sides (A) fits into the grooves in the back faces of the stiles (H). Then check that the center rail (L) sits directly over the front edge of the middle shelf (B). Adjust if necessary.

4 With the assembly still clamped together, use a square to mark the dowel-hole centerlines across each joint where shown on the Face Frame drawing.

continued

Shaker-Style Tall Chest

continued

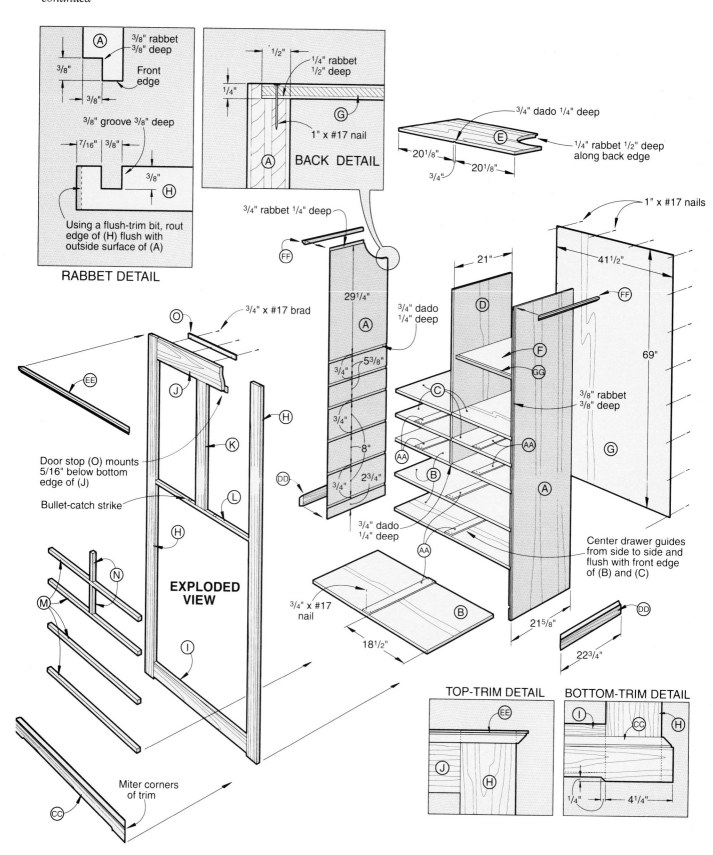

RABBET DETAIL

3/8" rabbet
3/8" deep

Front edge

3/8"

3/8"

Ⓐ

3/8" groove 3/8" deep

7/16"   3/8"

3/8"

Ⓗ

Using a flush-trim bit, rout edge of (H) flush with outside surface of (A)

BACK DETAIL

1/2"

1/4" rabbet 1/2" deep

1/4"

Ⓖ

1" x #17 nail

Ⓐ

3/4" dado 1/4" deep

Ⓔ

1/4" rabbet 1/2" deep along back edge

20 1/8"

20 1/8"

3/4"

1" x #17 nails

41 1/2"

ⒻⒻ

69"

3/8" rabbet 3/8" deep

Ⓖ

Ⓐ

3/4" rabbet 1/4" deep

ⒻⒻ

29 1/4"

Ⓐ

3/4" dado 1/4" deep

5 3/8"

3/4"

3/4"

8"

3/4"

2 3/4"

ⒹⒹ

3/4" dado 1/4" deep

21"

Ⓓ

Ⓕ

ⒼⒼ

Ⓒ

ⒶⒶ

ⒶⒶ

Ⓑ

ⒶⒶ

Center drawer guides from side to side and flush with front edge of (B) and (C)

21 5/8"

ⒹⒹ

22 3/4"

3/4" x #17 nail

18 1/2"

Ⓑ

Ⓞ

3/4" x #17 brad

ⒺⒺ

Ⓙ

Ⓗ

Ⓚ

Door stop (O) mounts 5/16" below bottom edge of (J)

Bullet-catch strike

Ⓛ

Ⓗ

EXPLODED VIEW

Ⓘ

Ⓝ

Ⓜ

Miter corners of trim

ⒸⒸ

TOP-TRIM DETAIL

ⒺⒺ

Ⓙ

Ⓗ

BOTTOM-TRIM DETAIL

Ⓘ

ⒸⒸ

Ⓗ

1/4"

4 1/4"

CUTTING DIAGRAM

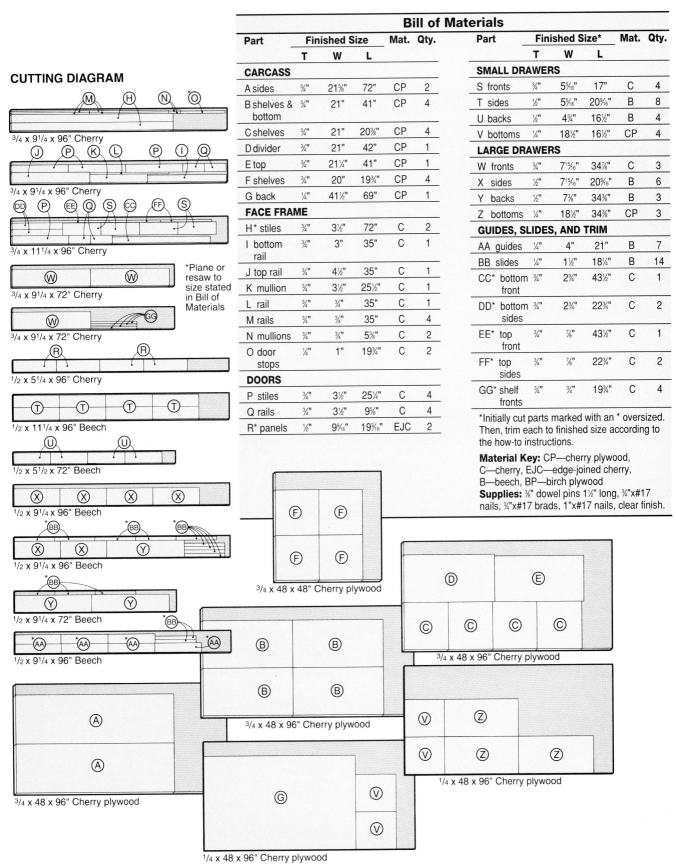

3/4 x 9 1/4 x 96" Cherry

3/4 x 9 1/4 x 96" Cherry

3/4 x 11 1/4 x 96" Cherry

*Plane or resaw to size stated in Bill of Materials

3/4 x 9 1/4 x 72" Cherry

3/4 x 9 1/4 x 72" Cherry

1/2 x 5 1/4 x 96" Cherry

1/2 x 11 1/4 x 96" Beech

1/2 x 5 1/2 x 72" Beech

1/2 x 9 1/4 x 96" Beech

1/2 x 9 1/4 x 96" Beech

1/2 x 9 1/4 x 72" Beech

1/2 x 9 1/4 x 96" Beech

3/4 x 48 x 96" Cherry plywood

3/4 x 48 x 48" Cherry plywood

3/4 x 48 x 96" Cherry plywood

3/4 x 48 x 96" Cherry plywood

3/4 x 48 x 96" Cherry plywood

1/4 x 48 x 96" Cherry plywood

1/4 x 48 x 96" Cherry plywood

Bill of Materials

Part	Finished Size			Mat.	Qty.
	T	W	L		
CARCASS					
A sides	3/4"	21 5/8"	72"	CP	2
B shelves & bottom	3/4"	21"	41"	CP	4
C shelves	3/4"	21"	20 3/8"	CP	4
D divider	3/4"	21"	42"	CP	1
E top	3/4"	21 1/4"	41"	CP	1
F shelves	3/4"	20"	19 3/4"	CP	4
G back	1/4"	41 1/2"	69"	CP	1
FACE FRAME					
H* stiles	3/4"	3 1/2"	72"	C	2
I bottom rail	3/4"	3"	35"	C	1
J top rail	3/4"	4 1/2"	35"	C	1
K mullion	3/4"	3 1/2"	25 1/2"	C	1
L rail	3/4"	3/4"	35"	C	1
M rails	3/4"	3/4"	35"	C	4
N mullions	3/4"	3/4"	5 3/8"	C	2
O door stops	1/4"	1"	19 3/4"	C	2
DOORS					
P stiles	3/4"	3 1/2"	25 1/4"	C	4
Q rails	3/4"	3 1/2"	9 5/8"	C	4
R* panels	1/2"	9 9/16"	19 9/16"	EJC	2

Part	Finished Size*			Mat.	Qty.
	T	W	L		
SMALL DRAWERS					
S fronts	3/4"	5 5/16"	17"	C	4
T sides	1/2"	5 5/16"	20 9/16"	B	8
U backs	1/2"	4 3/4"	16 1/2"	B	4
V bottoms	1/4"	18 1/2"	16 1/2"	CP	4
LARGE DRAWERS					
W fronts	3/4"	7 15/16"	34 7/8"	C	3
X sides	1/2"	7 15/16"	20 9/16"	B	6
Y backs	1/2"	7 3/8"	34 3/8"	B	3
Z bottoms	1/4"	18 1/2"	34 3/8"	CP	3
GUIDES, SLIDES, AND TRIM					
AA guides	1/4"	4"	21"	B	7
BB slides	1/4"	1 1/2"	18 1/4"	B	14
CC* bottom front	3/4"	2 3/4"	43 1/2"	C	1
DD* bottom sides	3/4"	2 3/4"	22 3/4"	C	2
EE* top front	3/4"	7/8"	43 1/2"	C	1
FF* top sides	3/4"	7/8"	22 3/4"	C	2
GG* shelf fronts	3/4"	3/4"	19 3/4"	C	4

*Initially cut parts marked with an * oversized. Then, trim each to finished size according to the how-to instructions.

Material Key: CP—cherry plywood, C—cherry, EJC—edge-joined cherry, B—beech, BP—birch plywood
Supplies: 3/8" dowel pins 1 1/2" long, 3/4"x#17 nails, 3/4"x#17 brads, 1"x#17 nails, clear finish.

continued

Shaker-Style Tall Chest

continued

5 Using a doweling jig and the marked centerlines, drill ⅜" holes to the depths marked on the drawing for the dowel pins.

6 Glue, dowel, and clamp the face frame, checking for square. Later, remove the clamps and excess glue. Sand the front and back of the face frame smooth.

7 Glue and clamp the face frame to the cabinet with the ends flush.

8 Later, remove the clamps. Mount a flush-trim bit in your router, and rout the protruding edges of the stiles (about ¹⁄₁₆") flush with the outside faces of the cabinet sides (A). See the Rabbet detail for reference.

9 Cut the remaining rails and mullions (M, N), and, using bar clamps, clamp them to the front of the cabinet where shown on the Exploded View drawing.

10 Cut the door stops (O) to size (we resawed thicker stock to ¼" thickness). Glue the stops in place behind the top rail (J) so the stop protrudes ⁵⁄₁₆" below the bottom edge of the top rail.

Cut a ¼" tenon ½" long across the ends of the door rails. Clamp a stop to the miter-gauge fence for consistent lengths.

THE FRAME-AND-PANEL DOORS COME NEXT

1 Cut the door stiles (P) and rails (Q) to size. Cut or rout a ¼" groove ½" deep along one edge of each stile and rail where shown on the Door drawing and accompanying Groove detail *above right*.

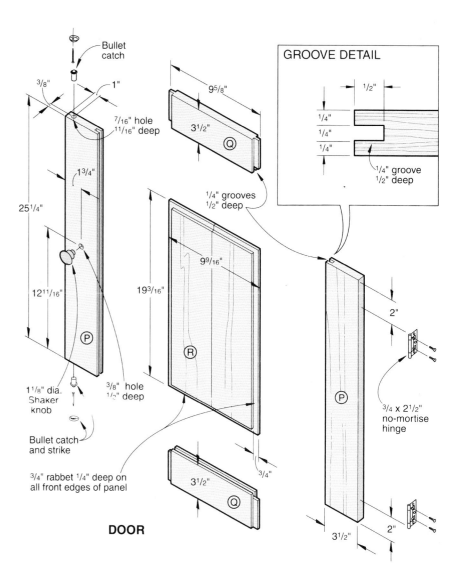

DOOR

GROOVE DETAIL

BULLET CATCH DETAIL
- Face frame
- Strike
- Catch
- ⅜" hole ½" deep

TENON AND GROOVE DETAIL
- ¼" groove ½" deep
- ¼" tenon ½" long

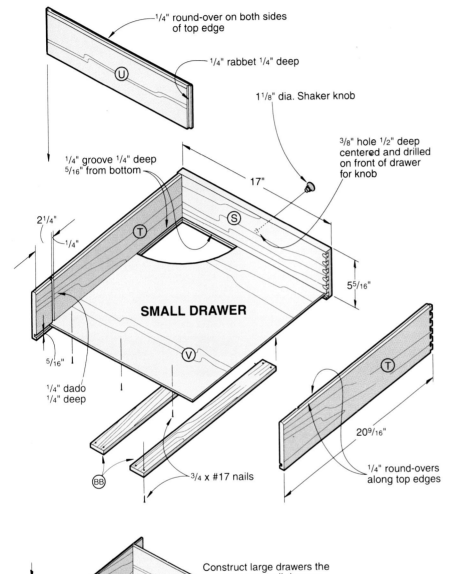

¹/₄" round-over on both sides of top edge

¹/₄" rabbet ¹/₄" deep

1¹/₈" dia. Shaker knob

³/₈" hole ¹/₂" deep centered and drilled on front of drawer for knob

U

¹/₄" groove ¹/₄" deep
⁵/₁₆" from bottom

17"

2¹/₄"

¹/₄"

S

T

5⁵/₁₆"

SMALL DRAWER

V

⁵/₁₆"

¹/₄" dado
¹/₄" deep

T

20⁹/₁₆"

¹/₄" round-overs along top edges

BB

³/₄ x #17 nails

2 Cut a ¼" tenon ½" long across each end of each rail. (We mounted a dado blade to our tablesaw and an auxiliary fence to our miter gauge. Then, we raised the blade ¼" above the saw table, clamped a stop to the miter-gauge auxiliary fence, and cut the ends to form the tenons as shown in the photo *opposite*.)

3 To achieve the wide width for the door panels (R), edge-join stock to form two ½×10×20" pieces. Then, trim each panel to finished size, keeping the joint line centered from side to side. We prefer to edge-join narrower stock for pieces this wide to diminish the chances of warpage.

4 Cut ¾" rabbets ¼" deep along the front edges of each panel as shown on the Door drawing.

5 Test-fit the door pieces. The panels should be ¹⁄₁₆" undersized in width to allow them to expand and contract within the frame. Applying glue to the rails and stiles only, assemble the door parts for each door and clamp. This allows the panel to float inside the frame without glue.

AND NOW FOR THE DRAWERS
Note: *See the drawer construction and the installation article on page 36 for an in-depth look at our drawer-making* continued

Construct large drawers the same as small drawers

7¹⁵/₁₆"

4"

X

Y

Z

7"

W

X

LARGE DRAWER

20⁷/₈"

21"

7"

³/₈" hole ¹/₂" deep

1¹/₈" dia. Shaker knob

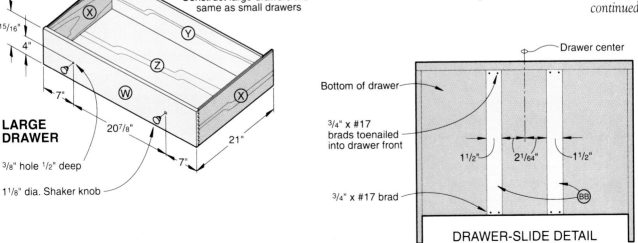

Drawer center

Bottom of drawer

³/₄" x #17 brads toenailed into drawer front

³/₄" x #17 brad

1¹/₂"   2¹/₆₄"   1¹/₂"

BB

DRAWER-SLIDE DETAIL

Shaker-Style Tall Chest

continued

techniques. Use these methods and the Drawer drawings to build the four small and three large drawers. The sizes for the drawers are listed in the Bill of Materials. For a continuous flow of grain across the side-by-side drawer-fronts, see the Cutting Diagram.

For stability, we used ½" beech for the drawer sides and back. Cherry or birch would also work.

FOR SMOOTH ACTION, ADD THE GUIDES AND SLIDES

1 Cut the drawer guides (AA) and slides (BB) to size. Sand a slight round-over along the top two edges of each guide.

2 Glue and nail a guide to each of the fixed shelves (B, C), accurately centered between the stiles of each drawer opening. (When attaching the guides, we used a framing square to keep the guides perpendicular to the front edge of the face frame. (To act as handles until the knobs are fastened later, we attached duct tape to the front of each drawer as shown in the photo *above right*.)

3 Find the center of each drawer bottom, and use ¾×#17 brads to toenail the front end of the slides to the drawer front (two brads per front end of each slide). See the Drawer-slide detail on *page 47* for reference. Slide the drawers into the openings, and square the front of the drawer with the face frame. Next, working from the back of the cabinet, mark the locations, and then, glue and brad-nail the back ends of the slides to the drawer bottoms. (We numbered each drawer and corresponding opening for a custom fit of the drawers to the openings and guides).

4 Reinsert the drawers, and check that the front faces of the drawers are flush with the face frame. If you find a drawer that is not flush, mark a line along its edges as shown in the photo *above right* to indicate the

If the front of a drawer protrudes beyond the face frame, mark the protrusion. Then, plane and sand it flush with the face frame.

protrusion. Now, plane and sand the drawer front even with the lines. Recheck against the face frame.

CUT AND APPLY THE TRIM

1 Cut one piece of ¾" cherry to 4" wide by 8' long for trim pieces (CC, DD, EE, FF).

2 Follow the six-cut sequence shown in the drawing *opposite* to form the trim pieces.

3 Miter-cut the top and bottom front and side trim pieces to lengths required by the actual dimensions of your cabinet's sides and front. Then, mark and cut the notch along the bottom edge of the front trim piece (CC) where dimensioned on the Bottom Trim detail accompanying the Exploded View drawing.

4 Clamp the bottom trim pieces (CC, DD) firmly in place with the mitered ends flush. Glue and clamp the trim pieces to the cabinet

and remove the clamps. Attach the top trim pieces (EE, FF).

5 Now, cut the shelf front trim pieces (GG) to size for each shelf. Glue and clamp the trim pieces to the fronts of the shelves (F). Later, sand the shelves smooth.

ADD THE SHELVES, DOORS, DRAWERS, AND FINISH

1 Make a shelf-hole template like that shown *opposite, far right*. Mark a B on the bottom end; this will prevent you from inadvertently flopping it end for end.

2 Using the shelf-hole template and a depth-stop on your drill bit, drill ¼" holes ⅜" deep into the sides (A) and divider (D) where shown on the Exploded View drawing.

3 Mark the center points, and drill the holes for the Shaker knobs in the drawers and doors.

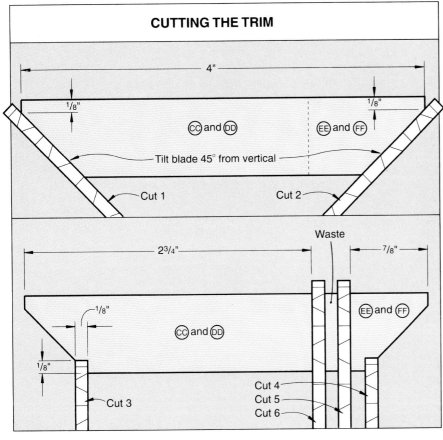

CUTTING THE TRIM

4"

1/8"

1/8"

CC and DD   EE and FF

Tilt blade 45° from vertical

Cut 1   Cut 2

2³/₄"   Waste   7/8"

1/8"

CC and DD   EE and FF

1/8"

Cut 3   Cut 4
Cut 5
Cut 6

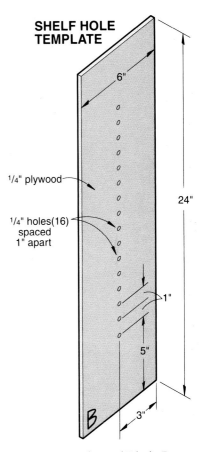

SHELF HOLE TEMPLATE

6"

1/4" plywood

1/4" holes(16)
spaced
1" apart

24"

1"

5"

B   3"

4 Mark the center points, and drill the holes for a pair of bullet catches in each door where shown on the Exploded View drawing and the bullet Catch detail accompanying the Door drawing. Do not insert the catches in the doors just yet.

5 Add the hinges to the doors where shown on the Door drawing. Next, with an equal gap at the top and bottom, fasten the hinged doors to the cabinet.

6 Remove the hinges from the doors and stiles. Sand the cabinet, back, drawers, doors, and adjustable shelves smooth. Add the finish to all parts, including the Shaker knobs, being careful not to get any finish into the holes for the knobs, the tenons on the end of each knob, and in the bullet-catch holes.

7 Insert the bullet catches and reattach the doors to the cabinet. Mark the mating bullet-catch strike locations on the face-frame rails (J, L). With the groove in the bullet-catch strike opening toward the front of the cabinet, nail the strikes to the top and bottom rails, centered over or under the protruding ball of each catch when the door is closed.

8 Position the back in the rabbeted opening, and nail it in place. Glue the shaker knobs in place. Insert the shelf clips and add the adjustable shelves.

BUYING GUIDE

• **Hardware.** 4—³/₈×½" bullet catches and strikes (#28464), 2 pairs ¾×2½" no-mortise hinges (#28696), 12—1⅛"-diameter cherry Shaker knobs (#78469), 16 shelf clips (#62067—4 sets). Kit No. 80870. For current prices, contact The Woodworkers' Store, 21801 Industrial Blvd., Rogers, MN 55374-9514, or call 612/428-2199 to order.

PROJECT TOOL LIST

- Tablesaw
- Dado blade or dado set
- Portable drill
- Doweling jig
- Bits: ¼", ⅜", ⁷/₁₆"
- Router
- Dovetail jig
- Bits: dovetail jig
- Bits: dovetail, ¼" round-over, flush-trimming
- Finishing sander

Note: *We built the project using the tools listed. You may be able to substitute other tools or equipment for listed items you don't have. Additional common hand tools and clamps may be required to complete the project.*

For the Young at Heart

They just don't build 'em like they used to. That's especially true of kids toys and furnishings, and it's why heirloom wooden toys are among today's most sought-after collectibles. When you build our Happy-Days High Chair—or any of the other designed-to-last projects in this section— you can be sure your work will be appreciated by generations of kids to come!

Wagons, Ho!

For the youngster who's always on the go

Whether hauling building blocks or giving teddy bear a ride, this handsome four-wheeler will help your youngster get the job done. And you'll appreciate the wagon for its box-jointed corners, walnut trim, and sturdy hardwood construction.

Note: *You'll need some thin stock for this project. You can either resaw or plane thicker stock to size. See the Buying Guide on page 55 for our wagon-hardware kit.*

START WITH THE WAGON-BOX SIDES

1 From ½"-thick maple, cut the box sides (A), and front and back (B) to the sizes listed in the Bill of Materials on *page 54*.

2 To box-joint the wagon-box pieces (A, B), start by fitting your tablesaw with a zero-clearance insert where shown in the Box-Joint Jig drawing on *page 52*. (Our Delta tablesaw requires a ½"-thick insert; we used plywood.)

3 Mount a ¼" dado blade to your tablesaw (we used a stackable blade). With the blade running, raise the rotating blade through the insert and ½" above the surface of the saw table. Elevate the

blade about ½" more (we found it is best to cut the fingers a bit long and sand them flush with the box sides after assembly).

4 Construct the jig and stopblock shown on the Box-Joint Jig drawing. The stopblock helps steady the long wagon sides, front, and back when cutting the box joints.

5 Carefully locate and cut a pair of ¼"-wide kerfs ¼" apart in the jig. For snug-fitting box joints, the kerfs and the distance between the guide pin and kerf must be exactly ¼". Cut the guide pin to the size stated on the Box-Joint Jig drawing, and glue it into the kerf where shown on the drawing.

6 To box-joint the sides (A) simultaneously, tape the pieces together face-to-face with double-faced tape. Check that the edges and ends are flush. Repeat the taping procedure with the front and back pieces (B).

7 Follow the drawings on the previous page to cut the notches in the side pieces, and then notch
continued

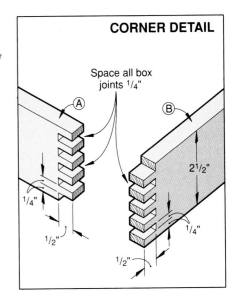

CORNER DETAIL

Space all box joints ¼"

Ⓐ   Ⓑ

2½"

¼"

½"

¼"

½"

Wagons, Ho!

continued

the front and back pieces. (To test the setup, we box-jointed scrap ½" stock before cutting the box pieces.) After notching the ends of each piece, separate the pieces, remove the tape, and sand smooth. (We used a thin, wedge-shaped piece of wood to pry apart the taped-together pieces. If necessary, use a splash of lacquer thinner to dissolve the adhesive on the tape.)

NOW, LET'S ADD THE BOX BOTTOM AND TRIM PIECES

1 Cut a ¼" groove ¼" deep along the inside bottom edge of the box front and back (B) where shown on the Box Assembly drawing and accompanying Groove detail *below*.

2 Edge-join ½" stock to form a 10×18" panel for the wagon bottom (C). Later, scrape off the excess glue, trim to size, sand smooth, and rout a ¼" rabbet ¼" deep along the ends (not the edges) of the wagon bottom.

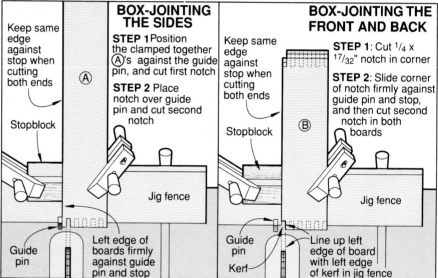

BOX-JOINT JIG

¼ x ½ x 1½" long guide pin

Stopblock

1½"

3"

19"

¼" saw kerf

Miter gauge screwed to jig

Dado blade set ¼" wide and 17/32" (½" plus 1/32") above saw table

2"

¼"

4"

Zero-clearance insert

¾"

BOX-JOINTING THE SIDES

Keep same edge against stop when cutting both ends

STEP 1 Position the clamped together (A)'s against the guide pin, and cut first notch

STEP 2 Place notch over guide pin and cut second notch

Stopblock

(A)

Jig fence

Guide pin

Left edge of boards firmly against guide pin and stop

BOX-JOINTING THE FRONT AND BACK

Keep same edge against stop when cutting both ends

STEP 1: Cut ¼ x 17/32" notch in corner

STEP 2: Slide corner of notch firmly against guide pin and stop, and then cut second notch in both boards

Stopblock

(B)

Jig fence

Guide pin

Kerf

Line up left edge of board with left edge of kerf in jig fence

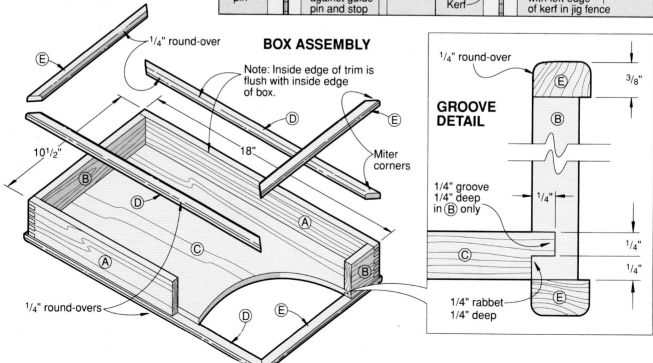

BOX ASSEMBLY

¼" round-over

Note: Inside edge of trim is flush with inside edge of box.

(E)

(D)

(E)

Miter corners

10½"

18"

(B)

(D)

(A)

(C)

(A)

(B)

¼" round-overs

(D)

(E)

GROOVE DETAIL

¼" round-over

(E)

3/8"

(B)

1/4" groove 1/4" deep in (B) only

¼"

(C)

¼"

¼"

(E)

1/4" rabbet 1/4" deep

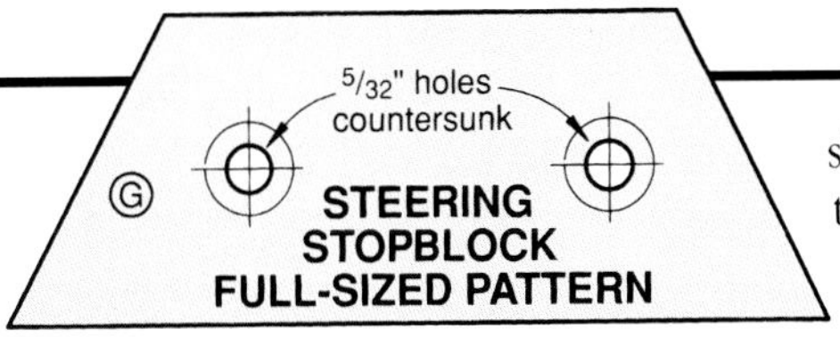
5/32" holes countersunk
G
STEERING STOPBLOCK FULL-SIZED PATTERN

3 Dry-fit the pieces (A, B, C) to check the fit.

4 Cover the mating surfaces of the box-joint fingers of pieces A and B with glue. (To allow the extended open time when applying the glue, we used white woodworker's glue and applied it with a ¼"-wide acid brush.) Glue and clamp the pieces (A, B, C), and check for square. Wipe off excess glue with a damp cloth.

5 Cut two pieces of ⅜" walnut to ⅝" wide by 5' long for trim pieces (D, E). Rout ¼" round-overs along the top edges of each strip. Miter-cut the top and bottom trim pieces (D, E) to length, and glue and clamp them to the box assembly with the inside edges flush where shown on the Box Assembly drawing and accompanying Groove detail.

NEXT, ADD THE FRONT AND REAR WHEEL SUPPORTS

1 Cut the lazy-Susan spacer (F) to size from ⅜" plywood. Glue and clamp it to the box bottom.

2 Using the Parts View drawing for reference, cut the steering stopblock (G) and axle-support spacer (H) to size. Cut the undercarriage tongue parts (I, J) to the sizes listed in the Bill of Materials.

3 Using the Parts View drawing for reference, mark the taper-cut lines on one edge of parts I and J. Bandsaw along the outside of each marked line, and then sand to the line to shape the pieces.

4 Referring to the Parts View drawing, mark the outlines and hole center points for the axle struts (K, L), and cut them to size. Note that part K is ¼" shorter in length than part L. Next, drill the axle holes where marked.

5 Cut the rear-axle spacer (M) to size. Drill the mounting holes, and glue and screw the rear-axle struts (L) to the spacer (M).

6 Drill the mounting holes and assemble the front undercarriage assembly (H, I, J, K) in the manner shown on the Front-Wheel Support drawing.

7 Drill pilot holes, and screw the lazy-Susan bearing to the support spacer (H). Rotate the bearing slightly, and fasten the other half of the bearing to the underside of the wagon box (F). You'll need to stick the end of your screw driver through the ½" hole in the axle-support spacer (H) to gain access to the screw heads when screwing to the underside of the wagon box.

ADD THE HANDLE FOR EASY PULLING

1 Cut the handle supports (N) to shape, using the five steps listed on the Handle-Support Blank drawing on *page 55*.

2 Cut the handle stem (O) to size. Drill a ½" hole ½" from one end where shown on the Exploded View drawing. Mark and cut a ½" radius on the same end as the hole for the handle dowel.

3 Glue the handle supports to the handle, being sure to keep the ¼" holes in the supports aligned with each other. Sand smooth.

4 Sand a slight round-over on all edges of the handle where shown on the Exploded View drawing.

5 Cut a ½" birch dowel to 5½" long. Sand a slight chamfer on the ends, and glue it in place in the ½" hole in the handle.

continued

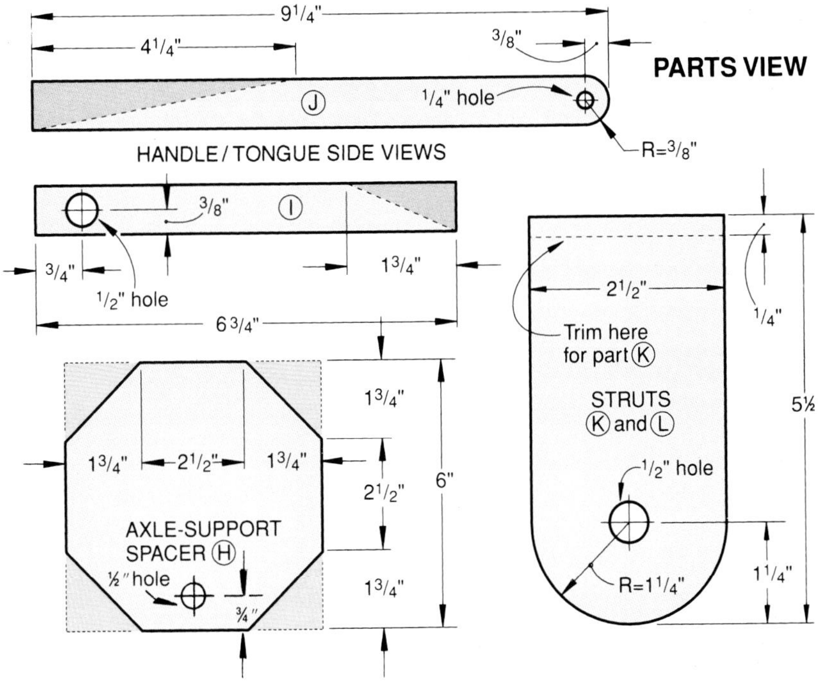
PARTS VIEW
9 1/4"
4 1/4"
3/8"
J
1/4" hole
R=3/8"
HANDLE / TONGUE SIDE VIEWS
3/8"
I
3/4"
1/2" hole
1 3/4"
6 3/4"
2 1/2"
1/4"
Trim here for part K
STRUTS K and L
5½"
1/2" hole
R=1 1/4"
1 1/4"
1 3/4"
2 1/2"
1 3/4"
6"
1 3/4"
AXLE-SUPPORT SPACER H
½" hole
¾"

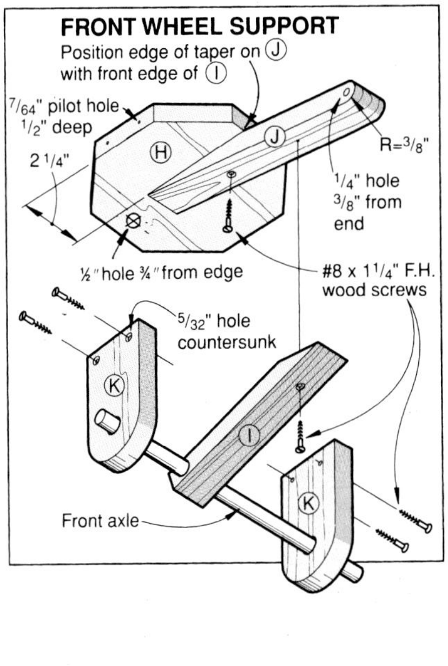
FRONT WHEEL SUPPORT
Position edge of taper on J with front edge of I
7/64" pilot hole 1/2" deep
2 1/4"
H
J
R=3/8"
1/4" hole 3/8" from end
½" hole ¾" from edge
#8 x 1 1/4" F.H. wood screws
5/32" hole countersunk
K
I
K
Front axle

Wagons, Ho!

continued

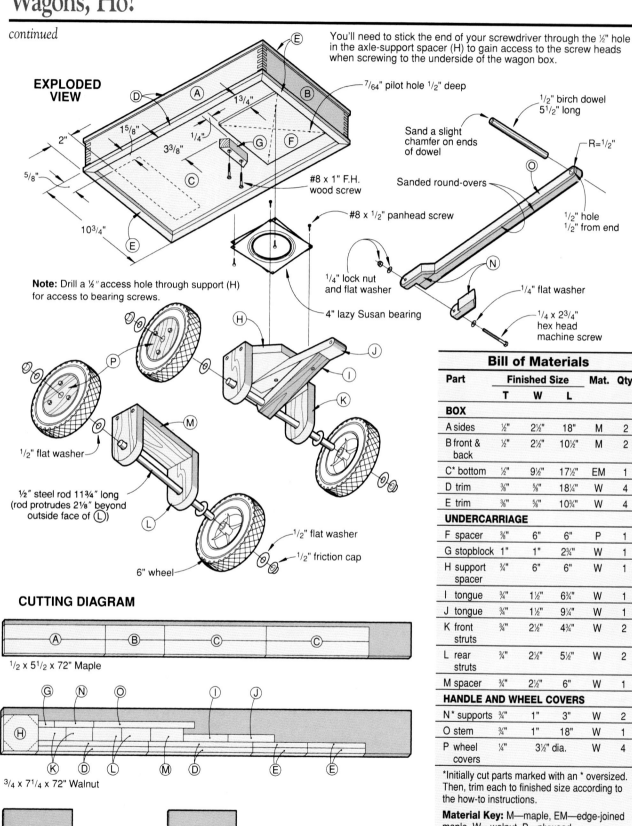

EXPLODED VIEW

2"

$1^{5}/_{8}$"

$1^{3}/_{4}$"

$1/_{4}$"

$3^{3}/_{8}$"

$5/_{8}$"

$10^{3}/_{4}$"

$7/_{64}$" pilot hole $1/_{2}$" deep

#8 x 1" F.H. wood screw

You'll need to stick the end of your screwdriver through the $1/_{2}$" hole in the axle-support spacer (H) to gain access to the screw heads when screwing to the underside of the wagon box.

$1/_{2}$" birch dowel $5^{1}/_{2}$" long

Sand a slight chamfer on ends of dowel

Sanded round-overs

R=$1/_{2}$"

$1/_{2}$" hole $1/_{2}$" from end

#8 x $1/_{2}$" panhead screw

$1/_{4}$" lock nut and flat washer

$1/_{4}$" flat washer

$1/_{4}$ x $2^{3}/_{4}$" hex head machine screw

4" lazy Susan bearing

Note: Drill a $1/_{2}$" access hole through support (H) for access to bearing screws.

$1/_{2}$" flat washer

$1/_{2}$" steel rod $11^{3}/_{4}$" long (rod protrudes $2^{1}/_{8}$" beyond outside face of (L))

$1/_{2}$" flat washer

$1/_{2}$" friction cap

6" wheel

CUTTING DIAGRAM

$1/_{2}$ x $5^{1}/_{2}$ x 72" Maple

$3/_{4}$ x $7^{1}/_{4}$ x 72" Walnut

$1/_{4}$ x 12 x 12" Walnut

$3/_{8}$ x 12 x 12" plywood

Bill of Materials

Part	Finished Size			Mat.	Qty.
	T	W	L		
BOX					
A sides	$1/_{2}$"	$2^{1}/_{2}$"	18"	M	2
B front & back	$1/_{2}$"	$2^{1}/_{2}$"	$10^{1}/_{2}$"	M	2
C* bottom	$1/_{2}$"	$9^{1}/_{2}$"	$17^{1}/_{2}$"	EM	1
D trim	$3/_{8}$"	$5/_{8}$"	$18^{1}/_{4}$"	W	4
E trim	$3/_{8}$"	$5/_{8}$"	$10^{3}/_{4}$"	W	4
UNDERCARRIAGE					
F spacer	$3/_{8}$"	6"	6"	P	1
G stopblock	1"	1"	$2^{3}/_{4}$"	W	1
H support spacer	$3/_{4}$"	6"	6"	W	1
I tongue	$3/_{4}$"	$1^{1}/_{2}$"	$6^{3}/_{4}$"	W	1
J tongue	$3/_{4}$"	$1^{1}/_{2}$"	$9^{1}/_{4}$"	W	1
K front struts	$3/_{4}$"	$2^{1}/_{2}$"	$4^{3}/_{4}$"	W	2
L rear struts	$3/_{4}$"	$2^{1}/_{2}$"	$5^{1}/_{2}$"	W	2
M spacer	$3/_{4}$"	$2^{1}/_{2}$"	6"	W	1
HANDLE AND WHEEL COVERS					
N* supports	$3/_{4}$"	1"	3"	W	2
O stem	$3/_{4}$"	1"	18"	W	1
P wheel covers	$1/_{4}$"		$3^{1}/_{2}$" dia.	W	4

*Initially cut parts marked with an * oversized. Then, trim each to finished size according to the how-to instructions.

Material Key: M—maple, EM—edge-joined maple, W—walnut, P—plywood
Supplies: (other than those listed in the Buying Guide): $1/_{2}$" birch dowel $5^{1}/_{2}$" long, double-faced tape, #8 x1" flathead wood screws, #8 x$1^{1}/_{4}$" flathead wood screws, clear finish.

NOW, FOR THE WHEEL COVERS

1 Use a compass or the full-sized wheel-cover pattern to mark four 3½" circles on ¼" walnut stock (we resawed thicker stock) for the wheel covers (P).

2 Cut the wheel covers to shape, cutting just outside the marked line. Now, sand to the line to finish the shaping. (We bandsawed the covers to shape, and then used our disc sander to sand to the line to finish the shaping.)

3 Transfer the ½" and 5⁄32" hole center points to each wheel cover, and then drill the holes where marked. (Using double-faced tape, we adhered the wheel covers together face-to-face with the edges flush. Then, we used spray adhesive to adhere a photocopy of the wheel-cover pattern to the top piece. Next, we drilled through all four wheel covers at one time to drill the ½" and 5⁄32" holes. Finally, we pried apart the pieces with a wooden wedge, and removed the tape.)

IT'S ALMOST PLAYTIME

1 Finish-sand, and apply the finish. For indoors use, we recommend polyurethane. For use outdoors, apply spar varnish.

2 Fasten the handle to tongue part (J). Fasten the wheel covers to the wheels where shown on the Wheel Assembly drawing.

3 Using the Exploded View drawing for reference, mount the wheels to the wagon.

BUYING GUIDE

• **Wagon-hardware kit.** 4—6"-diameter wheels; 2—½" steel rods 11¾" long with 4—½" friction caps and 8—½" flat washers; 4" lazy Susan bearing with 8—#8x½" panhead wood screws; ¼x2¾" hex-head machine screw with 2—¼" flat washers and a ¼" lock nut; 12—8-32x1¼" roundhead brass machine screws with 24—#8 brass flat washers and 12—#8 brass cap nuts. Kit No. WDWG. For current prices, contact Miller Hardware, 1300 M. L. King Pkwy., Des Moines, IA 50314, or call 515/283-1724 to order.

PROJECT TOOL LIST

• Tablesaw
• Dado blade or dado set
• Bandsaw
• Belt sander
• Disc sander
• Router
• ¼" round-over bit
• Portable drill
• Drill press
• Circle cutter
• Bits: 7⁄64", 5⁄32", ¼", ½"
• Finishing sander

Note: *We built the project using the tools listed. You may be able to substitute other tools or equipment for listed items you don't have. Additional common hand tools and clamps may be required to complete the project.*

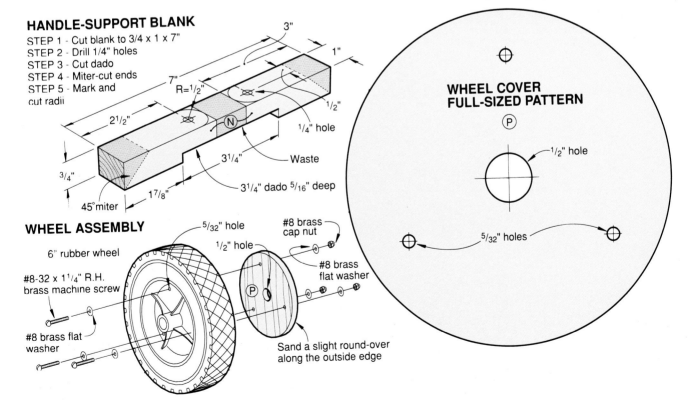

HANDLE-SUPPORT BLANK
STEP 1 - Cut blank to 3/4 x 1 x 7"
STEP 2 - Drill 1/4" holes
STEP 3 - Cut dado
STEP 4 - Miter-cut ends
STEP 5 - Mark and cut radii

3"
1"
7"
R=1/2"
2½"
1/2"
3/4"
45° miter
1 7/8"
3¼"
Waste
3¼" dado 5/16" deep
1/4" hole
N

WHEEL ASSEMBLY
5/32" hole
1/2" hole
#8 brass cap nut
6" rubber wheel
#8-32 x 1¼" R.H. brass machine screw
#8 brass flat washer
#8 brass flat washer
P
Sand a slight round-over along the outside edge

WHEEL COVER FULL-SIZED PATTERN
P
½" hole
5/32" holes

Rough 'n' Ready Wrecker

Every now and then, even the sturdiest toy vehicle "breaks down" somewhere and needs to go to the "shop" for repairs. When that happens at your house, we've got the truck your child needs to get the hauling job done. For heavy loads, simply have him lock the boom's lift bar in the up position just like the real McCoy, and off he'll go.

Note: *You'll need some thin stock for this project. You can either plane or resaw thicker stock to the sizes in the Bill of Materials.*

LAMINATE THE CAB

1 Cut a piece of ¾" pine to 2" wide by 12" long for the cab (A).

2 Measuring 1" from each end of the pine stock, mark the location for a 1⅜" dado. Cut the marked dadoes ½" deep where shown on *page 58, top*.

3 Crosscut the pine into two equal lengths. Mark the windshield location on one piece where shown on the Windshield detail accompanying the Tractor drawing. Align the top of the windshield flush with the top of the dado. Now, drill four ¼" holes inside the marked square. Cut the opening to shape with a scrollsaw or coping saw. Sand or file the edges of the opening.

4 Apply glue to the mating surfaces of cab parts (A), align the dadoes, and clamp. Remove excess glue before it dries.

5 Trim the top and bottom of the cab lamination to length where shown on the Windshield detail.

Bill of Materials

Part	Finished Size			Mat.	Qty.
	T	W	L		
A* cab	1½"	2"	3"	LP	1
B hood	¾"	2"	1½"	P	1
C chassis	¾"	2"	6¾"	P	1
D bed	¾"	¾"	4¼"	P	1
E boom	¾"	1¾"	5⅛"	P	1
F lift bar	¼"	½"	3⅝"	B	1
G hook	¼"	1"	1⅛"	B	1
H* inner wheels	¾"	2" dia.		P	4
I* outer wheels	¾"	2" dia.		P	6

*Initially cut parts marked with an * oversized. Then, trim each to finished size according to the how-to instructions.

Material Key: LP—laminated pine, P—pine, B—birch

Supplies: #8 finish nails, 10–⅜" flat washers, mason's line or $\frac{1}{16}$"-diameter cord, ⅜" dowel stock, ½" dowel stock, 7–½" wood buttons, ⅜" all-thread rod 5½" long with nuts and washers for sanding arbor, clear finish.

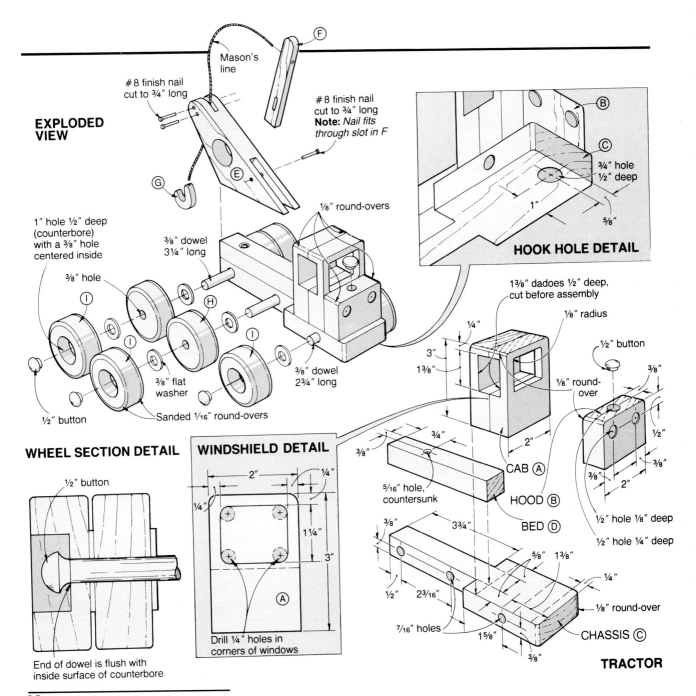

EXPLODED VIEW

Mason's line

#8 finish nail cut to ¾" long

#8 finish nail cut to ¾" long
Note: *Nail fits through slot in F*

1" hole ½" deep (counterbore) with a ⅜" hole centered inside

⅜" hole

⅜" dowel 3¼" long

⅛" round-overs

⅜" flat washer

½" button

Sanded ¹⁄₁₆" round-overs

⅜" dowel 2¾" long

HOOK HOLE DETAIL

¾" hole ½" deep

1"

5⁄8"

WHEEL SECTION DETAIL

½" button

End of dowel is flush with inside surface of counterbore

WINDSHIELD DETAIL

2"

¼"

¼"

1¼"

3"

Drill ¼" holes in corners of windows

1⅜" dadoes ½" deep, cut before assembly

⅛" radius

¼"

3"

1⅜"

⅛" round-over

½" button

⅜"

⅛" round-over

½"

⅜"

2"

⅜"

½" hole ⅛" deep

½" hole ¼" deep

¾"

⅜"

CAB Ⓐ

5⁄16" hole, countersunk

HOOD Ⓑ

BED Ⓓ

⅜"

3¾"

5⁄8"

1⅜"

¼"

⅛" round-over

½"

2³⁄16"

1⅝"

⅜"

7⁄16" holes

CHASSIS Ⓒ

TRACTOR

NOW, CUT THE BODY PARTS

1 Cut the hood (B), chassis (C), and bed (D), to the sizes listed in the Bill of Materials. Cut the chassis to the shape shown on the Tractor drawing.

2 Sand ⅛" round-overs on the hood, cab, and chassis where shown on the Tractor drawing.

3 Mark all the hole center points on the hood, chassis, and bed. One at a time, support each piece with a hand-screw clamp, and drill the holes (we used a drill press) to the sizes listed on the Tractor

drawing. Don't forget to drill a ¾" hole ½" deep on the bottom front of your other toys where shown in the Hook Hole detail accompanying the Exploded View drawing. The hole allows the wrecker hook (G) to fit into it for towing.

4 With the bottom and edges of the cab and hood flush, glue and clamp them together. Recessing the hood ¼" from the front end of the chassis to form the bumper, glue and clamp the cab assembly to the chassis. Later, glue and clamp the bed on top

of the chassis and against the back of the cab. Sand smooth, and glue a ½" button into the radiator-cap hole.

ADD THE BOOM AND LIFT BAR

1 From ¾" pine, cut a block 1¼×5⅛" for the boom (E).

2 Using carbon paper, transfer the boom outline, hole center points, and ⅛" and ¼" slot locations to the boom blank.

continued

Rough 'n' Ready Wrecker

continued

3 Drill the holes to the sizes stated on the Boom drawing.

4 With a bandsaw, cut the slots to size. (You also could use a push block, and cut the slots on the tablesaw.) Cut the boom to shape.

5 Glue the boom to the bed where shown on the Section View drawing.

6 Using carbon paper and the full-sized patterns, transfer the lift bar (F) and the hook (G) outlines, as well as the hole and slot locations for each to ¼" birch stock. Cut the two parts to shape.

7 Form the slot in the lift bar where marked. Using a hand-screw clamp to hold the parts steady, drill a ⅟₁₆" hole through the hook and lift bar where marked. Then, drill the ⅛" counterbores. These holes will hide the boom-line knots later.

8 Snip three #8 finish nails to ¾" long. Position the lift bar in the boom slot. Press the top two nails into the ³⁄₃₂" holes in the boom. (We used a drop of instant glue in each hole to secure the nails.) Align the slot in the lift bar with the lower ³⁄₃₂" hole in the boom, and press the bottom nail into position, trapping the lift bar in the boom slot.

9 Cut a piece of cord (we used mason's line) to about 7" long. Tie a knot on one end and thread the other end through the hole in the lift bar, pulling the knot into the counterbore. Pass the line between the nails in the boom, and thread it through the hole in the hook. Now, tie a knot on this end and tug the line to draw the knot into the hook's ⅛" hole.

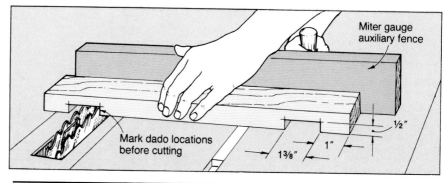

Miter gauge auxiliary fence

Mark dado locations before cutting

½"

1"

1⅜"

NEXT UP, THE WHEELS

1 To make 10 wheels (H, I), cut a piece of ¾"-thick pine to 4x36". Starting 3" from one end, mark 10 center points 3" apart.

2 With a compass, mark a 2"-diameter circle (1" radius) at each marked center point.

3 Chuck a 1" Forstner bit into your drill press. Attach a scrap work surface to your drill-press table. As shown in the photo *opposite, top right*, center the bit over a marked center point, and bore a ½"-deep hole in six of the

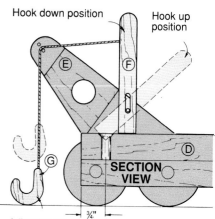

Hook down position

Hook up position

E

F

G

D

SECTION VIEW

¾"

Adjust length of line so hook just touches floor

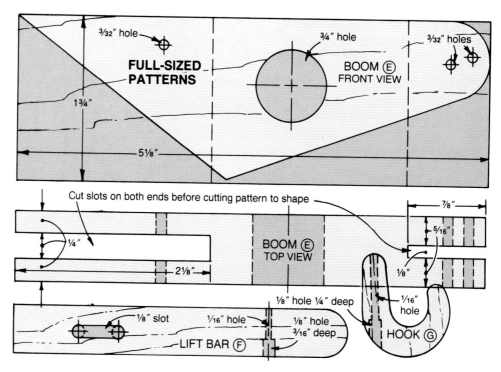

³⁄₃₂" hole

¾" hole

³⁄₃₂" holes

FULL-SIZED PATTERNS

BOOM Ⓔ FRONT VIEW

1¾"

5⅛"

Cut slots on both ends before cutting pattern to shape

⅞"

⁵⁄₁₆"

¼"

2⅛"

BOOM Ⓔ TOP VIEW

⅛"

⅟₁₆" hole

⅛" slot

⅟₁₆" hole

⅛" hole ¼" deep

⅛" hole ³⁄₁₆" deep

LIFT BAR Ⓕ

HOOK Ⓖ

Mark the wheel center points and radii, and use a 1" Forstner bit to drill holes ½" deep for each wheel.

marked circles. (We used the stop on our drill press to ensure a uniform depth.)

4 Chuck a circle cutter into your drill press. Using the drawing *below* for reference, turn the cutter blade so the pointed end is on the inside to cut a perfect wheel. Adjust the circle-cutter arm to cut the correct diameter.

5 Raise the cutter blade ⅝" higher than the bottom of the pilot bit. Center the pilot bit over the depression left by the Forstner bit in each 1" hole or over the marked center point on the four marked circles, and slowly cut the 10 wheels to shape as shown in the photo *above right.*

Center the circle-cutter pilot bit over the Forstner-bit depression, and cut the outside of the wheels to shape.

6 Remove the circle cutter, and chuck a ⅜" twist drill bit into your drill press. Secure a wheel in a small hand-screw clamp, and enlarge the ¼" pilot hole to ⅜". Repeat for each wheel.

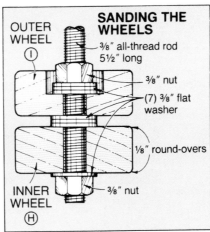

SANDING THE WHEELS

OUTER WHEEL (I)
⅜" all-thread rod 5½" long
⅜" nut
(7) ⅜" flat washer
⅛" round-overs
INNER WHEEL (H)
⅜" nut

7 Cut a piece of ⅜" all-thread rod to 5½" long, and chuck it into your drill press. Then, using nuts and washers, attach a pair of wheels to the work arbor where shown in the drawing *above.* With the drill press running at about 750 rpm, hand-sand a ⅛" round-over on the wheels where shown on the drawing. (We found

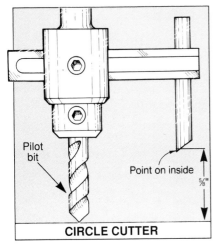

Pilot bit
Point on inside
⅝"

CIRCLE CUTTER

sanding the round-overs safer and easier than trying to rout them on a router table.)

MOUNT THE WHEELS

1 Cut two ⅜" axles to 3¼" long and one to 2¾" long.

2 Glue one wheel onto each dowel axle so the end of the dowel is flush with the inside of the counterbore where shown on the Wheel Section detail. After the glue dries, place ⅜" flat washers on the axles next to the glued wheels. Slide the front axle through the front-axle hole, and add a washer onto the protruding axle end. Glue on the remaining wheel, leaving enough free play so the wheels turn easily. Repeat the process with the back axles, adding an inside wheel and washer on each side of the chassis.

3 To add the hubcaps, set the wrecker on its side. Place a drop of glue on the ends of the axle dowels, and glue a ½" button on the ends of each dowel. After the glue dries, flip over the assembly and repeat for the other hubcaps.

4 Apply a clear finish to all the parts (for a durable finish, we used polyurethane).

PROJECT TOOL LIST
• Tablesaw
• Dado blade or dado set
• Scrollsaw
• Drill press
• Circle cutter
• Bits: 1/16", 3/32", 1/8", 1/4", 5/16", 3/8", 7/16", 1/2", 3/4", 1"
• Finishing sander

Note: *We built the project using the tools listed. You may be able to substitute other tools or equipment for listed items you don't have. Additional common hand tools and clamps may be required to complete the project.*

Happy-Days High Chair

It's super-safe and easy to clean

Happy-Days High Chair

Now, I could tell you all sorts of neat things about this hardwood high chair, but I'll let my son Slade, shown *opposite*, do the talking, or should I say babbling. If I understand him correctly, he's gaga over the sturdy wobble-free construction, and removable and adjustable rimmed tray (for catching those inevitable spills). But he's not cooing over the safety strap that, once buckled keeps him from slipping out to pull the dog's tail.

—*Marlen Kemmet*
How-To Editor

Note: *As shown opposite, we designed and built two contrasting high chairs— one traditional, and one featuring a colorful balloon backrest.*

START WITH THE SPLAYED BASE

1 From 1¹⁄₁₆"-thick stock (we used cherry), cut the legs (A) to the sizes listed in the Bill of Materials on *page 63*. From the same stock, cut the upper side rails (B), and lower side rails (C) to size plus 1" in length.

2 Set your sliding T-bevel at 10°, and mark the angles on the ends of the legs and rails where shown on the Leg Assembly drawing on *page 62*.

3 Miter-cut the rails to length.

4 Mark the four mounting-hole center points on the outside edge of each leg where located on the Leg Assembly drawing. (Don't mark the two footrest mounting holes; you'll drill them later.)

5 Clamp one of the upper side rails (B) to your workbench, and then glue and position one of the legs next to it where shown in Photo A. Drill the counterbored mounting holes through the leg and into the rail where marked and shown in Photo A. Drive the screws. Add the

continued

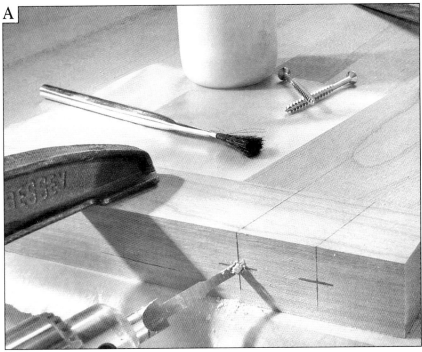

Drill counterbored mounting holes through the leg into the end of the top rail, and drive screws to join the pieces.

Using a miter gauge with a wooden auxiliary fence for support, bevel-rip the top edge of the leg assembly.

Happy-Days High Chair

continued

lower rail in the same manner. Next, glue and fasten the other leg to the two rails. Repeat the process to form the other leg assembly (A, B, C).

6 To obtain the proper angle along the top edges of the two leg assemblies, tilt the blade on your tablesaw 10° from vertical. Add an auxiliary wooden fence to your miter gauge, and angle the miter gauge 10° left of center. Hold one leg assembly outside facedown firmly against the miter gauge, and *check that the top rail is parallel to the miter gauge slot.* (This ensures a straight cut along the top edge of the top rail.) Adjust the miter gauge slightly if necessary.

7 As shown in Photo B, bevel-rip the top edge of each leg assembly. Trim just enough to angle the top edge without shortening the assembly. See the Side View portion of the Leg Assembly drawing *below right* for reference.

8 Reposition the miter gauge 10° right of center. With the outside face up and as shown in Photo C, miter-cut the bottom edges of the feet. Check that the leg assemblies are the same length.

JOIN THE LEG ASSEMBLIES WITH THE STRETCHERS AND FOOTREST

1 Cut the upper stretchers (D) and lower stretchers (E) to size plus 1" in length.

2 As shown in Step 1 of the two-step drawing *opposite top,* tilt the tablesaw blade 1° right of vertical. With the outside facedown, cut an 11° miter across one end of each stretcher. (For tight-fitting joints the 1° angle is necessary.) Miter-cut the opposite end as shown in Step 2.

3 Using masking tape, tape the stretchers between the leg assemblies to check the fit. Trim the stretchers if necessary.

4 Drill mounting holes, and glue and screw the stretchers between the leg assemblies.

C

Adjust the miter gauge 10° right of center, and bevel-rip the bottom edge of the leg assembly parallel to the top edge.

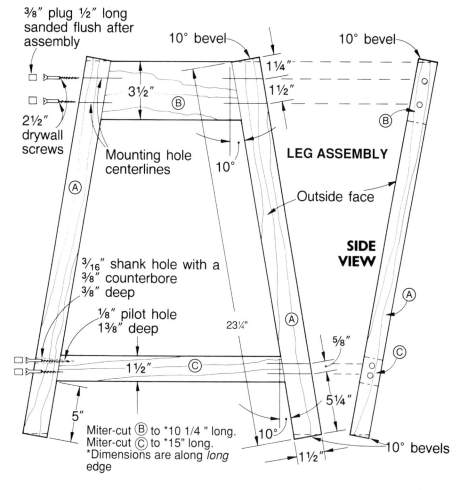

⅜" plug ½" long sanded flush after assembly

10° bevel

10° bevel

1¼"

3½"

1½"

B

B

2½" drywall screws

Mounting hole centerlines

10°

LEG ASSEMBLY

A

Outside face

³⁄₁₆" shank hole with a
⅜" counterbore
⅜" deep

⅛" pilot hole
1⅜" deep

23¼"

SIDE VIEW

A

A

C

5⁄8"

1½"

C

5¼"

5"

Miter-cut Ⓑ to *10 1/4 " long.
Miter-cut Ⓒ to *15" long.
*Dimensions are along *long* edge

10°

1½"

10° bevels

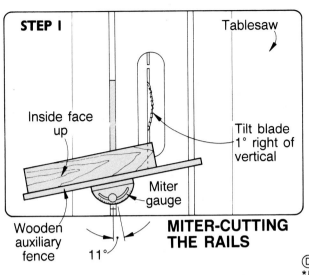

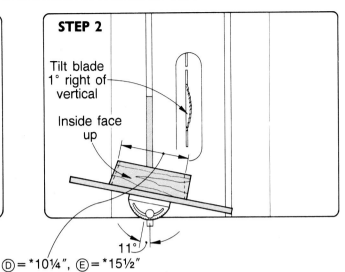

STEP 1

Tablesaw

Inside face up

Tilt blade 1° right of vertical

Miter gauge

Wooden auxiliary fence

11°

MITER-CUTTING THE RAILS

STEP 2

Tilt blade 1° right of vertical

Inside face up

11°

Ⓓ = *10¼", Ⓔ = *15½"
*Dimensions along *short* edge.

CUTTING DIAGRAM

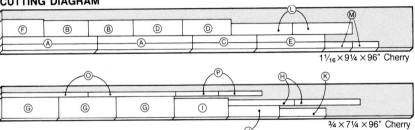

1¹/₁₆ × 9¼ × 96" Cherry

¾ × 7¼ × 96" Cherry

Ⓝ is cut from ¾" cherry plywood

Bill of Materials				
Part	**Finished Size**		**Mat.**	**Qty.**
	T	**W**	**L**	
BASE				
A legs	1¹/₁₆"	1½"	23¼"	C	4
B* upper side rails	1¹/₁₆"	3½"	10¼"	C	2
C* lower side rails	1¹/₁₆"	1½"	15"	C	2
D* upper stretchers	1¹/₁₆"	3½"	11½"	C	2
E* lower stretchers	1¹/₁₆"	1½"	16¹/₁₆"	C	2
F footrest	1¹/₁₆"	4"	13"	C	1
G* seat	¾"	14"	13¼"	EJC	1
BACKREST				
H stiles	¾"	1½"	14⅜"	C	2
I top	¾"	4"	12¾"	C	1
J middle	¾"	2½"	11¾"	C	1
K bottom	¾"	2"	10⅞"	C	1
L armrests	1¹/₁₆"	2½"	14½"	C	2
M supports	1¹/₁₆"	1½"	5⅜"	C	2
TRAY				
N panel	¾"	8¼"	18½"	CP	1
O* trim	¾"	1"	20"	C	2
P* trim	¾"	1"	9¾"	C	2

*Initially cut parts marked with an * oversized. Then, trim each to finished size according to the how-to instructions.

Material Key: C—cherry, EJC—edge-joined cherry, CP—cherry plywood
Supplies: 2" drywall screws, 2½" drywall screws, double-faced tape, #4x½" roundhead wood screws, #8x⅝" flathead wood screws, #8 finish (countersunk) washers, ¼" flat washers, clear finish, acrylic paint for balloon and landscape pattern.

5 Sand ⅛" round-overs along the edges of the base parts where shown on the Base drawing.

6 Cut the footrest (F) to size, bevel-cutting the ends at 10° and then radiusing the front corners. Rout ¼" round-overs on the footrest, stopping where shown on the Base drawing.

7 Position the footrest so it's parallel to the floor and snug between the front legs. Then, drill the mounting holes, and glue and screw it in place.

8 Plane a piece of cherry to ½" thick. Using a ⅜" plug cutter, cut seventy ⅜" plugs from the ½" stock. Plug the holes, matching the grain direction of the plug with the piece being plugged. Save the remaining plugs.

MAKE THE PLATFORM SEAT

1 Edge-join pieces of ¾"-thick stock to form a 14"-square blank for the seat. Crosscut the ends of the blank for a 13¼" length.

2 Mark the location and drill the holes for all of the mounting-hole center points where dimensioned on the Seat Assembly drawing. Note that the three holes used for attaching the backrest to the seat are drilled at 10°. See the Backrest detail accompanying the Seat Assembly drawing on *page 66* for reference.

3 Mark the center points and drill a pair of ¼" holes for each of the three strap slots. With a scrollsaw or coping saw, cut between the ¼" holes to form the slots.

4 Rout ¼" round-overs where shown on the Seat Assembly drawing.

5 Clamp the seat to the base, centered from side to side and front to back. Use the previously drilled mounting holes

continued

continued

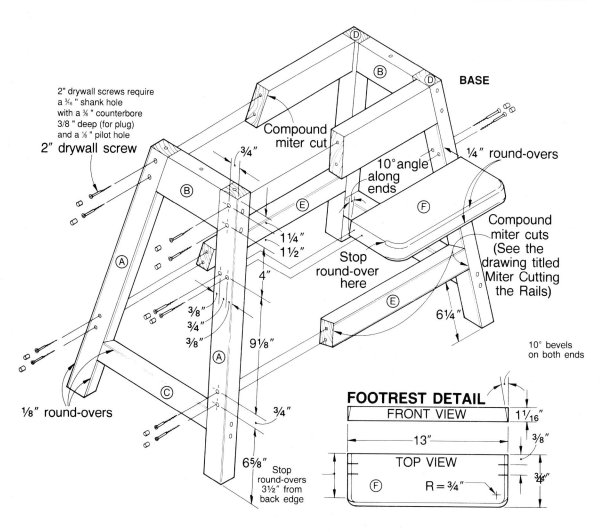

2" drywall screws require a ³⁄₁₆ " shank hole with a ⅜ " counterbore 3/8 " deep (for plug) and a ⅛ " pilot hole

2" drywall screw

Compound miter cut

¾ "

BASE

10°angle along ends

¼ " round-overs

Compound miter cuts (See the drawing titled Miter Cutting the Rails)

1¼ "
1½ "

4 "

Stop round-over here

6¼ "

⅜ "
¾ "
⅜ "

9⅛ "

10° bevels on both ends

¾ "

6⅝ " Stop round-overs 3½" from back edge

⅛ " round-overs

FOOTREST DETAIL

| FRONT VIEW | 1¹⁄₁₆ " |

— 13" —

⅜ "

TOP VIEW

R = ¾ "

¾ "

---

in the seat as guides to drill pilot holes into the base. Do not screw the seat to the base just yet.

NOW, LET'S ADD THE BACKREST

1 Cut the pair of backrest stiles (H) to size. Now, cut the backrest rails (I, J, K) to size, miter-cutting the ends at 5°.

2 Mark and cut a 1" radius at each top corner of the backrest top (I) where shown on the Backrest drawing *opposite*.

3 Mark the hole center points, drill the holes, and screw the backrest assembly (H, I, J, K) together. Plug the holes.

4 Rout ⅜" round-overs along the top edge of the backrest top (I)

where shown on the Seat Assembly drawing on *page 66*. Do not rout the 1" radiused corners. Switch bits, and rout (or sand) ⅛" round-overs along the edges of the back-rest assembly, but not its bottom edge where noted on the Backrest drawing.

5 Tilt your tablesaw blade 10° from vertical, and set your miter gauge 5° from center. Check that the bottom backrest rail (K) is parallel to the miter-gauge slot. Cut the bottom edge of the backrest assembly at 10° where shown on the Backrest detail accompanying the Seat Assembly drawing.

ADD THE ARMRESTS TO SUPPORT THE TRAY

1 Cut the armrests (L) to the size listed in the Bill of Materials, bevel-cutting the back end at 10°.

2 Using the dimensions on the Seat Assembly drawing for reference, mark the radii on the top surface of one armrest. Using double-faced tape, adhere the armrests together face-to-face with the ends and edges flush. Bandsaw the armrests to shape, sand the cut edges smooth, and pry the pieces apart with a wooden wedge. Remove the tape.

3 Rout ¼" round-overs along all but the *back* edges of each armrest as shown on *page 66*.

continued

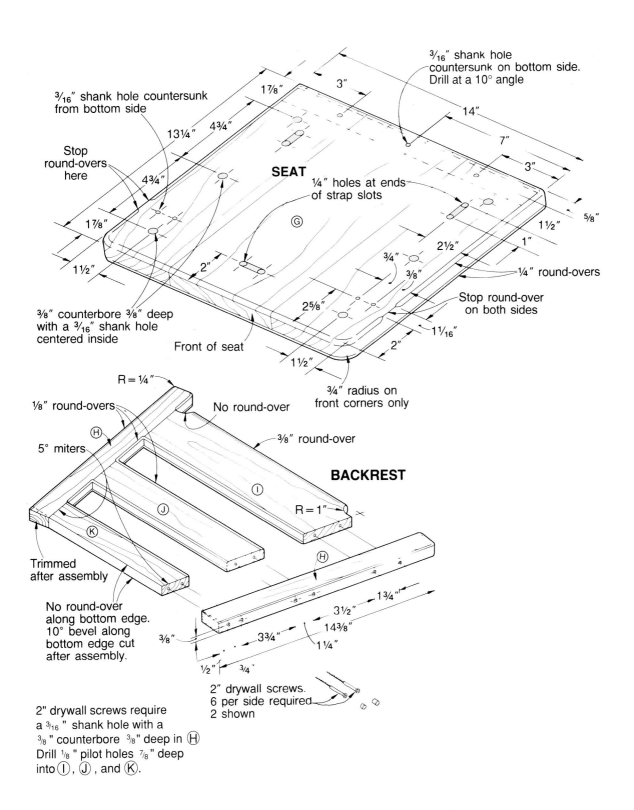

3/16" shank hole countersunk
from bottom side

3/16" shank hole
countersunk on bottom side.
Drill at a 10° angle

Stop
round-overs
here

SEAT

1/4" holes at ends
of strap slots

13¼" 4¾"

14"

7"

3"

1⅞" 3"

1⅞"

G

5/8"

1½"

1½"

2"

¾"

2½"

1"

3/8"

¼" round-overs

⅜" counterbore ⅜" deep
with a 3/16" shank hole
centered inside

2⅝"

Stop round-over
on both sides

Front of seat

1 1/16"

2"

1½"

¾" radius on
front corners only

R = ¼"

No round-over

⅛" round-overs

⅜" round-over

H

BACKREST

5° miters

I

J

R = 1"

K

H

Trimmed
after assembly

13¾"

3½"

14⅜"

No round-over
along bottom edge.
10° bevel along
bottom edge cut
after assembly.

⅜"

3¾"

1¼"

½" ¾

2" drywall screws.
6 per side required
2 shown

2" drywall screws require
a 3/16 " shank hole with a
⅜ " counterbore ⅜" deep in H
Drill ⅛ " pilot holes ⅞" deep
into I, J, and K.

Happy-Days High Chair

continued

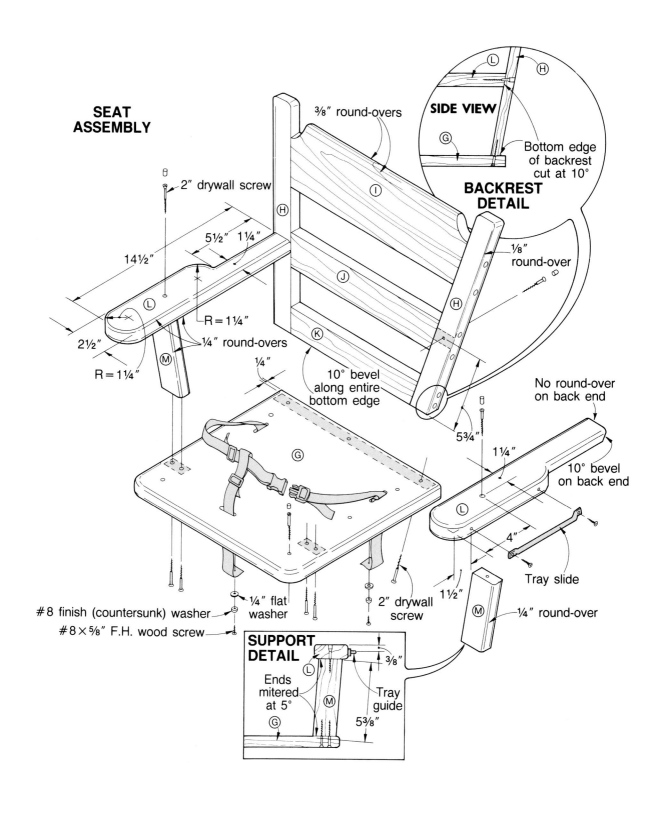

SEAT ASSEMBLY

2″ drywall screw

14½″

5½″ 1¼″

2½″

R = 1¼″

R = 1¼″

¼″ round-overs

¼″

#8 finish (countersunk) washer
#8 × ⅝″ F.H. wood screw

¼″ flat washer

10° bevel along entire bottom edge

2″ drywall screw

1½″

⅜″ round-overs

SIDE VIEW

Bottom edge of backrest cut at 10°

BACKREST DETAIL

⅛″ round-over

5¾″

No round-over on back end

1¼″

10° bevel on back end

4″

Tray slide

¼″ round-over

SUPPORT DETAIL

Ends mitered at 5°

⅜″

Tray guide

5⅜″

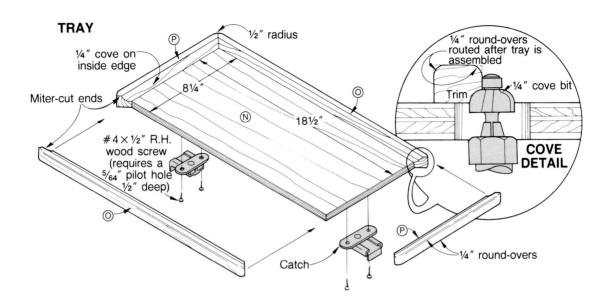

TRAY

½" radius

¼" cove on inside edge

Miter-cut ends

8¼"

18½"

#4 × ½" R.H. wood screw (requires a 5/64" pilot hole ½" deep)

Catch

¼" round-overs routed after tray is assembled

¼" cove bit

Trim

COVE DETAIL

¼" round-overs

4 Cut the armrest supports (M) to size, miter-cutting each end at 5° where shown on the Support detail accompanying the Seat Assembly drawing. Rout a ¼" round-over along all edges (but not the ends) of both supports.

5 Drill mounting holes in each armrest where shown on the Seat Assembly drawing.

A TRAY FOR TINY TOTS

1 Cut the tray panel (N) to size.

2 Cut a pair of ¾×1" cherry strips 32" long (enough stock for two O's and two P's).

3 Rout a ¼" cove along the top inside edge of each strip where shown on the Cove detail accompanying the Tray drawing.

4 Miter-cut one part O and one part P from each strip. Glue and clamp the four trim pieces to the tray panel.

5 Rout ¼" round-overs along the top and bottom edges of the assembled tray. Sand the tray.

ASSEMBLE THE PIECES, AND ADD THE FINISH

1 Glue and screw the backrest to the seat.

2 Glue and screw the armrest supports to the seat, and then glue and screw the armrests to the backrest and supports. Now, drill the mounting holes, and glue and screw the armrests to the backrest.

3 Next, glue and screw the seat/backrest assembly to the base.

4 Glue the remaining plugs in place. Finish-sand the entire chair, and add the finish.

5 If you've decided to go with the balloon backrest, rough-up the finish with 00 steel wool. Then, using acrylics, paint the balloon and landscape pattern.

6 Attach the tray glides to the armrests where shown on the Seat Assembly drawing. Position the tray on the armrests so the back edge of the tray is 5½" from the front edge of the backrest. Center the tray from side to side and lightly clamp to the armrests. Position the catches and screw them to the underside of the tray. The catches should fit into the rearmost notches in the tray glides in this position.

7 Finally, to keep the little one safely strapped in place (and they do love to try and get out when you're not looking), add the three straps shown on the Seat Assembly drawing. See the Buying Guide for our source of strapping material and fasteners.

BUYING GUIDE

• **Tray-support hardware.** Tray glide and catch, made of cold rolled steel and zinc plated. Catalog No. 30866. For current prices, contact Woodworkers' Store, 21801 Industrial Blvd., Rogers, MN 55374-9514, or call 612/428-3200 to order.

• **Strap and buckles.** Six feet of 1"-wide blue nylon webbing and plastic buckles. Contact Miller Hardware, 1300 M.L. King Pkwy, Des Moines, IA 50314, or call 612/428-3200 or 515/283-1234 to order.

PROJECT TOOL LIST

• Tablesaw
• Scrollsaw
• Bandsaw
• Portable drill
• Bits: 5/64", 7/64", 5/32", ¼", 3/8" 3/8" plug cutter
• Router
• Router table
• Bits: ⅛" round-over, ¼" round-over, 3/8" round-over, ¼" cove
• Finishing sander

Note: *We built the project using the tools listed. You may be able to substitute other tools or equipment for listed items you don't have. Additional common hand tools and clamps may be required to complete the project.*

Standing-Tall Blocks Box

For kids living in a grown-up world

There comes a time in every child's life when being just a few inches taller would open up great new possibilities. Whether it's getting a drink of water or turning off the light, many kids wobble through this stage balancing on chairs or other precarious perches. Here's a better plan: let them stand taller on this sturdy box of blocks.

1 Rip and crosscut the front and back (A), ends (B), and top and bottom (C) to the dimensions shown in the Bill of Materials. Cut the trim strips (D and E) and eight 5¼" squares for the numbers and letters from ⅛" plywood or tempered hardboard. Refer to the Exploded View drawing, *opposite*, and then assemble the sides and ends with screws and woodworker's glue.

2 Place the front and back between the ends. Attach the top and bottom, and then sand the box smooth and the corners flush. Now, add the trim strips. Place a long strip (D) on one end face, flush with the top edge of the box. Cut or sand the ends flush

with the front and back of the box, and attach the strip with woodworker's glue and brads (we used ½"×#18 brads).

3 Place another long strip along the bottom. Then, complete the square frame on the end by fitting short trim strips (E) vertically

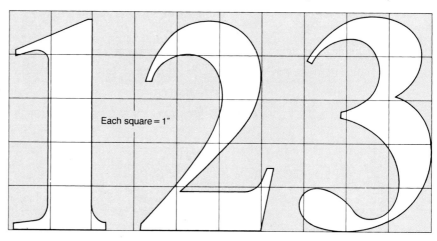

Each square = 1"

between the horizontal pieces. Keep the edges flush at the front and back of the box.

4 Attach strips to the other end, then to the front and back, and lastly to the top. Leave a ⅛" space where shown on the top, front, and back to create the look of two separate blocks.

5 Enlarge the letter and numeral patterns *below* with gridded paper or an enlarging photocopier. Enlarge at 129 percent, again at 129 percent, and then at 121 percent. Separate the patterns, and then affix one to each of six of the squares with spray adhesive.

6 Because you need a total of eight figures, stack-cut two copies of the "A" and "B." To do this, adhere one of the remaining squares to the back of the piece with the "A" pattern and the other to the piece with the "B" pattern using double-faced tape. Drill blade start holes where indicated on the "A" and "B" patterns. Then, cut out the letters and numerals, starting with the inside cuts. (We drilled ¼" blade start holes and used a .110 x.022" blade with 15 teeth per inch.) Center a letter or numeral in each square, and attach with glue and brads.

7 Fill the brad holes and trim-strip joints as necessary. Sand, rounding over the corners slightly, and apply white latex primer.

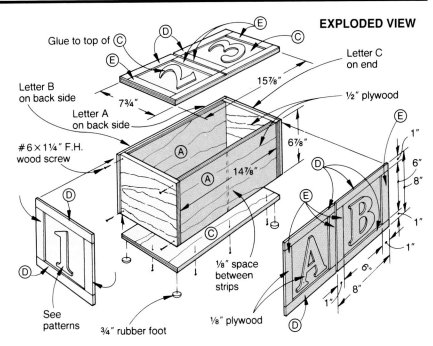

EXPLODED VIEW

Glue to top of Ⓒ

Letter C on end

½" plywood

Letter B on back side

Letter A on back side

15⅞"

7¾"

#6 × 1¼" F.H. wood screw

6⅞"

14⅞"

1"

6"

8"

1"

1"

See patterns

¾" rubber foot

⅛" space between strips

⅛" plywood

6"

8"

1"

8 Paint the step stool with white latex enamel, and accent the raised faces with brightly colored enamels. Apply two coats of clear acrylic after the paint dries. Attach ¾" rubber bumpers to the bottom to prevent skidding.

PROJECT TOOL LIST
- Tablesaw
- Scrollsaw
- Portable drill or drill press
- ¼" bit
- Finishing sander

Note: *We built the project using the tools listed. You may be able to substitute other tools or equipment for listed items* *you don't have. Additional common hand tools and clamps may be required to complete the project.*

Part	Finished Size			Mat.	Qty.
	T	**W**	**L**		
A side	½"	6⅞"	14⅞"	P	2
B end	½"	6⅞"	7¾"	P	2
C top and bottom	½"	7¾"	15⅞"	P	2
D* long trim	⅛"	1"	8¼"	P	16
E* short trim	⅛"	1"	6¼"	P	16

Bill of Materials

*Initially cut parts marked with an * oversized. Then, trim each to finished size according to the how-to instructions.

Material Key: P—plywood

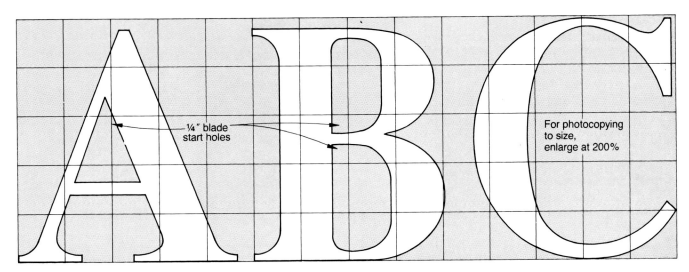

¼" blade start holes

For photocopying to size, enlarge at 200%

All Aboard the Wood Express

Another last-a-lifetime winner from the Build-a-Toy™ contest

When reader Richard Zichos of Pasadena, Maryland, entered his creation in our 1991 contest, his primary aim was to make some lucky child happy at Christmas. Little did he know that he also would walk away with $1,850 worth of merchandise—a $1,600 Shopsmith Mark V multipurpose woodworking machine and $250 in power tools from Seven Corners Ace Hardware. And who said it doesn't pay to be a nice guy?

Note: *You'll need some thin stock for this project. You can resaw or plane thicker stock to the thickness listed in the Bill of Materials. For our source of wheels, pegs, people, cup hooks, screw eyes, and dry-transfer labels, see the Buying Guide on page 75.*

START WITH THE BOILER AND TANK LAMINATION

1 Cut four pieces of ¾"-thick maple to 3x15½" for the boiler/tank lamination. Plane or resaw two of the pieces to ⅝" thick.

2 With the edges and ends flush, glue the four pieces face-to-face in the configuration shown on the Boiler/Tank Lamination drawing *below*. Later, remove the clamps, scrape off the excess glue from one edge, plane that edge smooth, and then rip the opposite edge for a 2¾" finished width.

3 Using the Boiler/Tank Lamination drawing for dimensions, mark all the hole center points (top and front) on the boiler portion, and drill the holes. (We used Forstner bits.)

4 Tilt your tablesaw blade 45° from vertical, and bevel-rip each corner of the lamination at 45° where shown on the Boiler/Tank Lamination drawing. Crosscut the boiler (A) and tanker-car tank (C) to length.

5 Rout a ¼" round-over along the edges of the front end of the boiler where shown on the Locomotive drawing on *page 72*. Sand smooth.

BOILER/TANK LAMINATION

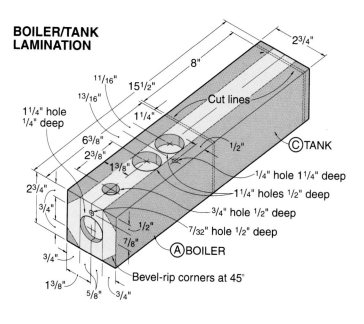

CUT THE PARTS AND ASSEMBLE THE LOCOMOTIVE

1 Cut a ¾"-thick piece of maple to 3½×12¼" for the pilot/chassis (B).

2 Using the dimensions on the drawing *below*, lay out the angled front end, notches, and hole center points on the chassis.

3 Drill the ⁵⁄₁₆" axle-pin holes centered along the edges.

4 To cut the pilot/chassis front end to shape, tilt your tablesaw blade 45° from vertical. Attach an auxiliary fence to your miter gauge, and angle the gauge 45° from center. Following the previously marked lines, miter-cut one edge of the pilot/chassis as shown in the photo at *right*. Readjust the miter gauge to cut 45° on the opposite side of center, and angle-cut the opposite edge.

5 Being careful to sand an equal amount from both edges, sand a ⅛" flat across both bevel-cut front edges of the pilot/chassis to remove the sharp edge.

6 From ¾" maple, cut the cab base (C) to size. Then, from ¼"-thick maple (we resawed ¾" stock), cut the cab floor (D), side walls (E), front cut the two side bars (H) to size.

7 Drill a ⅛" hole through the cab floor (D) where located on the Locomotive drawing. Using the Cab detail accompanying the Locomotive drawing for reference, cut a window in both side walls, and sand a chamfer across the bottom back surface of the roof.

8 With the back edges flush, glue and clamp the cab base (C) to the pilot/chassis (B).

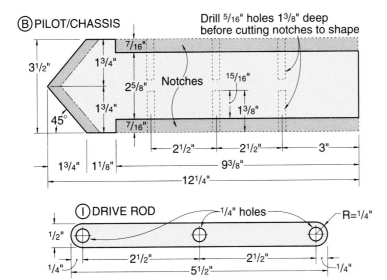

PARTS VIEW

continued

All Aboard the Wood Express

continued

9 Dry-clamp the cab assembly (D, E, F), and check that the outside surfaces of the cab are flush with the outside edges of the boiler. Trim if necessary. The sides must be flush for adding the side bars (H) later. Glue and clamp the cab assembly together, and later glue the roof on.

10 With the front edge of the base (C) flush with the front edge of the cab assembly, glue and clamp the cab to the base. Next, glue and clamp the boiler to the chassis and to the front of the base and cab.

ADD THE WHEELS (DRIVERS) AND DECORATIVE ACCESSORIES

1 Drill a ⁷⁄₃₂" hole ⁹⁄₁₆" deep and ⅝" from the center point of each of the six drivers (2¼"-diameter wheels)

where shown on the Wheel detail accompanying the Locomotive drawing. (We used a brad-point bit to eliminate bit wander.)

2 Either sand or rout a ¼" round-over on both ends of a long length of 1¼" dowel stock. Then, cut the headlamp and front sand dome to length. (Railroaders used the sand domes to hold sand that they could deposit onto the track for extra traction.) Round-over another end of the dowel and cut the rear sand dome to length.

3 Stain the locomotive parts as shown in the opening photo. (We used a walnut gel stain.) Glue the parts in place, wiping off excess glue with a damp cloth.

4 Using the Parts View drawing for reference, transfer the drive rod (I) outline and hole center points to a piece of ⅛" stock. Repeat to make another pattern. Drill the holes, and then cut the two drive rods to shape.

5 To make six brass bushings for the locomotive wheels (drivers), use a pipe cutter or hacksaw to cut six pieces of ¼" brass or copper tubing to ⁵⁄₁₆" long. Hand-sand the cut ends smooth (we did this with 220-grit sandpaper).

6 Using toy axle pegs, pin the 2¼"-diameter wheels to the chassis, and then pin the drive rod and bushings to the wheels.

7 Glue the engineer in the hole in the cab.

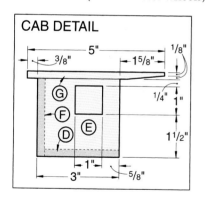

CAB DETAIL

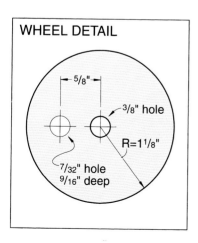

WHEEL DETAIL

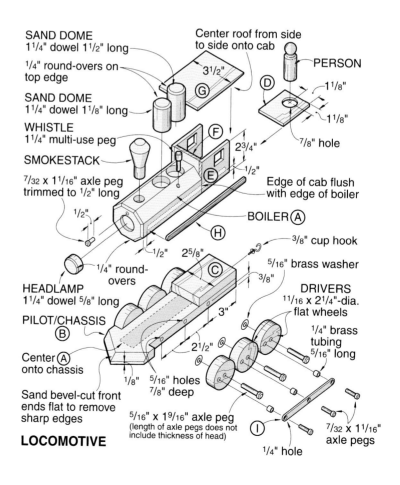

Build a chassis that fits all the cars

1 To form the trucks (A), cut two pieces of ¾" maple and one piece of ½" maple to 1⅜x24". With the edges and ends flush, glue and clamp the pieces face-to-face. Scrape and plane both edges for a 1¼" finished thickness.

2 For each car, cut a pair of trucks (A) to length from the lamination. Cut and sand ⅜" round-overs on the ends of each where shown on the Chassis drawing and accompanying Truck detail. (We held the trucks with a hand-screw clamp when band-sawing the ends; do not try to hand-hold these small pieces when cutting.)

3 Mark the center points on each truck where located on the Truck detail. Hold the pieces steady with a hand-screw clamp, and drill the holes on the drill press. (We used a depth gauge to ensure consistent depth from hole to hole.)

4 Cut a chassis (B) to size for each car, cutting a ¼" radius on each corner. Rout ⅛" round-overs along all edges of each chassis.

5 Drill a 1/16" pilot hole ⅜" deep centered in each end of each chassis and back end of the locomotive for adding the cup hooks and screw eyes later. The caboose needs only one hole.

6 Glue and clamp a pair of trucks to each chassis where located on the Chassis drawing. Do not add the wheels until each car has been fully assembled.

7 Using the Exploded View drawings and accompanying Bill of Materials, cut the pieces and assemble each car.

8 After assembling the entire train, finish-sand each car, and peg the wheels to the trucks.

continued

Bill of Materials

Part	Finished Size T	W	L	Mat.	Qty.
LOCOMOTIVE					
A* boiler	2¾"	2¾"	6⅜"	LM	1
B pilot/ chassis	¾"	3½"	12¼"	M	1
C base	¾"	2⅝"	4"	M	1
D floor	¼"	2¼"	2¾"	M	1
E sides	¼"	2¾"	3"	M	2
F front	¼"	2¼"	2¾"	M	1
G roof	¼"	3½"	5"	M	1
H side bars	⅛"	½"	8½"	M	2
I drive rods	⅛"	½"	5½"	M	2

*Initially cut part marked with an * oversized. Then, trim it to finished size according to the how-to instructions.

Material Key: LM—laminated maple, M—maple

Supplies: 1¼" dowel stock, 5/16" brass flat washers, ¼" brass tubing, stain, polyurethane.

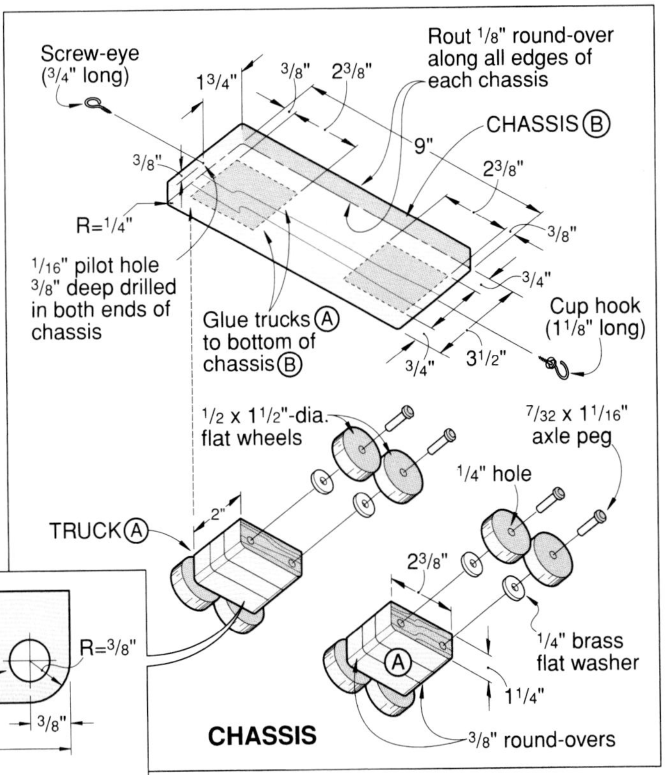
Screw-eye
(3/4" long)
1 3/4"
3/8"
2 3/8"
Rout 1/8" round-over along all edges of each chassis
CHASSIS (B)
9"
2 3/8"
3/8"
R=1/4"
3/8"
1/16" pilot hole 3/8" deep drilled in both ends of chassis
Glue trucks (A) to bottom of chassis (B)
3/4"
Cup hook
(1 1/8" long)
3/4"
3 1/2"
1/2 x 1 1/2"-dia. flat wheels
7/32 x 1 1/16" axle peg
1/4" hole
TRUCK (A)
2"
2 3/8"
1/4" brass flat washer
(A)
1 1/4"
3/8" round-overs
CHASSIS

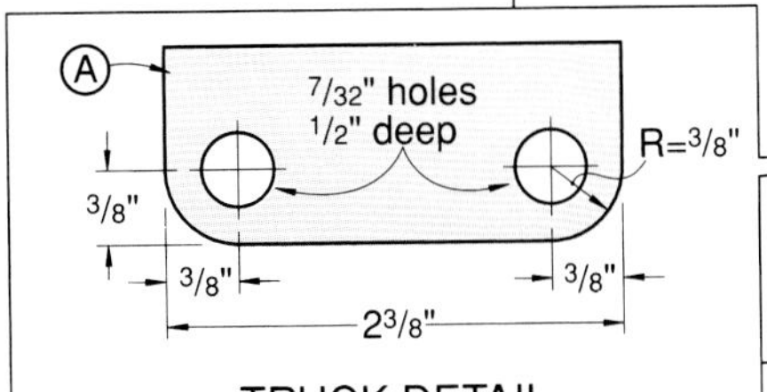
(A)
7/32" holes
1/2" deep
R=3/8"
3/8"
3/8"
3/8"
2 3/8"
TRUCK DETAIL

All Aboard the Wood Express

continued

9 To apply the dry-transfer decals, see the Buying Guide *opposite* for our source of the dry-transfer decals, burnishing tool, and application instructions. Use the opening photo and the wording on our train. Finish with a clear polyurethane. Do not use lacquer over the dry-transfer labels. Lacquer will dissolve the labels and adhesive.

To form the grooves for the car doors (E), cut a pair of 1/8" grooves 1/8" deep in the top face of the chassis (B) and bottom face of the roof (F). Cut 1/8" rabbets 1/8" deep along the top and bottom edges of each door. Glue the door stops (H) in place after assembly.

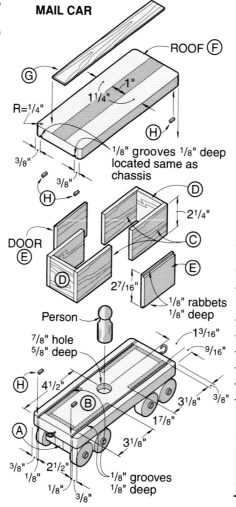

Bill of Materials

Part	Finished Size			Mat.	Qty.
	T	W	L		
MAIL CAR					
A* trucks	1¼"	2"	2⅜"	LM	2
B chassis	¾"	3½"	9"	M	1
C sides	¼"	2¼"	3⅛"	M	4
D ends	¼"	2¼"	1⅞"	M	2
E doors	¼"	2⁷⁄₁₆"	2¾"	M	2
F roof	½"	3½"	9"	M	1
G top	⅛"	1"	9"	M	1
H stops	⅛"	⅛"	⅜"	M	8

*Initially cut part marked with an * oversized. Then, trim it to finished size according to the how-to instructions.

Material Key: LM—laminated maple, M—maple

Supplies: ¼" brass screws, polyurethane.

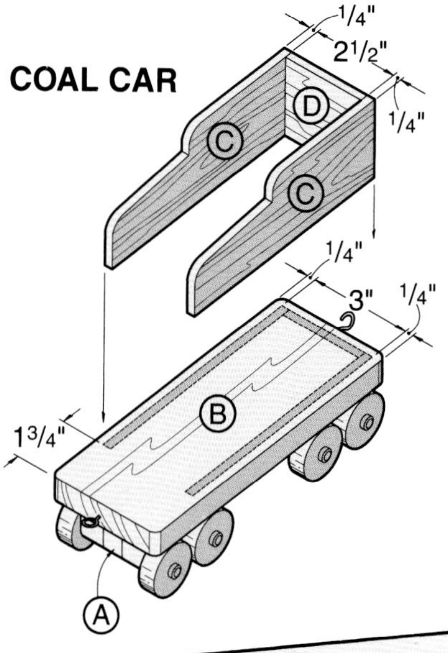

Bill of Materials

Part	Finished Size			Mat.	Qty.
	T	W	L		
COAL CAR					
A* trucks	1¼"	2"	2⅜"	LM	2
B chassis	¾"	3½"	9"	M	1
C side walls	¼"	2½"	7"	M	2
D rear wall	¼"	2½"	2½"	M	1

*Initially cut part marked with an * oversized. Then, trim it to finished size according to the how-to instructions.

Material Key: LM—laminated maple, M—maple

Supplies: ¼" brass flat washers, stain, polyurethane.

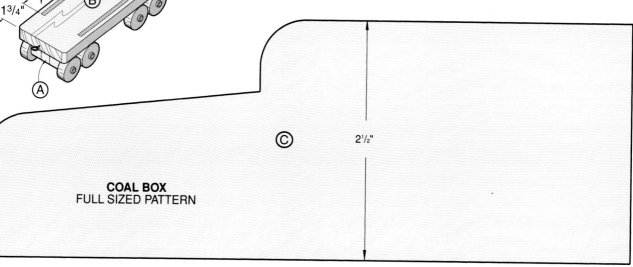

COAL BOX
FULL SIZED PATTERN

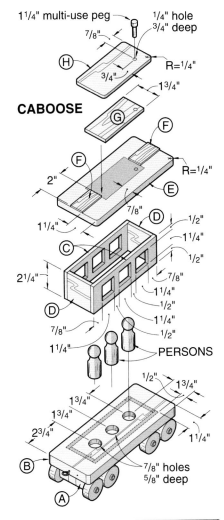

CABOOSE

1¼" multi-use peg

¼" hole
¾" deep

⅞"

¾"

1¾"

R=¼"

Ⓗ

Ⓖ

Ⓕ

Ⓕ

2"

R=¼"

Ⓔ

⅞"

1¼"

Ⓓ

½"

1¼"

½"

Ⓒ

⅞"

1¼"

2¼"

Ⓓ

½"

1¼"

Ⓓ

½"

⅞"

1¼"

PERSONS

½"

1¾"

1¾"

1¾"

2¾"

1¼"

Ⓑ

⅞" holes
⅝" deep

Ⓐ

Bill of Materials

Part	Finished Size			Mat.	Qty.
	T	W	L		
CABOOSE					
A* trucks	1¼"	2"	2⅜"	LM	2
B chassis	¾"	3½"	9"	M	1
C sides	¼"	2¼"	6½"	M	2
D ends	¼"	2¼"	2"	M	2
E roof	½"	3½"	8"	M	1
F tops	⅛"	1"	2"	M	2
G support	¼"	1¾"	4"	M	1
H roof	¼"	2½"	5"	M	1

*Initially cut part marked with an * oversized.
Then, trim it to finished size according to the
how-to instructions.

Material Key: LM—laminated maple,
M—maple
Supplies: ¼" brass flat washers, stain,
polyurethane.

Bill of Materials

Part	Finished Size			Mat.	Qty.
	T	W	L		
TANKER					
A* trucks	1¼"	2"	2⅜"	LM	2
B chassis	¾"	3½"	9"	M	1
C* tank	2¾"	2¾"	8"	LM	1
D tops	⅛"	1"	2⅝"	M	2
E tank dome	¼"	2"	2"	M	1

*Initially cut parts marked with an * oversized.
Then, trim each to finished size according to the
how-to instructions.

Material Key: LM—laminated maple,
M—maple
Supplies: ¼" brass flat washers, 1" dowel
stock, stain, polyurethane.

TANK CAR

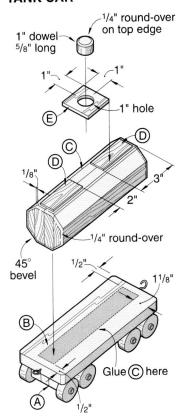

1" dowel
⅝" long

¼" round-over
on top edge

1"

1"

1"

Ⓔ

1" hole

Ⓓ

⅛"

Ⓒ

Ⓓ

3"

2"

¼" round-over

45°
bevel

½"

1⅛"

Ⓑ

Glue Ⓒ here

Ⓐ

½"

Drill a trio of ⅞" holes in the chassis (B) where shown for the passengers. Glue the passengers (called "persons" by toy-part companies) in place. Next, add the walls (C, D) and roof assembly (E, F, G, H) to the caboose chassis.

BUYING GUIDE

• **Train kit.** Includes all the flat wheels, axle pegs, smokestack, multi-use pegs, persons, 1" and 1¼" birch dowel stock, brass-plated cup hooks, and brass-plated screw eyes to make the train. Kit No. WM1292-A. For current prices, contact Cherry Tree Toys, P.O. Box 369, Belmont, OH 43718, or call 800/848-4363 to order.

• **Labels and tool.** Sheet of dry-transfer train labels (plus extras, allowing you room for error), burnishing tool, and application instructions. For current prices, contact The Art Store, 600 M. L. King Pkwy., Des Moines, IA 50312 or call 515/244-7000 or 800/652-2225 to order.

PROJECT TOOL LIST

• Tablesaw
• Bandsaw
• Scrollsaw
• Drill press
• Bits: 1/16", 7/32" ¼", 5/16" ⅜", ¾", ⅞", 1", 1¼"
• Router
• Bits: ⅛" round-over, ¼" round-over
• Disc or belt sander
• Finishing sander

Note: *We built this project using the tools listed. You may be able to substitute other tools and equipment for listed items you don't have. You'll also need various common hand tools and clamps to complete the project.*

Sneak-a-Peek Periscope

A "fun-tastic" plaything for your favorite private eye

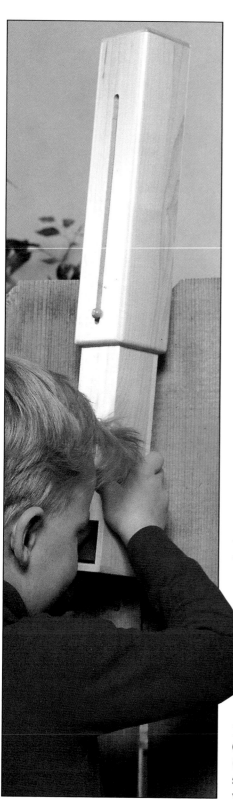

Your little investigator will enjoy peering over sofas and around corners searching for his buddies with this expandable project. Solidly built to take plenty of espionage work, this toy should offer years of spying fun.

Note: You'll need some ¼"-thick stock for this project. You can either resaw or plane thicker stock to the correct thickness. Have the mirrors cut to size at your local glass shop, or use our Buying Guide source listed opposite.

START WITH THE TOP SECTION

1 From ¼"-thick stock (we used maple), cut the sides (A), front (B), back (C), and top (D) to the sizes listed in the Bill of Materials.

2 Keeping the edges and ends of the pieces flush and square to each other, glue and clamp them together. See the Periscope Top Section drawing for reference.

3 Scrape off the excess glue, and sand smooth. Fit your table-mounted router with a ¼" round-over bit and a fence. Align the outside edge of the fence with the outside edge of the round-over bit pilot bearing. (The fence prevents the bit from dipping into the mirror opening when routing.) Rout the edges of the top section where shown on the Top Section drawing.

4 Tilt your tablesaw blade to 45° from vertical, and bevel-rip both edges of a ¼"-thick piece of 12"-long maple to 2⅜" wide. Crosscut the angled mirror block (E) to length (2") from the 2⅜×12" strip. Save the remaining piece; you'll use it for part (J) later.

TURN TO THE BOTTOM SECTION

1 Cut the bottom-section back (F), front (G), sides (H), and bottom cap (I) to size.

2 Dry-clamp the bottom section together, and test-fit it into the top section. The fit should be snug, yet slide easily. Glue and clamp the bottom section in the same manner as the top.

3 Bevel-rip one edge of the piece remaining when you cut mirror block (E) earlier to 2⅛" wide. Then, crosscut the bottom mirror block (J) to 1½" long.

FINAL ASSEMBLY AND CLEANUP

1 Glue the mirror blocks (E, J) into the periscope sections where shown in the drawings.

2 Fit your table-mounted router with a ¼" straight bit. Position the router table fence 1¼" from the center of the bit. Now, start the router, lower the top section down onto the bit, and rout a ¼" slot 8¼" long in the front piece (B) where shown on the Top Section drawing. (We clamped stops to the router fence to ensure an 8¼"-long slot.)

Bill of Materials				
Part	Finished Size		Mat.	Qty.
	T	W	L	
TOP SECTION				
A	¼"	2½"	11¼"	M	2
B	¼"	2"	11¼"	M	1
C	¼"	2"	9¾"	M	1
D	¼"	2½"	2½"	M	1
E	¼"	2⅜"	2"	M	1
BOTTOM SECTION				
F	¼"	2"	11"	M	1
G	¼"	1½"	7⅞"	M	1
H	¼"	1¾"	9⅜"	M	2
I	¼"	2"	2"	M	1
J	¼"	2⅛"	1½"	M	1

Material Key: M—maple

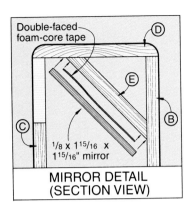

Double-faced foam-core tape

$1/8$ x $1^{15}/_{16}$ x $1^{15}/_{16}$" mirror

MIRROR DETAIL (SECTION VIEW)

3 Sand both sections smooth, and mask mirror blocks (E, J). The foam-core tape sticks better to an unfinished surface. Apply a clear finish to both sections, and remove the masking from the mirror blocks.

4 Drill a $7/32$" hole in part G where shown on the Bottom Section drawing. Before drilling, double-check that the hole aligns directly beneath the slot in part (B).

5 Insert the bottom periscope section into the top. Slide the axle peg through the slot in the top section, and glue it in place in the $7/32$" hole in the bottom section. To prevent the two pieces from sliding too freely, snug the peg head against the top section when periscope gluing it in place. For a bit more strength, you might want to use epoxy to secure the peg in place.

6 Using double-faced foam-core tape, adhere the mirrors to the mirror blocks (E, J). See the Mirror detail for locating the mirror in the top section.

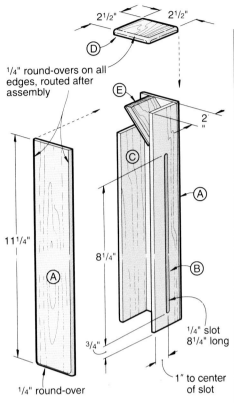

$1/4$" round-overs on all edges, routed after assembly

$11^{1}/_4$"

$8^{1}/_4$"

$3/4$"

$1/4$" round-over

$2^{1}/_2$" $2^{1}/_2$"

2"

$1/4$" slot $8^{1}/_4$" long

1" to center of slot

TOP SECTION

BUYING GUIDE

• **Mirrors, tape, peg.** One $1/8$x$1^{15}/_{16}$x$1^{15}/_{16}$" mirror, one $1/8$x$1^3/_8$x2" mirror, axle peg, and double-faced foam-core tape. For current prices, contact The Stained Glass Store, 3617 Ingersoll, Des Moines, IA 50312, or call 515/279-4855.

PROJECT TOOL LIST

• Tablesaw
• Router
• Router table
• Bits: $1/4$" straight, $1/4$" round-over,
• Portable drill
• Bits: $7/32$" bit
• Finishing sander

Note: We built this project using the tools listed. You may be able to substitute other tools and equipment for listed items you don't have. You'll also need various common hand tools and clamps to complete the project.

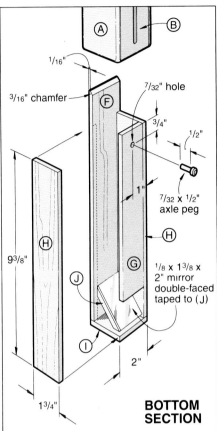

$1/16$"

$3/16$" chamfer

$7/32$" hole

$3/4$"

$1/2$"

$7/32$ x $1/2$" axle peg

$9^3/8$"

1"

$1/8$ x $1^3/8$ x 2" mirror double-faced taped to (J)

2"

$1^3/4$"

BOTTOM SECTION

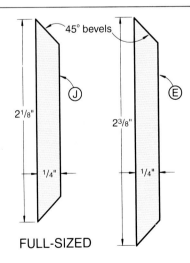

45° bevels

$2^{1}/8$"

$1/4$"

$2^3/8$"

$1/4$"

FULL-SIZED

MIRROR BLOCKS (SIDE VIEW)

Pride of the Shop

If you see a project in our WOOD® Magazine Idea Shop™,
you can pretty much bet that it's the best we know how
to make it. Whether it's an innovative wall-cabinet storage
system, or just a practical workshop clock, all the Idea
Shop projects in this section are surefire winners. Put a few of
them to work in your shop and see what we mean!

Universal Wall-Cabinet System

The be-all, end-all solution to shop clutter

When we decided to build the *Idea Shop*™, we wanted every component to be fresh, new, and above all practical. With that in mind, I put my engineering background to work and designed a wall-cabinet system that works great for organizing hand tools, safety equipment, power-tool accessories, and much more. The cabinets go together quickly, they won't cost you an arm and a leg, and the acrylic inserts in the doors allow you to spot your well-organized tools in a jiffy, and keep dust away from them, too.

On the following pages, we'll show you how to build a 2×4' cabinet. (For cabinets with different dimensions, see the sizing guidelines on *page 80.*) On *page 83*, we'll explain the method Jim Boelling, our Project Builder, used to design the tool holders in our cabinets. Turn to *page 85* for plans to build the Forstner-bit holders.

—*Marlen Kemmet*
How-To Editor

START WITH THE BACK AND THE MOUNTING STRIPS

1 From ½" plywood, cut the back (A) to the size listed in the Bill of Materials.

2 Using the drawing on *page 80*, bevel-rip the 29 mounting strips (B) to size from ½"-thick stock. Crosscut the strips to length.

3 Mark the screw-hole center points where dimensioned on the Exploded View drawing, and then drill and countersink a trio of shank holes in each strip.

4 To ensure consistent spacing between the strips and smooth-sliding components, build a spacing jig like that shown on *page 80*.

5 Clamp the back (A) to your workbench. Cut a piece of scrap

continued

Universal Wall-Cabinet System

continued

How to size cabinets to suit your needs

The cabinet we show on *page 79* measures 2x4'. But we've also built various-sized cabinets for such things as our measuring and marking tools, lathe tools, air-powered tools, and hand planes, to name a few. To help size your custom cabinets, follow these planning guidelines:

• Gather together the tools or other items you want to store in a special-purpose cabinet. Then, lay out the items on a large piece of plywood. This will give you a rough idea of how large to make the cabinet's back.

• If making your cabinet shorter or longer than the model shown, do so in 1½" increments to allow for each mounting strip and a ¼" gap added or subtracted.

• Also, if you widen a cabinet and the door becomes wider than it is tall, we recommend using two doors.

• Finally, make the depth of the cabinet equal to the width of the widest tool to be stored in the cabinet plus 1½".

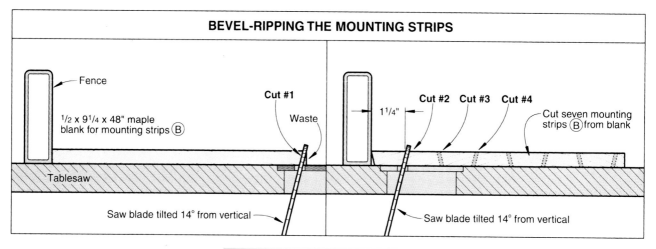

BEVEL-RIPPING THE MOUNTING STRIPS

Fence

½ x 9¼ x 48" maple blank for mounting strips (B)

Cut #1
Waste

Tablesaw

Saw blade tilted 14° from vertical

1¼"
Cut #2 Cut #3 Cut #4

Cut seven mounting strips (B) from blank

Saw blade tilted 14° from vertical

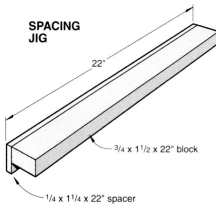

SPACING JIG

22"

¾ x 1½ x 22" block

¼ x 1¼ x 22" spacer

Glue and screw the maple mounting strips to the plywood back, using the spacing jig for consistent gaps.

measuring 2¼x22". With the top edges flush, clamp the scrap piece to the top of the back where shown in the photo *above right*.

6 Starting flush with the bottom edge of the scrap strip (2¼" from the top edge of the back), glue and screw the first mounting strip (B) to the back where shown in the photo. See the Mounting detail accompanying the Exploded View drawing

opposite for reference. Check that the ends of the mounting strip are flush with the outside edges of the back. Use only a small amount of glue to avoid squeeze-out. Immediately wipe off excess glue with a damp cloth. *Caution: Glue left between the mounting strips can prevent the tool holders from sliding easily in the dovetail grooves later.*

7 To ensure consistent gaps between the mounting strips, use the spacing jig as shown at *left*. Working from the top down, glue and screw all the mounting strips to the back.

NOW, CONSTRUCT THE BASIC CABINET ASSEMBLY

1 Cut the cabinet sides (C) and top and bottom (D) to the sizes listed in the Bill of Materials from ¾" birch plywood.

2 Cut a ¾" rabbet ½" deep across both ends of each side piece. Glue and clamp the pieces (C, D). Check for square, and wipe off excess glue. So the cabinet will easily fit onto the back (A) later, the opening is 1⁄16" larger in length and width than the back.

3 Cut the hanger strip (E) to size. For mounting the strip to the back later, mark the locations, and drill and countersink a pair of mounting holes through the front

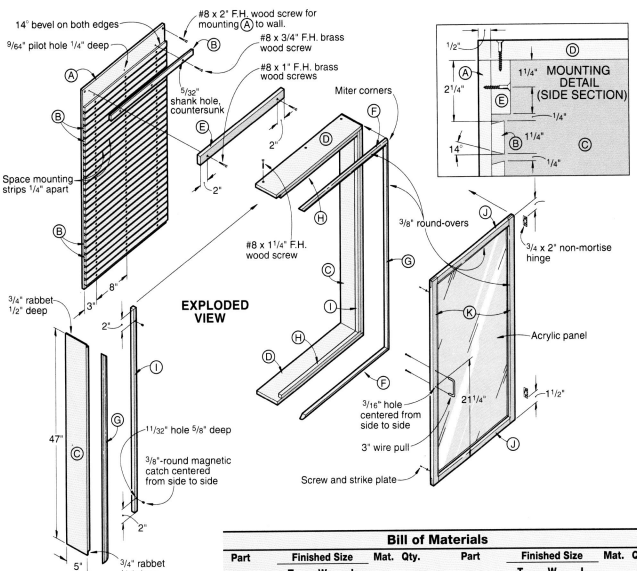

14° bevel on both edges

⁹/₆₄" pilot hole ¼" deep

#8 x 2" F.H. wood screw for mounting Ⓐ to wall.

#8 x ¾" F.H. brass wood screw

#8 x 1" F.H. brass wood screws

⁵/₃₂" shank hole, countersunk

Miter corners

Space mounting strips ¼" apart

#8 x 1¼" F.H. wood screw

2"

¾" rabbet ½" deep

8"

3"

2"

EXPLODED VIEW

¾" round-overs

¾ x 2" non-mortise hinge

Acrylic panel

47"

¹¹/₃₂" hole ⅝" deep

⅜"-round magnetic catch centered from side to side

³/₁₆" hole centered from side to side

3" wire pull

21¼"

1½"

Screw and strike plate

5"

¾" rabbet ½" deep

2"

MOUNTING DETAIL (SIDE SECTION)

½"

1¼"

2¼"

¼"

1¼"

14°

¼"

Bill of Materials

Part	Finished Size			Mat.	Qty.
	T	W	L		
BACK AND STRIPS					
A back	½"	22"	45½"	BP	1
B mounting strips	½"	1¼"	22"	M	29
CABINET FRAME					
C sides	¾"	5"	47"	BP	2
D top/ bottom	¾"	5"	23"	BP	2
E hanger strip	¾"	2"	22"	M	1
F face strips	¾"	¾"	23½"	M	2
G face strips	¾"	¾"	47"	M	2
H door stops	¾"	¾"	22"	M	2
I door stops	¾"	¾"	44"	M	2

Part	Finished Size			Mat.	Qty.
	T	W	L		
DOOR					
J rails	¾"	1½"	21⅞"	M	2
K stiles	¾"	1½"	45⅜"	M	2
L stops	¼"	¼"	19⅜"	M	2
M stops	¼"	¼"	42⅞"	M	2

Material Key: BP—birch plywood, M—maple
Supplies: #8x1¼" flathead wood screws, #8x2" flathead wood screws, #8x1" flathead brass wood screws, #8x¾" flathead brass wood screws, ⅛" clear acrylic, ½"x#18 brads, paint, clear finish.

face of E where shown on the Exploded View drawing.

4 Glue and clamp the hanger strip to the bottom of the cabinet top (D), ½" in from the back edge. See the Mounting detail accompanying the Exploded View drawing for reference. Drill three mounting holes through the cabinet top, centered into the top edge of the hanger strip (E). Drive a #8x1¼" wood screw through each hole just drilled.

5 Rip and miter-cut the face-frame strips (F, G) to size. Glue and clamp them to the front of the

continued

Universal Wall-Cabinet System

continued

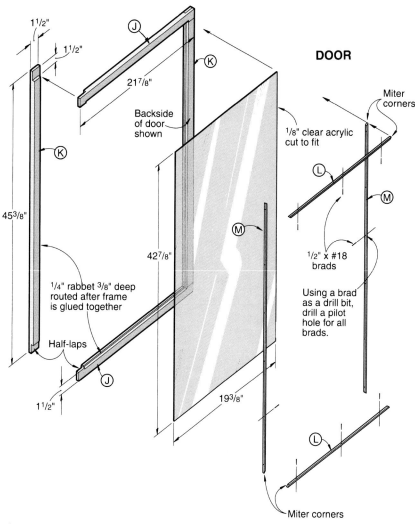

DOOR

Backside
of door
shown

1¹/₂"

1¹/₂"

21⁷/₈"

45³/₈"

42⁷/₈"

¹/₄" rabbet ³/₈" deep
routed after frame
is glued together

Half-laps

1¹/₂"

¹/₈" clear acrylic
cut to fit

Miter
corners

¹/₂" x #18
brads

Using a brad
as a drill bit,
drill a pilot
hole for all
brads.

19³/₈"

Miter corners

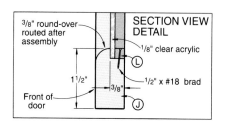

SECTION VIEW DETAIL

³/₈" round-over
routed after
assembly

¹/₈" clear acrylic

1¹/₂"

³/₈"

¹/₂" x #18 brad

Front of
door

panying the Door drawing for reference.

6 Using the Wire Pull drawing *below* for dimensions, drill the mounting holes in the left-hand stile for the pull. (For a flush-closing door, we drilled ⅜" holes ¹/₁₆" deep on the back of the door for the screw heads. Then, we used a combination bolt cutter/ wire stripper to snip ⅛" off the end of each screw so the wire pull would draw tight to the door front.) See the Buying Guide on page 84 for our hardware source.

7 Drill the pilot holes, and fasten a pair of no-mortise hinges to the right-hand door stile. Center the door top to bottom in the opening, and mark the mating hinge locations on the cabinet side. Drill mounting holes, and attach the hinges and door to the cabinet.

8 Cut the acrylic-panel stops (L, M) to size. Snip the head off a ½"×#18 brad, chuck the headless brad into your portable drill, and drill pilot holes through the stops. Do not install the acrylic yet.

continued

---

cabinet. Sand the strips flush with the cabinet frame.

6 Rout a ⅜" round-over along the outside front edge of the cabinet assembly (parts F and G).

7 Cut the door stops (H, I) to size.

8 For mounting the magnetic catches later, drill a pair of ¹¹/₃₂" holes ⅝" deep in one door stop (H) where shown on the Exploded View and Catch drawings. Hold off installing the door stops until final assembly.

FOR AN OPEN AND SHUT CASE, ADD THE DOOR

1 Cut the maple door rails (J) and stiles (K) to size.

2 Cut 1½"-long half-lap joints on the ends of each rail and stile.

3 Glue and clamp the door frame members together, checking for square and making sure the frame clamps flat. Later, remove the clamps and sand the door smooth.

4 Rout a ¼" rabbet ⅜" deep along the back inside edge of the door frame for the acrylic panel and stops. Using a chisel, square the curved corners left by the router.

5 Fit your router with a ⅜" round-over bit, and rout along the front inside edge of the door frame. See the Section View detail accom-

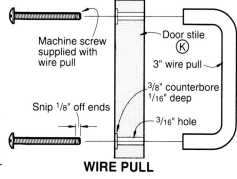

Machine screw
supplied with
wire pull

Door stile
K

3" wire pull

³/₈" counterbore
¹/₁₆" deep

³/₁₆" hole

Snip ⅛" off ends

WIRE PULL

How to design and make your own customized tool holders

Now that you've built a cabinet or two using our wall-cabinet design, it's time to add some customized holders. But before you begin, familiarize yourself with a holder's parts.

ANATOMY OF A TOOL HOLDER

As shown *below*, we call the horizontal part that supports the tool the *shelf*. For heavier items, the shelf fits into a groove in the support. The *dovetail strip* attaches to the back of a shelf or support and slides between the mounting strips. The *banding strips* protect tools from falling off the front or ends of the shelf.

MAKE YOUR HOLDERS TO FIT

To make the shelf, start by laying the item you want to store on a piece of stock. (We used ½"- and ¾"-thick maple for most shelves.) If the bottom of the tool is square or rectangular, cut the shelf about ⅛" oversize. Or, for

screwdrivers, router bits, and other shanked items, cut the shelf to size, and drill holes for the tool shanks where shown on the Screwdriver Holder drawing. The distance between holes depends on the items you intend to store.

NEXT, ADD THE BANDING STRIPS

These should extend high enough above the shelf (usually about ¼") to keep the tool from being bumped off. We used banded shelves for planes, sharpening stones, drill-bit index boxes, and other flat-bottomed items. If the tool's outline is irregular, like that of the caliper holder *below right*, mark a portion of the tool's outline on ¾" stock. Then, cut the outline to shape.

NOW, ADD THE DOVETAIL STRIPS

Bevel-rip long lengths of dovetail-strip stock at 14°. See the

Dovetail Strip detail accompanying the drawing *below left* for reference. Crosscut the dovetail strips to length. Drill and countersink mounting holes in the back edge of the strip. Glue and screw the dovetail strip to the back edge of the shelf, support, or holder.

Slide the dovetail strip of the holder between the mounting strips in the cabinet back. If the dovetail strip fits too tightly between the mounting strips, sand it slightly for a smooth sliding action. Remove and finish holders.

Once dry, slide your holders between the mounting strips in the cabinet back (attached to the wall at this point). Arrange the holders as needed, and secure the cabinet back to the wall. You're ready to add your tools and accessories.

SCREWDRIVER HOLDER

Dovetail strip · 2" · R=½" · Shelf (¾" stock) overall length=12" · ¼" round-overs · ¾" · 1½" · 1" · Holes to fit screwdrivers

TOOL HOLDER ANATOMY

½" · ½" · 14 · DOVETAIL STRIP DETAIL · Shelf · Dovetail strip · Support · Banding strips

SCREW-HOLE DETAIL

Banding · Dovetail strip · #6 x 1" F.H. wood screw · 9/64" shank hole, countersunk · Shelf · Support

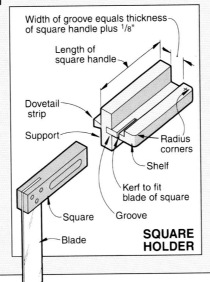

Width of groove equals thickness of square handle plus ⅛" · Length of square handle · Dovetail strip · Support · Radius corners · Shelf · Kerf to fit blade of square · Square · Groove · Blade · **SQUARE HOLDER**

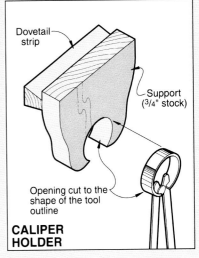

Dovetail strip · Support (¾" stock) · Opening cut to the shape of the tool outline · **CALIPER HOLDER**

Universal Wall-Cabinet System

continued

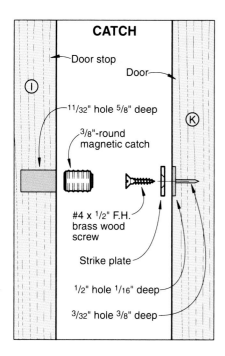

CATCH

Door stop

Door

11/32" hole 5/8" deep

3/8"-round
magnetic catch

#4 x 1/2" F.H.
brass wood
screw

Strike plate

1/2" hole 1/16" deep

3/32" hole 3/8" deep

COMPLETE THE ASSEMBLY, ADD THE FINISH, AND HANG

1 Insert a pair of magnetic catches into the holes in the left-hand door stop.

2 Fasten the door stops (H, I) to the cabinet so when swung shut, the front of the door is flush with the front of the cabinet.

3 Close the door tightly against the catches to mark their mating position on the back edge of the door stile (K). Next, using a brad-point bit, drill a ½" hole ⅟₁₆" in the door stile where indented for each strike plate. Using the centered depression left by the brad-point bit

when drilling the ½" hole, drill a ³⁄₃₂" pilot hole ⅜" deep centered inside the ½"-diameter counterbore. Screw the strike plates in place.

4 Remove the hardware (except for the magnetic catches) from the cabinet and door. Finish-sand the cabinet assembly, back, door, and acrylic panel stops.

5 Mask the surrounding areas and catches, and apply a clear finish to the face strips, door stops, mounting strips, and door.

6 Mask the maple face strips (F, G), and then paint the cabinet.

7 Measure the openings, and have an acrylic panel cut to fit. Secure the panel with the stops (L, M).

8 Reattach the wire pull and hinges to the door. Reattach the door to the cabinet.

9 To mount the back (A) to the wall, locate the stud(s), and position the back. Drill mounting holes through the top and bottom of the back, centered over the stud(s). Check for plumb and level, and secure the back to the wall. Fit the cabinet assembly onto the back, and secure it to the back by driving a set of screws through the hanger strip (E) and into the back. After you've built your organizers, remove the cabinet from the back, slide the organizers in place, and reattach the cabinet to the back. For ease in removing the cabinet frame from the back (A, B, E) we've used only the

three # 8 wood screws along the top of the cabinet (D) to secure the two assemblies. This allows you to easily separate the two assemblies for rearranging the tool holders.

Note: *To remove the basic cabinet surround from the back board assembly to adjust the tool holders, simply remove the three #8x1¼" wood screws from the cabinet top D. Remove the cabinet, adjust the tool holders, and reattach the cabinet to the back board assembly.*

BUYING GUIDE

- **Hardware.** 3" polished-brass wire pull, two magnetic catches with strike plates, and two ¾x2" no-mortise hinges. Kit No. 71159 (enough for one cabinet). For current prices, contact Klockit, P.O. Box 636, Lake Geneva, WI 53147, or call 800/556-2548 to order.

PROJECT TOOL LIST

- Tablesaw
- Drill press
- Portable drill
- Bits: ³⁄₃₂", ⁹⁄₆₄", ³⁄₁₆", ¹¹⁄₃₂", ⅜", ½"
- Router
- Bits: ¼" rabbet, ⅜" round-over
- Finishing sander

Note: *We built the project using the tools listed. You may be able to substitute other tools or equipment for listed items you don't have. Additional common hand tools and clamps may be required to complete the project.*

Forstner-Bit Holders

For the drill-press cabinet

Here's a handy pair of holders to fit inside our universal wall-cabinet system shown on *page 79*. To make each holder, bevel-rip the dovetail strips (A, D) to size. Next, cut the top and bottom shelf pieces (B, C, and E, F) to size and shape for each holder. Bore the holes in each top piece (B and E). Laminate the mating pieces together for each holder. Cut the slots for the bit shank with a bandsaw or scrollsaw. Drill the mounting holes through the dovetail strips, and glue and screw them to the back edge of each laminated shelf.

PROJECT TOOL LIST
• Tablesaw
• Bandsaw or scrollsaw
• Drill press
• Portable drill
• Bits: ³⁄₃₂", ⁹⁄₆₄", Forstner bits
• Finishing sander

Note: *We built the project using the tools listed. You may be able to substitute other tools or equipment for listed items you don't have. Additional common hand tools and clamps may be required to complete the project.*

Bill of Materials

Part	Finished Size			Mat.	Qty.
	T	W	L		
A	½"	½"	8¾"	M	1
B	½"	2½"	8¾"	M	1
C	¼"	2½"	8¾"	M	1
D	½"	½"	14"	M	1
E	½"	3"	14"	M	1
F	¼"	3"	14"	M	1

Material Key: M—maple
Supplies: #6 x ¾" F.H. wood screws, finish.

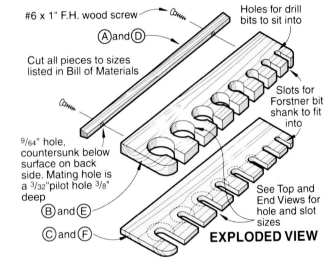

#6 x 1" F.H. wood screw

Ⓐ and Ⓓ

Cut all pieces to sizes listed in Bill of Materials

Holes for drill bits to sit into

Slots for Forstner bit shank to fit into

⁹⁄₆₄" hole, countersunk below surface on back side. Mating hole is a ³⁄₃₂" pilot hole ³⁄₈" deep

Ⓑ and Ⓔ

Ⓒ and Ⓕ

See Top and End Views for hole and slot sizes

EXPLODED VIEW

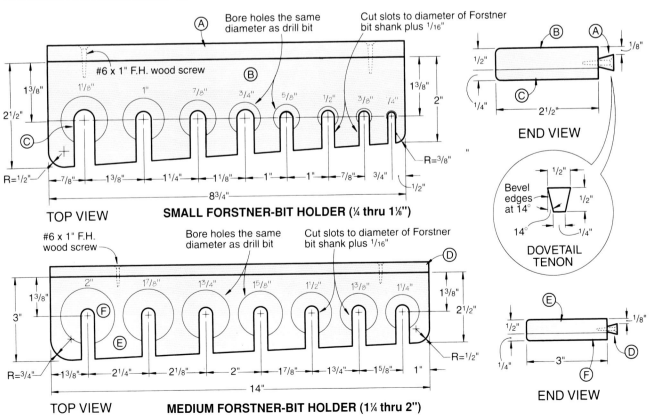

Bore holes the same diameter as drill bit

Cut slots to diameter of Forstner bit shank plus ¹⁄₁₆"

#6 x 1" F.H. wood screw

TOP VIEW   **SMALL FORSTNER-BIT HOLDER (¼ thru 1⅛")**

END VIEW

Bevel edges at 14°

DOVETAIL TENON

#6 x 1" F.H. wood screw

Bore holes the same diameter as drill bit

Cut slots to diameter of Forstner bit shank plus ¹⁄₁₆"

TOP VIEW   **MEDIUM FORSTNER-BIT HOLDER (1¼ thru 2")**

END VIEW

Collector's-Edition Angle Bevel

For more than 30 years now, going back to the time when I cut my first board, I've loved the heft, feel, accuracy, and rich look of fine hand tools. If you, too, share the same passion for hand tools, then let me talk you into making my brass and walnut angle bevel.

Whether you're a novice or an advanced woodworker, you'll find that this tool serves its purposes well and makes an attractive addition to your tool ensemble.

—*Jim Boelling*
Project Builder

Note: *You'll need ⁵⁄₁₆" walnut for this project. You can either resaw or plane thicker stock to size.*

START BY MACHINING THE HANDLE BLANK

1 Cut a piece of walnut to ⁵⁄₁₆"×1×18" (we planed ¼" stock to ⁵⁄₁₆"thick).

2 Cut or rout a 1⅝" rabbet ³⁄₁₆" deep across both ends of the stock where shown on the Handle Blank drawing, *opposite.*

3 Fit your table-mounted router with a ⅜" core box bit and raise it ⅛" above the surface of the table. Clamp a fence to your router table, and clamp a start and stop block to the fence where shown on the drawing *below.*

4 With the rabbeted ends facing down, position one end of the handle blank against the start block, and lower the blank onto the spinning cove bit. Holding the handle blank firmly against the fence, push the stock until the opposite end of the blank reaches the stop block. Keeping the same surface down, turn the handle blank end for end and repeat the routing process to form the second cove where shown on the Handle Blank drawing.

5 Crosscut two 7¼"-long pieces from the 18" blank where shown on the Handle Blank drawing.

ADD THE BRASS AND LAMINATE THE HANDLE PIECES

1 To form the brass side caps, start by scribing a ½" radius on both ends of one of the 12" lengths of ¹⁄₁₆"-thick brass. (See the Buying Guide for our source of brass.) Cut the radii to shape (we used a bandsaw fitted with a ¼" blade). File the cut edges smooth.

2 Crosscut each end of the brass strips to obtain the two 1⅝"-long brass side caps. Next, cut a third piece to ¹¹⁄₁₆"×1" for the end cap.

3 For better adhesion to the epoxy in the next step, use 60-grit sandpaper to rough up one surface of each piece of brass.

4 Spread an even coat of epoxy on the sanded surfaces, and *lightly* clamp the brass side caps into the rabbets in the handle pieces where shown on the Handle Blank drawing.

continued

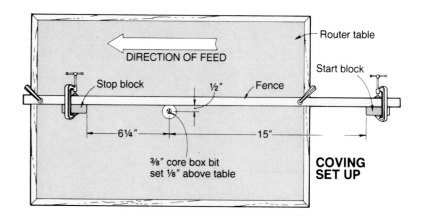

DIRECTION OF FEED

Stop block   ½"   Fence

Router table

Start block

6¼"   15"

³⁄₈" core box bit
set ⅛" above table

COVING SET UP

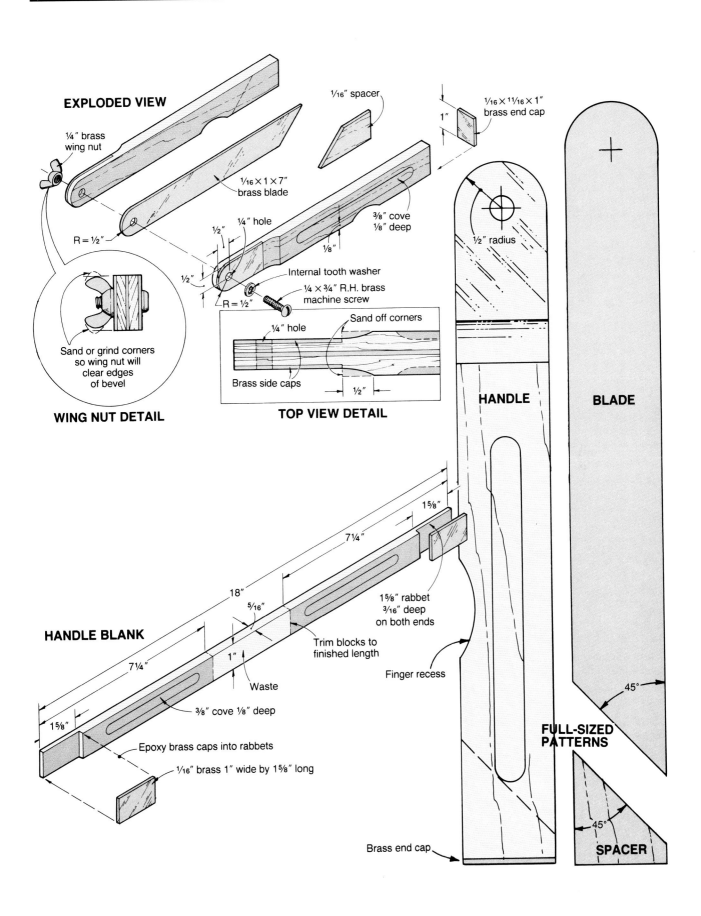

EXPLODED VIEW

¼" brass
wing nut

R = ½"

1/16 × 1 × 7"
brass blade

1/16" spacer

1/16 × 11/16 × 1"
brass end cap

1"

¼" hole

½"

½"

3/8" cove
1/8" deep

1/8"

R = ½"

Internal tooth washer

¼ × ¾" R.H. brass
machine screw

Sand or grind corners
so wing nut will
clear edges
of bevel

WING NUT DETAIL

¼" hole

Sand off corners

Brass side caps

½"

TOP VIEW DETAIL

½" radius

HANDLE

BLADE

HANDLE BLANK

18"

5/16"

7¼"

7¼"

1"

Waste

3/8" cove 1/8" deep

1 5/8"

Epoxy brass caps into rabbets

1/16" brass 1" wide by 1 5/8" long

1 5/8"

1 5/8" rabbet
3/16" deep
on both ends

Trim blocks to
finished length

Finger recess

Brass end cap

FULL-SIZED
PATTERNS

45°

45°

SPACER

Collector's-Edition Angle Bevel

continued

(**Note:** *Excessive clamping will force all or most of the epoxy to squeeze out and result in a weak bond.*) After the epoxy has cured, cut and sand the walnut flush with the brass.

5 Cut a ¹⁄₁₆"-thick piece of walnut to the shape shown on the Pattern drawing for the spacer.

6 With the ends and edges flush, glue and clamp the spacer between the handle pieces; see the Exploded View drawing for reference. Later, trim the end of the handle square.

7 Epoxy the remaining piece of brass to the trimmed end of the laminated handle.

8 Mark the finger recess on the walnut handle where shown on the Patterns drawing. Using a drum sander, sand the recess to shape.

9 Mark the slight radius on the walnut next to the brass side caps where shown on the Top View detail accompanying the Exploded View drawing. Drum-sand to the line and even with the brass but not into the brass, as shown in the photo *above right*. Sand the handle smooth.

NEXT, ADD THE BRASS BLADE

1 To form the blade (also called a tongue), miter-cut one end and radius the other end of a piece of ¹⁄₁₆X1" brass to the shape shown on the Pattern drawing.

2 Slide the brass blade into the handle assembly with the rounded ends of the blade and handle flush. Tape the blade firmly in place. Punch a center point on

Mark the radii on the handle, and then sand to the line, being careful not to sand the brass.

one of the brass side caps. Now, using a twist bit, drill a ¼" hole through the handle/blade assembly. Remove the tape, and remove the blade from the handle.

ASSEMBLE THE PARTS AND ADD THE FINISH

1 Sand or file the wings of a ¼" brass wing nut to the shape shown on the Wing Nut detail accompanying the Exploded View drawing. For accurate measuring later, the wings on the nut must not protrude beyond the edges of the handle assembly where shown on the detail.

2 For a better finished appearance, sand or file the slotted head of a

¼X¾" roundhead brass machine screw to remove the slot.

3 Insert the ¼" brass machine screw though an internal tooth washer and the handle assembly. Add the wing nut.

4 Polish the brass with 400-grit sandpaper to remove any filing or sanding marks. Remove the blade from the walnut handle.

5 Mask the brass, and add the finish to the handle. (We applied Watco Danish oil.) After the finish dries, re-move the masking and add the blade.

BUYING GUIDE
• **Angle bevel kit.** Two pieces of ¹⁄₁₆X1x12" brass, ¼X¾" brass machine screw, ¼" internal-tooth washer, ¼" brass wing nut. Kit No. AB895. For current prices, contact Puckett Electric Tools, 841 11th St., Des Moines, IA 50309, or call 800/544-4189 or 515/244-4189 to order.

PROJECT TOOL LIST
• Tablesaw
• Bandsaw
• Drill press
• Drum sander
• ¼" bit
• Router
• Router table
• ⅜" core box bit

Note: *We built this project using the tools listed. You may be able to substitute other tools and equipment for listed items you don't have. You'll also need various common hand tools and clamps to complete the project.*

Sanding-Supplies Organizer

Six smooth solutions for your shop

Looking for that single location where you can store all of your sanding supplies? This **WOOD**® magazine original, featuring a half-dozen easy-to-build projects, may be just the ticket. It includes holders for belts, sanding discs and accessories, stick sanders and strips, hand sanders, and rolls of adhesive-backed sandpaper.

GUIDE TO OUR SIX GREAT ORGANIZERS
1. Sanding-stick and sandpaper-strip organizer
2. 5" sanding-disc holder
3. Hand-sander rack and tote
4. Disc-sander center
5. Roll-sandpaper dispenser
6. Belt-sander belt divider

ORDERING INFORMATION
For our center, we used mostly 3M products, which you can find at home centers, hardware stores, contractor-supplies outlets, and through woodworking mail-order catalogs. Or, order them from:
  Puckett Electric Tools
  841 11th Street
  Des Moines, IA 50309
Call 800/544-4189 or 515/244-4189 to order.

continued

Sanding-Supply Organizer

continued

1 Sanding-Stick and Sandpaper-Strip Organizer

When that handcrafted project requires precision sanding, this trio of sanding sticks and adhesive-backed sandpaper strips performs admirably. Build the solid-maple organizer to divide the coarse-, medium-, and fine-grit sandpaper strips, using the drawing *below right* and the Bill of Materials. Then, refer to the full-sized pattern to make the contour-handled sticks.

Bill of Materials

Part	Finished Size			Mat.	Qty.
	T	W	L		
SANDING STICK AND SAND PAPER-STRIP ORGANIZER					
A	½"	2"	5¾"	M	2
B	½"	5¾"	15½"	BP	1
C	¼"	1½"	15½"	M	4
D	¼"	1½"	20"	M	3

Material Key: BP—birch plywood, M—maple
Supplies: 3M adhesive-backed 1½x14⅝" sandpaper strips; fine, cat. no. 9125; medium, cat. no. 9126; coarse, cat. no. 9127; ¼" birch dowel.

2 5" Sanding-Disc Holder

Adhered to a shanked disc pad and powered by your portable drill, a sanding disc allows you to sand contours with minimum effort. The discs press on and peel off, making for quick changes to the next grit. For larger-sized discs, simply increase the depth and width of the holder.

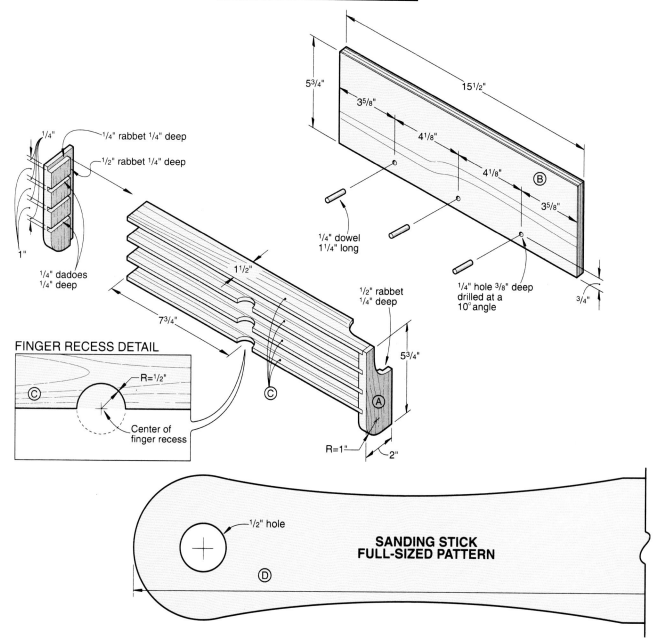

FINGER RECESS DETAIL

SANDING STICK
FULL-SIZED PATTERN

1/2" dowel 12 3/4" long

Bill of Materials

Part	Finished Size			Mat.	Qty.
	T	W	L		
5" DISC-SANDER HOLDER					
A	1/2"	5 1/4"	7"	M	2
B	1/2"	5 1/4"	5 3/4"	M	2
C	1/4"	5 3/4"	6 1/2"	BP	1
D	1/4"	5"	5 3/4"	M	4

Material Key: BP—birch plywood, M—maple
Supplies: 3M adhesive-backed 5" discs; fine grit, cat. no. 9170; medium grit, cat. no. 9171; coarse grit, cat. no. 9172.

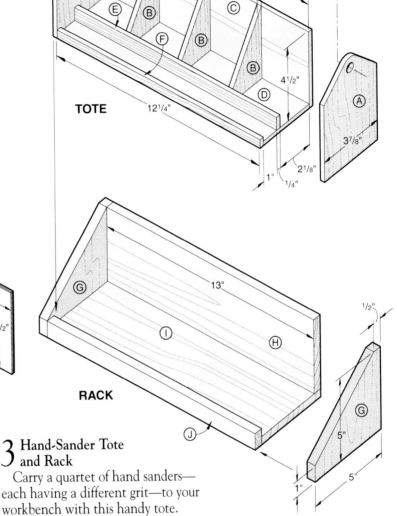

TOTE

12 1/4"

1/4"
2 7/8"
1/4"
2 7/8"
1/4"
2 7/8"
4 1/2"
2 1/8"
1"
1/4"
3 7/8"

RACK

13"
5 3/4"
1/2"
5"
1"
5"

DISC-SANDER HOLDER

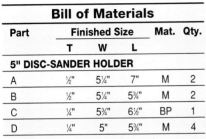

1/4" rabbet
1/4" deep
5 1/4"
5 3/4"

1/2" rabbets
1/4" deep
1/2"
1"
1"
1/4"
1"
1/2"

1/4" dadoes
1/4" deep
5 3/4"
6 1/2"
5"
7"

2 7/8"

Note:
See Finger Recess detail on the Sandpaper-Strip Organizer drawing for finger-recess size

1/4" rabbets
1/4" deep

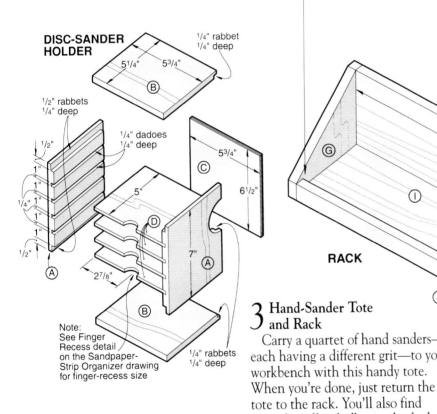

3 Hand-Sander Tote and Rack

Carry a quartet of hand sanders—each having a different grit—to your workbench with this handy tote. When you're done, just return the tote to the rack. You'll also find room for rolls of adhesive-backed sandpaper behind the hand sanders in the tote.

continued

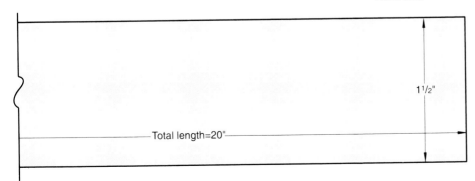

1 1/2"
Total length=20"

Sanding Supplies Organizer

continued

Bill of Materials

Part	Finished Size			Mat.	Qty.
	T	W	L		
HAND-SANDER TOTE					
A	¼"	3⅛"	6⅛"	M	2
B	¼"	2⅛"	4¼"	M	3
C	¼"	4½"	12¼"	M	1
D	¼"	3⅜"	12¼"	M	1
E	¼"	¾"	12¼"	M	1
F	¼"	½"	12¼"	M	1
TOTE RACK					
G	½"	5"	5"	M	2
H	½"	4½"	13"	M	1
I	½"	4½"	13 "	M	1
J	½"	1"	13 "	M	1

Material Key: M—maple
Supplies: 3M Hand Ease sander, cat. no. 45204. Sandpaper roll refills; very fine 2½x90", cat. no. 10124; fine 2½x80", cat. no. 10125; medium 2½x55", cat. no. 10126.

Bill of Materials

Part	Finished Size			Mat.	Qty.
	T	W	L		
DISC-SANDER CENTER					
A	½"	3½"	15½"	M	2
B	½"	3½"	7¼"	M	2
C	½"	3¼"	7¼"	M	4
D	¼"	3¼"	2½"	M	4
E	¼"	3¼"	1¾"	M	1
F	¼"	3¼"	3½"	M	4
G	¼"	7¼"	15"	BP	1

Material Key: BP—birch plywood, M—maple
Supplies: Disc-sanding kits available through most woodworking mail-order suppliers. We got ours from Industrial Abrasives Co., 642 N. 8th St., Box 14955, Reading, PA, 19612.

4 Disc-Sander Center

You can't beat small-diameter disc sanders for sanding the contours of shapely projects and the inside and outside of turned bowls. Here's a slick way to get your sanding-adhesive drill attachments and various discs in order and divided by grit.

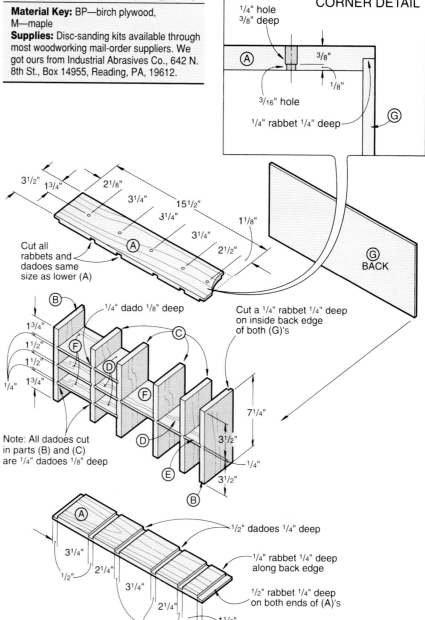

CORNER DETAIL

¼" hole ⅜" deep
⅜"
A
1/8"
3/16" hole
¼" rabbet ¼" deep
G

Cut all rabbets and dadoes same size as lower (A)

3½" 1¾" 2⅛" 3¼" 15½" 3¼" 3¼" 1⅛" 2½"

G BACK

Cut a ¼" rabbet ¼" deep on inside back edge of both (G)'s

¼" dado ⅛" deep

1¾" 1½" 1½" ¼" 1¾"

B F D C F D E B

Note: All dadoes cut in parts (B) and (C) are ¼" dadoes ⅛" deep

7¼" 3½" ¼" 3½"

A
3¼" 2¼" ½" 3¼" 2¼" ½" 1½"

½" dadoes ¼" deep
¼" rabbet ¼" deep along back edge
½" rabbet ¼" deep on both ends of (A)'s

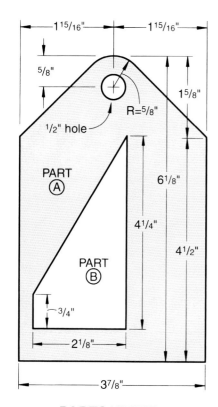

1 15/16" 1 15/16"
5/8"
1 5/8"
R=5/8"
½" hole
6⅛"
PART A
PART B
4¼"
4½"
¾"
2⅛"
3⅞"

PARTS VIEWS

Bill of Materials

Part	Finished Size			Mat.	Qty.
	T	**W**	**L**		
ROLL-SANDPAPER DISPENSER					
A	½"	3½"	9"	M	2
B	½"	4½"	21"	M	1
C	½"	4"	20"	M	1
D	½"	3"	20"	M	1
E	⅛"	3"	20½"	M	1
F	½"		3" dia.	M	3
G	½"	3½"	20"	M	1
H	¼"	1⅜"	2¼"	M	1

Material Key: M—maple
Supplies: 3M adhesive-backed sandpaper rolls 4½" wide by 10 yards long, 80-grit, cat. no. 00395; 100-grit, 00396; 120-grit, 00397; 220-grit, 00399; ¾" dowel, #8 x ⅝" flathead wood screws, ¾" x #17 brads.

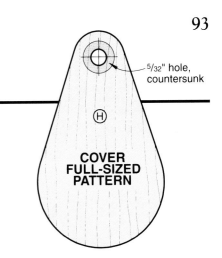

5/32" hole, countersunk

COVER FULL-SIZED PATTERN

5 Roll-Sandpaper Dispenser

This handy dispenser lets you store up to four 4½"-wide rolls of sandpaper. It loads from the bottom, and is dimensioned to let you tear off 4" pieces, perfect for the palm sander.

To remove a needed piece, pull the end of the sandpaper roll flush with the front top edge of part C. Fold a crease in the sandpaper along the back edge of part C (4" from the front). Pull the paper out until the crease aligns with the front edge of C. Adhere the paper back to part C so the crease is flush with the front edge. Just pull down on the paper to tear off a 4"-long piece.

6 Belt-Sander Belt Divider

We sized our divider for holding 3"-wide sanding belts. For wider belts, just increase the width of pieces B and C.

PROJECT TOOL LIST
- Tablesaw
- Dado blade or dado set
- Bandsaw
- Scrollsaw
- Drill press
- Portable drill
- Bits: 5/32", 7/64", 3/16", ¼", ½", ¾"
- Circle cutter
- Router
- ¼" rabbet bit
- Finishing sander

Note: *We built the project using the tools listed. You may be able to substitute other tools or equipment for listed items you don't have. Additional common hand tools and clamps may be required to complete the project.*

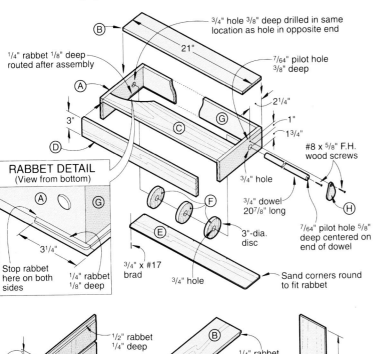

3/4" hole 3/8" deep drilled in same location as hole in opposite end
1/4" rabbet 1/8" deep routed after assembly
21"
7/64" pilot hole 3/8" deep
2¼"
1"
1¾"
3"
#8 x ⅝" F.H. wood screws
3/4" hole
3/4" dowel 20⅞" long
3"-dia. disc
7/64" pilot hole ⅝" deep centered on end of dowel

RABBET DETAIL
(View from bottom)
3¼"
Stop rabbet here on both sides
1/4" rabbet 1/8" deep
3/4" x #17 brad
3/4" hole
Sand corners round to fit rabbet

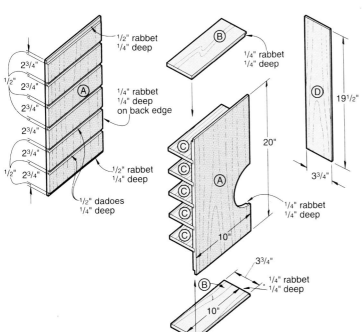

1/2" rabbet 1/4" deep
2¾"
½"
1/4" rabbet 1/4" deep on back edge
1/2" rabbet 1/4" deep
1/2" dadoes 1/4" deep
1/4" rabbet 1/4" deep
20"
19½"
3¾"
1/4" rabbet 1/4" deep
10"
3¾"
1/4" rabbet 1/4" deep
10"

Bill of Materials

Part	Finished Size			Mat.	Qty.
	T	**W**	**L**		
BELT-SANDER BELT DIVIDER					
A	½"	10"	20"	M	2
B	½"	3¾"	10"	M	2
C	½"	3¾"	9¾"	M	5
D	¼"	3¾"	19½"	BP	1

Material Key: BP—birch plywood, M—maple

A Workhorse of a Workbench

LET'S BUILD THE SUPER-STURDY LEGS FIRST

1 From 1½"-thick, straight-grained pine, rip and crosscut eight pieces 3¼" wide by 33¼" long for the leg blanks. Plane the edges of the stock before ripping it to finished width to re-move the rounded corners. (See the Design Notes *below left* for our method of obtaining straight-grained pieces from common lumberyard 2x10 stock.)

2 Cut a 3" dado ½" deep 18¾" from the bottom end of each leg blank where shown on the Mortise detail accompanying the End-Frame Assembly drawing.

3 Cut a 1x3x6" spacer to temporarily fit in the mating dadoes of two leg blanks where shown on the drawing on *page 96*. With the spacer between the pair of dadoes and the edges of the leg blanks flush, glue and clamp the pieces together. Then, remove the spacer before the glue dries. (We used pieces of scrap-wood stock between the clamp jaws and legs to prevent the metal jaws from denting the softwood.) Repeat the clamping process for each leg.

4 Remove the clamps, scrape the glue from one edge, and plane ⅛"
continued

Our *Idea-Shop*™ workbench may be the design you've waited years for. It's simple to build and super-strong. We relied on inexpensive lumberyard stock and rugged mortise-and-tenon joinery to construct the base. For the benchtop, we laminated maple to handle a lifetime of workshop activity. And we added bench dogs and a bench vise to expand the usefulness of our workbench, making it a fitting centerpiece for any home workshop. Plus, see the matching stool on *page 100*.

bow, and chose the straightest and driest pieces available. (If you have a moisture meter, take it with you when you shop.)

After getting the stock back to the *WOOD*® magazine shop, we stickered the boards, and let them acclimate to our indoor environment for several weeks before cutting the parts (A, B, C, D) from along the edges where shown in the sketch at *right*. This allowed us to use the straightest grain possible and achieve the best results.

—*J.R. Downing*
Design Editor

DESIGN NOTES

To keep costs down on this project, we hand-picked straight-grained pine 2x10s for the workbench base at a local lumberyard. In addition, we checked each 2x10 for twist and

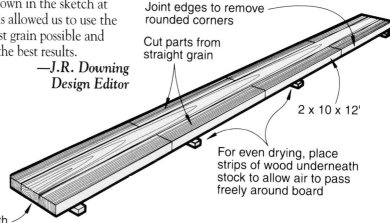

Joint edges to remove rounded corners

Cut parts from straight grain

2 x 10 x 12'

For even drying, place strips of wood underneath stock to allow air to pass freely around board

Pith

60"

29³/₄"

Center benchtop over base

Drill ³/₁₆" pilot holes 1" deep on bottom of benchtop to mate with lag screws

Do not chamfer top edges

¹/₄" flat washer

¹/₄ x 2¹/₂" lag screw

33¹/₂"

8"

38"

¹/₄" chamfers

¹/₄" chamfers

EXPLODED VIEW

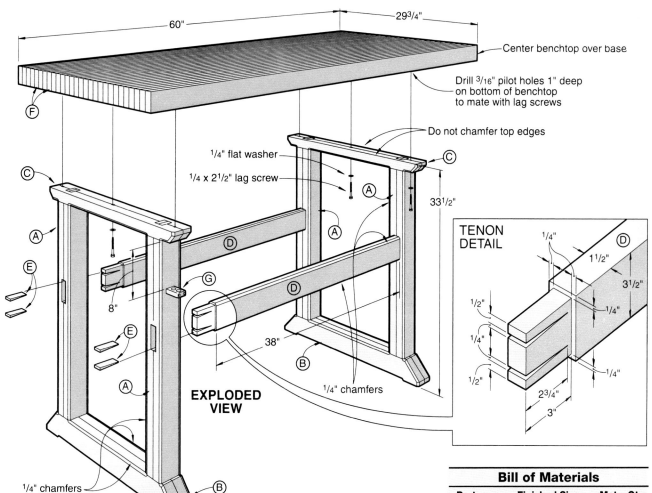

TENON DETAIL

¹/₄"

1¹/₂"

3¹/₂"

¹/₄"

¹/₂"

¹/₄"

¹/₂"

¹/₄"

2³/₄"

3"

CUTTING DIAGRAM

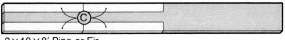

2 × 10 × 12' Pine or Fir

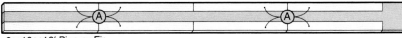

2 × 10 × 8' Pine or Fir

2 × 10 × 12' Pine or Fir

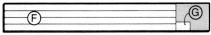

1¹/₁₆ x 9¹/₄ x 72" Maple (7 pieces)

Bill of Materials

Part	Finished Size			Mat.	Qty.
	T	W	L		
A* legs	3"	3"	33¹/₄"	LP	4
B* feet	3"	3¹/₄"	29¹/₂"	LP	2
C* rails	3"	1¹/₂"	28"	LP	2
D stretchers	1¹/₂"	3¹/₂"	44"	P	2
E* wedges	³/₈"	1"	3¹/₄"	DH	8
F* top pieces	1¹/₁₆"	2¹/₄"	60"	M	28
G dog holder	1¹/₁₆"	1³/₄"	2⁵/₈"	M	1

*Initially cut parts marked with an * oversized. Then, trim each to finished size according to the how-to instructions.

Material Key: LP—laminated pine, P—pine, DH—dark hardwood, M—maple
Supplies: 3—¹/₂" all-thread rods 27¹/₄" long, 6—¹/₂" nuts, 6—¹/₂" washers, 6—¹/₄ x 2¹/₂" lag screws, ¹/₄" flat washers, clear finish.

A Workhorse of a Workbench

continued

from the scraped edge to get it flat. Rip the opposite edge for a 3¹⁄₁₆" width. Next, plane ¹⁄₁₆" from the cut edge to remove the saw marks and to obtain the 3" finished width. Repeat for each leg.

NOW, ADD THE FEET AND RAILS FOR A WOBBLE-FREE BASE

1 For the feet (B) and the rails (C), see the End-Frame Assembly and Parts View drawings, follow the same method described to form the legs (A). Cut the pieces oversized in width, cut the dadoes, glue the pieces together with the dadoes and edges of the boards aligned, and then trim to finished width.

2 Clamp the two feet (B) bottom edge to bottom edge. Mark a center point 3¼" from each end of the clamped-together feet. Now, use a compass to mark a ½" hole (¼" radius) at each center point. Draw straight lines to connect the edges of each circle where shown in Photo A *opposite*.

3 Mark a 45° cutline across the end of each leg where shown on the Parts View drawing. Do the same thing to the ends of the rails where shown on the End-Frame Assembly drawing.

4 As shown in Photo A, drill a ½" hole at each marked center point. Remove the clamps, and bandsaw between the holes along the inside edge of the marked line. Sand to the line to remove saw marks.

5 Using the dimensions on the End-Frame Assembly and Parts View drawings, miter-cut (we used a bandsaw) both ends of each foot (B) and both ends of each rail (C). Sand smooth.

6 Drill a trio of ⅜" holes in each rail (C) where shown on the Parts View drawing.

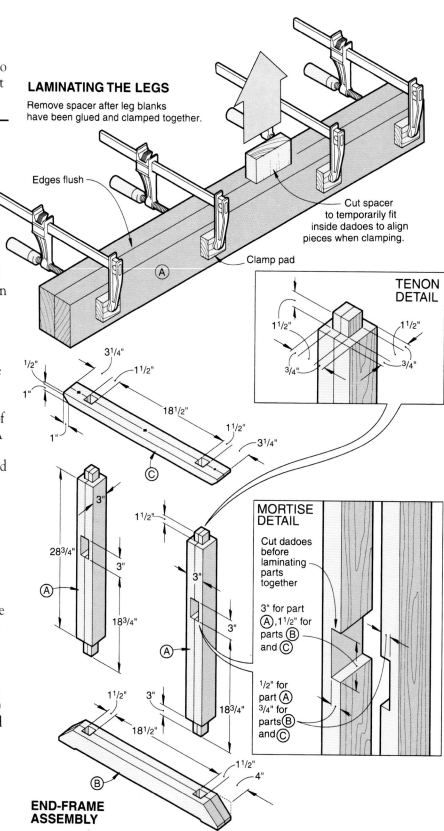

LAMINATING THE LEGS
Remove spacer after leg blanks have been glued and clamped together.

Edges flush

Cut spacer to temporarily fit inside dadoes to align pieces when clamping.

Clamp pad

Ⓐ

TENON DETAIL
1¹⁄₂"   1¹⁄₂"
³⁄₄"   ³⁄₄"

½"
1"
3¹⁄₄"
1¹⁄₂"
18¹⁄₂"
1"
1¹⁄₂"
3¹⁄₄"
Ⓒ

3"
28³⁄₄"
3"
18³⁄₄"
Ⓐ
Ⓐ

1¹⁄₂"
3"
3"
3"
18³⁄₄"
Ⓐ

MORTISE DETAIL
Cut dadoes before laminating parts together

3" for part Ⓐ, 1¹⁄₂" for parts Ⓑ and Ⓒ

½" for part Ⓐ
³⁄₄" for parts Ⓑ and Ⓒ

1¹⁄₂"
3"
18¹⁄₂"
1¹⁄₂"
4"
Ⓑ

END-FRAME ASSEMBLY

A

Clamp the feet together, and drill a ½" hole at the marked center points to form the radiused bottoms.

B

Tap the hardwood wedges into the notches. After the glue dries, trim the wedges flush with the legs.

NEXT, LET'S ASSEMBLE THE BASE

1 Mount an auxiliary wood fence to your miter gauge and a dado blade to your table-saw. Cut tenons to the sizes shown on the End-Frame Assembly drawing and accompanying Tenon detail.

2 Glue and clamp each end frame together, checking for square.

3 Rout ¼" chamfers along the edges of the end frames where shown on the Exploded View drawing.

4 Cut the stretchers (D) to size. Cut a 3"-long tenon at each end of each stretcher to fit snugly through the leg mortises.

5 Rout a ¼" chamfer along the edges of the stretchers between the tenons.

6 Using the Tenon detail accompanying the Exploded View drawing, bandsaw a pair of V-shaped notches in each tenon.

7 Cut eight wedges (E) to the size shown on the Parts View drawing. (For contrast against the light pine, use a dark-colored hardwood for the wedges; we choose genuine mahogany.)

8 Glue and clamp the stretchers in place between the end frame assemblies. Inject a bit of glue in each notch, and using a mallet, tap the wedges into the notches, and check for square.

9 Being careful not to mar the surface of the leg, trim the wedges flush as shown in Photo B.

BUILD A TOP THAT CAN TAKE A POUNDING

Note: *You either can laminate your own maple top as described below or substitute a solid-core door from a local lumberyard or home center. Ask to find out if the company has any doors that customers have rejected because of mistakes in staining or cutting. You can*
continued

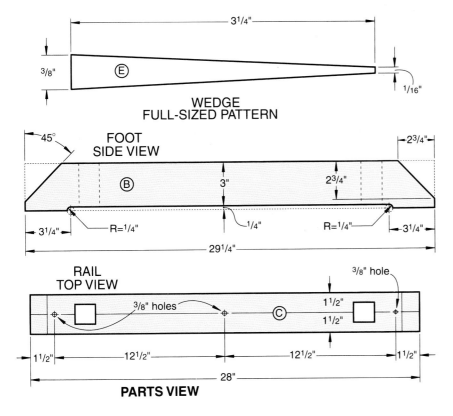

3¼"

3/8"

Ⓔ

1/16"

**WEDGE
FULL-SIZED PATTERN**

45°

**FOOT
SIDE VIEW**

Ⓑ

2¾"

3"

2¾"

R=¼"

¼"

R=¼"

3¼"

3¼"

29¼"

**RAIL
TOP VIEW**

3/8" hole

3/8" holes

Ⓒ

1½"

1½"

1½"

12½"

12½"

1½"

28"

PARTS VIEW

A Workhorse of a Workbench

continued

purchase these for a fraction of their retail cost. Avoid doors rejected because of warpage.

1 Cut 28 pieces of 1¹⁄₁₆"-thick maple (F) to 2¼×61" for the laminated top. For reference when drilling and laminating later, mark an X on the best (defect-free) edge (not face) of each strip.

2 Using the drawing *below right* for reference, construct and attach a long fence to your drill press to ensure consistently spaced holes. Add a support to each end. Mark the reference marks on the fence where shown on the drawing.

3 With the marked edge facing out, align the ends with the reference marks on the fence, and drill three ⅝" holes in 24 of the 28 benchtop pieces.

4 Still using the fence and your marks, drill three 1½" holes ¾" deep with a ½" hole centered inside each 1½" hole in two of the remaining four pieces.

5 Glue and clamp eight of the predrilled pieces (F) face-to-face, with the edges and ends flush, the ⅝" holes aligned, and the Xs facing up. Next, glue and clamp two nine-piece sections together in the same manner. Each of the nine-piece sections should have a strip with the 1½" holes on one outside edge. See the Top Assembly drawing for reference. (We found it easier to laminate three sections, and then glue and clamp the three sections together to form the top.) You should still have two maple strips (F) with no holes in them.

6 Using a hacksaw, cut three pieces of ½"-diameter all-thread rod to 27¼" long.

7 Spread glue on the mating edges, and clamp the three sections edge-to-edge, using pipe clamps and the all-thread rod with nuts and flat washers attached. Check that the surfaces are flush. (We used a ratchet to tighten the ½" nuts on the all-

thread rod.) Alternate back and forth between the clamps and the nuts on the threaded rods for even clamping pressure.

8 Glue the remaining two top pieces (F) to the edges of the top assembly to hide the holes and threaded rods.

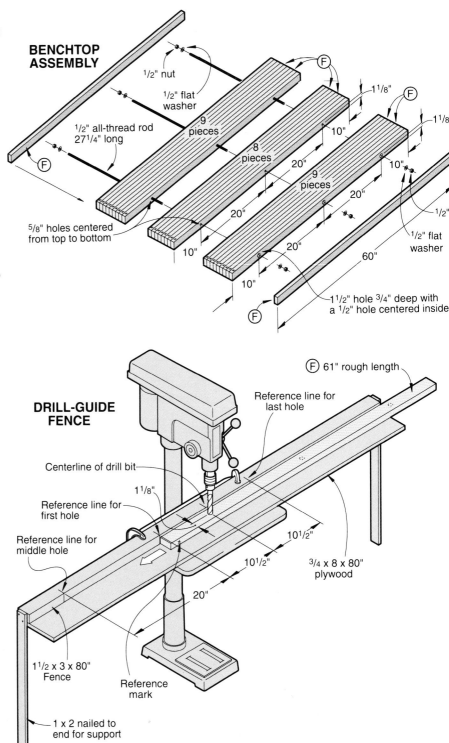

BENCHTOP ASSEMBLY

½" nut
½" flat washer
½" all-thread rod 27¼" long
9 pieces
8 pieces
9 pieces
1¹⁄₈"
1¹⁄₈"
10"
10"
20"
20"
20"
20"
½" nut
½" flat washer
60"
⅝" holes centered from top to bottom
10"
10"
1½" hole ¾" deep with a ½" hole centered inside
F

DRILL-GUIDE FENCE

(F) 61" rough length
Reference line for last hole
Centerline of drill bit
1¹⁄₈"
Reference line for first hole
Reference line for middle hole
10½"
10½"
20"
¾ x 8 x 80" plywood
1½ x 3 x 80" Fence
Reference mark
1 x 2 nailed to end for support

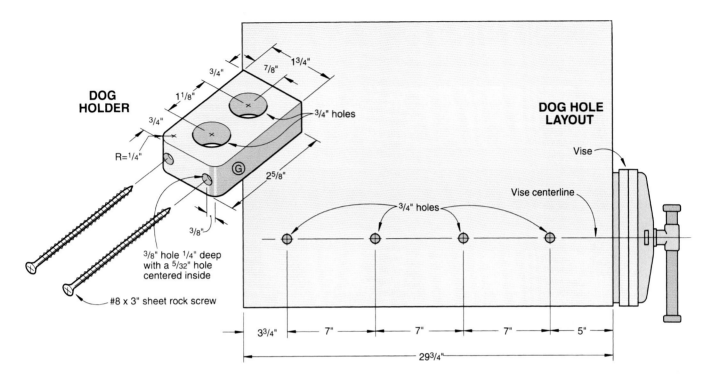

DOG HOLDER

3/4"
7/8"
1 3/4"
1 1/8"
3/4"
3/4" holes
R=1/4"
2 5/8"
3/8"
3/8" hole 1/4" deep with a 5/32" hole centered inside
#8 x 3" sheet rock screw

DOG HOLE LAYOUT

Vise
Vise centerline
3/4" holes
3 3/4" — 7" — 7" — 7" — 5"
29 3/4"

9 Scrape off the excess glue, and then belt-sand both surfaces of the benchtop flat.

10 Fit your portable circular saw with a carbide-tipped blade. Clamp a straightedge to the benchtop, and trim ½" off one end of the benchtop. Repeat at the other end.

FINISHING UP

1 Finish-sand the base and top.

2 Center the benchtop assembly on the base. Clamp the top to the base. Using the previously drilled holes in the rails (C) as guide, drill six 5/16" pilot holes 1" deep into the bottom side of the benchtop assembly. The holes in the rail are slightly oversized to allow the lag screws to move with the expansion and contraction of the benchtop. Using ¼" lag screws and flat washers, fasten the base to the top.

3 Add the finish to all surfaces. (We applied three coats of Watco Natural Danish Oil Finish.)

4 Drill the mounting holes, and add a vise using the instructions provided with the vise (see the Buying Guide for our source).

5 Mark and drill ¾" dog holes through the benchtop where shown in the drawing *above*.

6 If you use the same type of round bench dogs we did, mark the layout for the dog holder (G) on a piece of 1 1/16" maple. Mark the center points for the dogs and the mounting screws. Bore the holes for the dogs, and then cut the dog hold to shape. Next, drill the mounting holes, sand smooth, and apply the finish. Finally, screw the dog hold to the leg nearest the vise.

BUYING GUIDE

• **Woodworker's Vise.** Cast-iron jaws, predrilled mounting holes, 34 lbs., with retractable "dog." Catalog No. 9GT51875. Available to order through Sears stores nationwide.

• **Round bench dogs.** Two, with wire springs allowing for height adjustment. Catalog No. 827116. For current prices, contact Woodworker's Supply, Inc., 11 Glenn Rd., Casper, WY 82601, or call 800/645-9292 to order.

PROJECT TOOL LIST
• Tablesaw
• Dado blade or dado set
• Bandsaw
• Portable circular saw
• Jointer
• Drill press
• Portable drill
• Bits: 5/32", 3/16", 3/8", ½", 5/8", ¾", 1½"
• Router
• Chamfer bit
• Belt sander
• Finishing sander

Note: We built the project using the tools listed. You may be able to substitute other tools or equipment for listed items you don't have. Additional common hand tools and clamps may be required to complete the project.

Sit-a-Spell Shop Stool

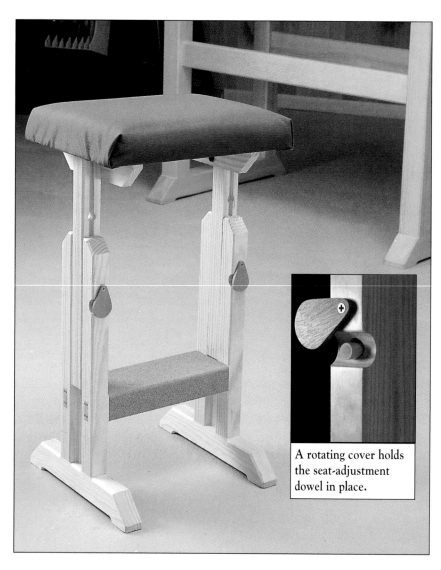

A rotating cover holds the seat-adjustment dowel in place.

If you're one of those wood-workers who spends every spare minute working in your shop, you're going to love this shop stool. The padded seat makes it a joy to sit on. And with the special height-adjustment system we've designed into it, you can raise or lower the seat to suit your height and the surface you're working at.

CUT AND LAMINATE PIECES FOR THE LEGS, FEET, AND STRETCHERS

1 To form the laminated legs (A), cut eight pieces of ¾"-thick, straight-grained pine (we used 1×4s) to 1¾" wide by 19" long for the leg blanks.

2 Cut a 1½" dado ¼" deep 8" from the bottom of each leg where shown on the Leg drawing on *page 102*.

3 Cut a ⅜×1½×3" spacer to temporarily fit in the mating dadoes of two leg blanks. With the spacer between the dadoes and the edges of the leg blanks flush, glue and clamp the pieces. Immediately after clamping, remove the spacer. Repeat for the other three legs.

4 Remove the clamps, scrape the glue from one edge, and plane the scraped edge to get it flat. Then, rip the opposite edge for a 1⁵⁄₁₆" width.

Next, plane ⅟₁₆" from the cut edge to remove the saw marks and obtain the 1½" finished width. Repeat for the other legs.

5 Follow the method described in Steps 1–4 to make the feet (B). Cut the pieces oversized in width, cut the dadoes, glue the pieces together, and then trim. Repeat the process (minus the dadoes) for the stretchers (C).

FINISH MACHINING THE LEGS, FEET, AND STRETCHERS

1 Mount an auxiliary wood fence to your miter gauge and a dado blade to your tablesaw. Using the dimensions on the Tenon detail accompanying the Stretcher Assembly drawing on *page 102*, cut tenons on the bottom ends of the legs and both ends of the stretchers.

2 Using the dimensions on the Tenon detail, bandsaw a pair of V-shaped notches in each tenon in the stretchers and legs.

3 With the dimensions on the Leg drawing, angle-cut the top end of each leg. Use the dimensions on the Foot drawing and accompanying Foot End detail to angle-cut both ends of each foot.

4 Clamp (without glue) the feet (B) bottom edge to bottom edge. Mark a center point 2¼" from each end of the legs. Use a compass to mark a ½" hole at each center point. Draw lines to connect the edges of each marked circle.

5 Drill a ½" hole at each marked center point. Remove the clamps, and bandsaw out the waste between the holes, cutting just inside the marked lines. Sand to the lines to remove the saw marks and finish shaping each recess.

IT'S TIME TO ASSEMBLE THE STOOL BASE

1 Cut the four guides (D) to the size stated in the Bill of Materials.

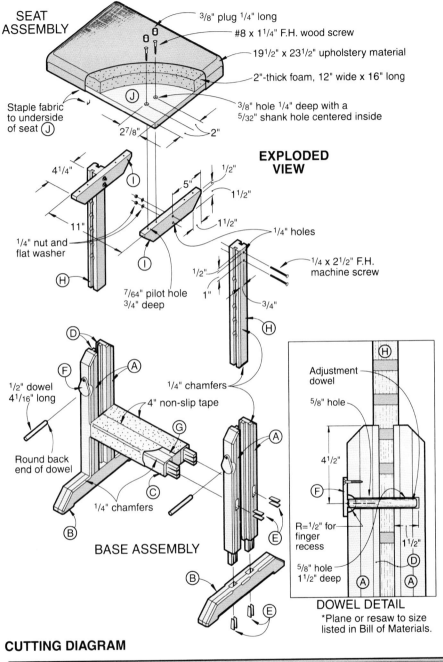

SEAT ASSEMBLY

3/8" plug 1/4" long

#8 x 1 1/4" F.H. wood screw

19 1/2" x 23 1/2" upholstery material

2"-thick foam, 12" wide x 16" long

3/8" hole 1/4" deep with a 5/32" shank hole centered inside

Staple fabric to underside of seat J

2 7/8"

2"

EXPLODED VIEW

4 1/4"

5"

1/2"

1 1/2"

1 1/2"

11"

1/4" holes

1/4" nut and flat washer

1/4 x 2 1/2" F.H. machine screw

1/2"

1"

3/4"

H

7/64" pilot hole 3/4" deep

1/2" dowel 4 1/16" long

1/4" chamfers

4" non-slip tape

Round back end of dowel

1/4" chamfers

BASE ASSEMBLY

DOWEL DETAIL
*Plane or resaw to size listed in Bill of Materials.

Adjustment dowel

5/8" hole

4 1/2"

R=1/2" for finger recess

5/8" hole 1 1/2" deep

1 1/2"

Bill of Materials

Part	Finished Size			Mat.	Qty.
	T	W	L		
BASE ASSEMBLY					
A* legs	1½"	1½"	19"	LP	4
B* feet	1½"	2¼"	14"	LP	2
C* stretchers	1½"	2"	14"	LP	2
D guides	⅜"	⅜"	17"	P	4
E wedges	³⁄₁₆"	½"	2¼"	DH	16
F covers	¼"	1⅜"	2¼"	DH	2
G* spacer	1½"	2"	11"	LP	1
SEAT ASSEMBLY					
H* posts	1½"	1½"	17"	LP	2
I rails	¾"	2"	10"	P	2
J* seat	¾"	12"	16"	EJP	1

*Initially cut parts marked with an * oversized. Then, trim each to finished size according to the how-to instructions.

Material Key: LP—laminated pine, P—pine, DH—dark hardwood, EJP—edge-joined pine
Supplies: #8x1¼" flathead wood screws, 4—¼x2½" flathead brass machine screws with flat washers and nuts, ½" dowel stock, non-slip tape, 2"-thick foam, upholstery material, staples, clear finish.

With the ends flush and the guide centered from side to side, glue and clamp one guide to each leg. See the Guide detail accompanying the Leg drawing for reference.

2 Transfer the full-sized wedge pattern (E) to ½"-thick dark hardwood (we chose mahogany), and cut 16 wedges to shape.

continued

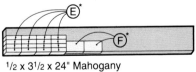

1/2 x 3 1/2 x 24" Mahogany

CUTTING DIAGRAM

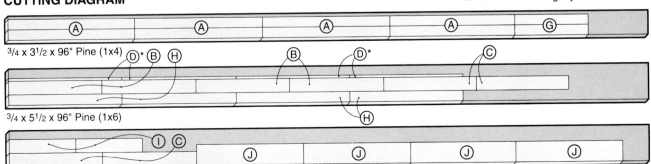

3/4 x 3 1/2 x 96" Pine (1x4)

3/4 x 5 1/2 x 96" Pine (1x6)

3/4 x 5 1/2 x 96" Pine (1x6)

Sit-a-Spell Shop Stool

continued

3 Next, transfer the hole cover pattern (F) and hole center point to 1/4"-thick stock. Cut the covers to shape, drill and countersink a 5/32" mounting hole in each, and set them aside for now. Fastened to the legs later, the covers prevent the dowels from sliding out when you move the stool around.

4 To bore the adjustment-dowel holes, dry-clamp a pair of legs together with the tenoned ends flush and the guides (D) mating and flush. Using a brad-point bit, bore a 5/8" hole where shown in the Dowel detail accompanying the Exploded View drawing and the Leg drawing. Drill through the first leg/guide and 1 1/2" into the second leg/guide.

5 To form the finger recesses, clamp the two front legs with the bored sides face-to-face, holes aligned, and the tenoned ends flush. Drill a 1" hole 4 1/2" from the top end and centered over the 5/8" adjustment-dowel holes as shown in the photo *opposite*.

6 Glue and clamp the stretchers (C) between the legs (A), checking for square. Inject a bit of glue in each notch, and using a mallet, tap the wedges into the notches. Again, check for square.

7 Glue and clamp the feet (B) to the bottom ends of the legs (A). Glue and drive the wedges.

8 Being careful not to mar the surfaces of the leg, trim and sand the wedges flush.

9 Measure the opening between the stretchers (C), and cut the spacer (G) to fit. (Since we were already using 3/4" stock, we laminated two pieces and then trimmed the laminated piece to size.) Glue the spacer in place.

10 Rout 1/4" chamfers along the edges of the base pieces where shown on the Exploded View drawing.

LET'S ADD THE ADJUSTABLE SEAT

1 Laminate 3/4" stock, and trim the adjustment posts (H) to size.

2 Mark the center points for the 5/8" holes on the surface (not edge) where shown on the Adjustment Post drawing, and bore the five holes through each post.

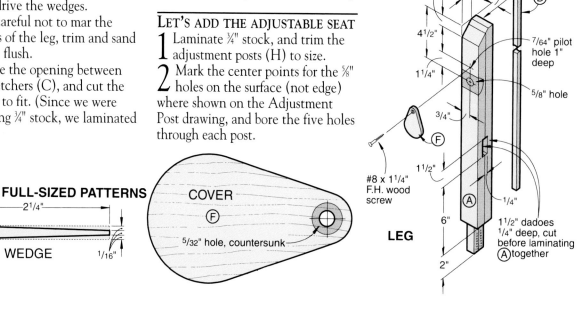

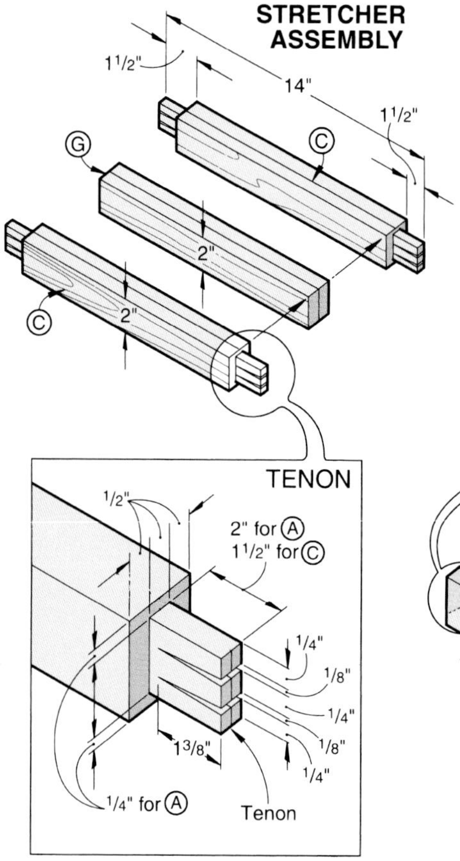
STRETCHER ASSEMBLY
1 1/2"
14"
1 1/2"
G
C
2"
2"
C
TENON
1/2"
2" for A
1 1/2" for C
1/4"
1/8"
1/4"
1/8"
1/4"
1 3/8"
1/4" for A
Tenon

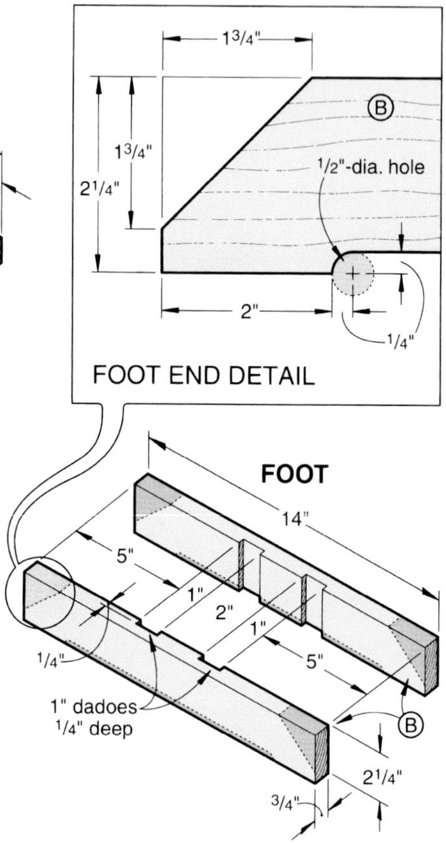
1 3/4"
B
1 3/4"
2 1/4"
1/2"-dia. hole
2"
1/4"
FOOT END DETAIL
FOOT
14"
5"
1"
2"
1"
5"
1/4"
1" dadoes
1/4" deep
B
2 1/4"
3/4"

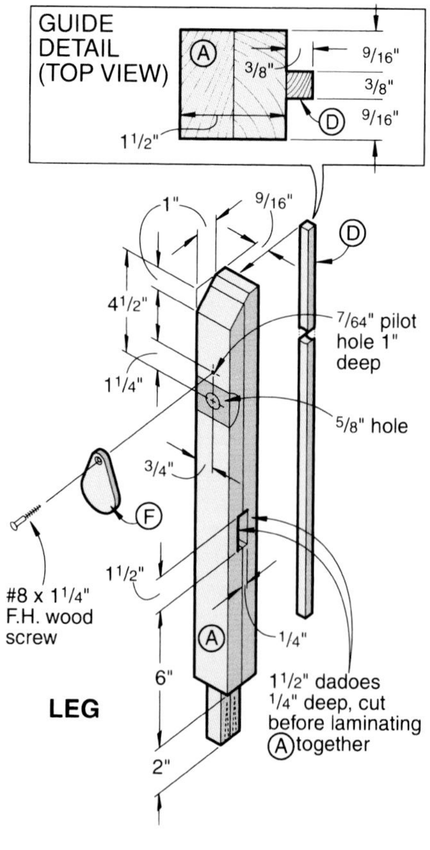
GUIDE
DETAIL
(TOP VIEW)
A
3/8"
9/16"
3/8"
9/16"
D
1 1/2"
1"
9/16"
D
4 1/2"
7/64" pilot
hole 1"
deep
1 1/4"
5/8" hole
3/4"
F
1 1/2"
#8 x 1 1/4"
F.H. wood
screw
A
1/4"
6"
1 1/2" dadoes
1/4" deep, cut
before laminating
A together
LEG
2"

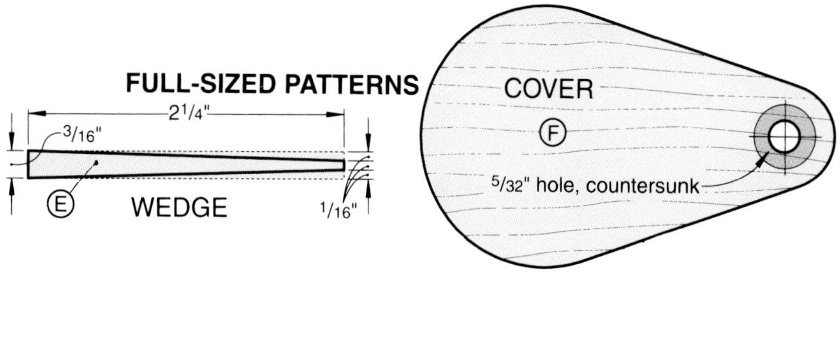
FULL-SIZED PATTERNS
2 1/4"
3/16"
E
WEDGE
1/16"
COVER
F
5/32" hole, countersunk

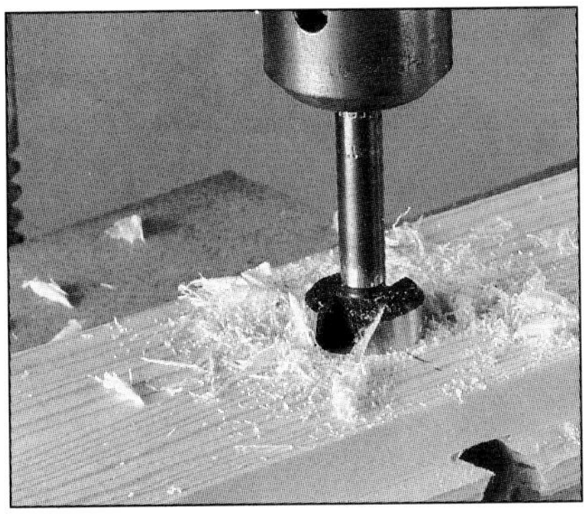

With the stool legs clamped together and the adjustment-dowel holes aligned, bore a 1" hole through both legs to form the finger recesses.

3 Rout 1/4" chamfers along the edge and bottom ends where shown on the Exploded View drawing.

4 Cut or rout a 3/8" groove 3/8" deep centered over the 5/8" holes on both sides of each post. Test the fit of each post on the guides between each pair of legs; the posts should slide easily up and down on their mating guides. If not, slightly enlarge the grooves.

5 Cut the seat rails (I) to size, angle-cutting the ends where dimensioned on the Exploded View drawing. Drill a pair of 1/4" holes through each rail where shown on the Adjustment Post drawing.

6 Edge-join 3/4" stock, and cut the seat (J) to size.

7 With the top edges flush, glue a rail to the inside face of each post (H), checking for square. Using the previously drilled 1/4" holes in the rails as guides, drill 1/4" holes through the posts. Strengthen each rail/post joint with a pair of 1/4x2 1/2" flathead machine screws.

8 Cut a pair of 1/2" dowels 4 1/16" long. For easy insertion into the legs later, sand a round-over on one end of each dowel.

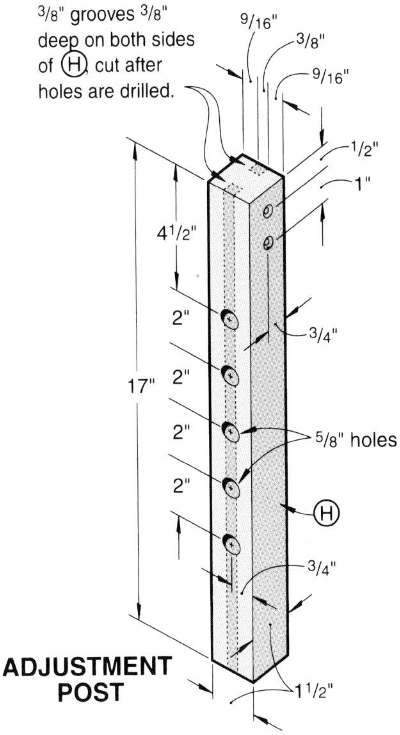
3/8" grooves 3/8" deep on both sides of (H) cut after holes are drilled.
9/16"
3/8"
9/16"
1/2"
1"
4 1/2"
2"
17"
2"
2"
2"
3/4"
5/8" holes
H
3/4"
1 1/2"
ADJUSTMENT POST

FASTEN THE SEAT TO THE ADJUSTABLE POSTS

1 Insert the adjustment posts between the legs, adjust to the same level, and insert the dowels.

2 Center, then glue and clamp the seat to the rails.

3 To further secure the seat to the rails, drill eight 3/8" holes 1/4" deep where shown on the Exploded View drawing, centered over the rails. Drill a shank hole through the seat and a pilot hole into the rail as dimensioned on the Exploded View drawing. Drive #8x1 1/4" wood screws through the holes.

4 Using a 3/8" plug cutter, cut eight plugs from 5/16" stock. Glue the plugs in place, and sand the protruding ends of the plugs flush with the top surface of the seat.

CLEAN UP BEFORE TAKING A SEAT

1 Disassemble the loose parts and sand the base, seat assembly, and covers (F) smooth.

2 To protect the stretchers, apply nonslip tape.

3 Mask the nonslip tape, and apply a clear finish to the parts (we used satin polyurethane).

4 For an exposed wood seat, rout a 3/8" round-over along the seat's top edge. Or, for a cushioned seat, have a piece of 2"-thick foam cut to size, cover it with upholstery material, and staple the material to the bottom of the seat.

5 Slide the seat assembly's adjustment posts into the base. Fasten the covers (F) to the base. Raise the stool to a comfortable seating height, insert the dowels, and give yourself a well-deserved break.

PROJECT TOOL LIST

- Tablesaw
- Dado blade or dado set
- Bandsaw
- Jointer
- Drill press
- Portable drill
- Bits: 7/64", 5/32", 1/4", 3/8", 1/2", 5/8", 1"
- 3/8" plug cutter
- Router
- Bits: chamfer, 3/8" straight
- Belt sander
- Finishing sander

Note: *We built the project using the tools listed. You may be able to substitute other tools or equipment for listed items you don't have. Additional common hand tools and clamps may be required to complete the project.*

C-Clamp Coatrack

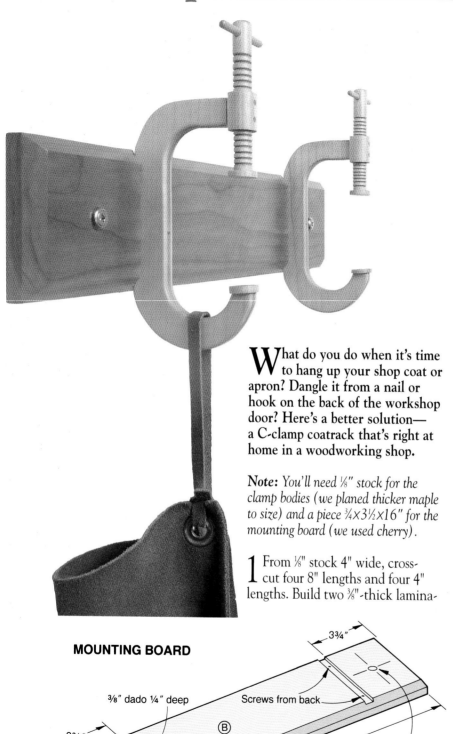

W hat do you do when it's time to hang up your shop coat or apron? Dangle it from a nail or hook on the back of the workshop door? Here's a better solution— a C-clamp coatrack that's right at home in a woodworking shop.

Note: *You'll need ⅛" stock for the clamp bodies (we planed thicker maple to size) and a piece ¾×3½×16" for the mounting board (we used cherry).*

1 From ⅛" stock 4" wide, cross-cut four 8" lengths and four 4" lengths. Build two ⅜"-thick lamina-tions, each with two 4" pieces laid edge to edge between two 8" pieces. Run the grain in the center layer at a right angle to the grain on the sides. Glue with epoxy, and clamp.

2 Stack the two laminations together with double-faced tape. Trace the pattern for the clamp body (A) onto the stack, and then cut with a bandsaw (use a ⅛" blade) or scrollsaw. Sand ¹⁄₁₆" round-overs where shown.

3 For the mounting board (B), rout ⅜" chamfers and ⅜" dadoes ¼" deep where shown. Glue a clamp body (A) into each dado with epoxy, and secure each from the back with two countersunk #6×1" flathead wood screws.

4 Drill a ½" hole 2⅛" deep centered on one end of a ¾" dowel 3" long. To do so, nail two 2×3" pieces of scrap wood together into a 3"-tall right angle. Secure the dowel into the corner with double-faced tape. Hold the jig with a hand-screw clamp as you drill.

5 Bandsaw or scrollsaw two ⅞" lengths of the drilled-out dowel for parts C. Sand a ⅜"-wide flat side on each. Glue parts C to parts A where shown.

6 On two 5" lengths of ½" dowel, mark the simulated thread lines for parts E where shown on the full-sized pattern. Chuck each length into your drill press. Run the machine at its slowest speed as you cut ¹⁄₁₆" deep at each mark with a hacksaw or triangular file. Then, sand a ¹⁄₁₆" chamfer on the end. Drill the ³⁄₁₆" hole where shown. Trim to 3⅝".

7 Round the ends of two 2" lengths of ³⁄₁₆" dowel, and glue one into the hole on each part E. Glue part E into part C, with 1" extending from the bottom of part C and the handle crosswise.

MOUNTING BOARD

3¾"

⅜" dado ¼" deep

Screws from back

3¾"

Ⓑ

3½"

16"

Locate mounting hole where needed

⅜" chamfer on all edges

8 Next, drill ⅛" holes 1⅛" deep where indicated. Glue ⅛" dowels 1¼" long into the holes, and sand the ends flush. Cut four pieces of ¾" dowel ¼" long for pads (D), and glue them in place. Finish-sand, and apply a clear oil finish followed by two coats of satin polyurethane varnish.

PROJECT TOOL LIST
- Tablesaw
- Bandsaw or scrollsaw
- Drill press
- Bits: ⅛", ³⁄₁₆", ½"
- Router
- Bits: ⅜", straight, chamfer
- Disc or belt sander
- Finishing sander

Note: *We built the project using the tools listed. You may be able to substitute other tools or equipment for listed items you don't have. Additional common hand tools and clamps may be required to complete the project.*

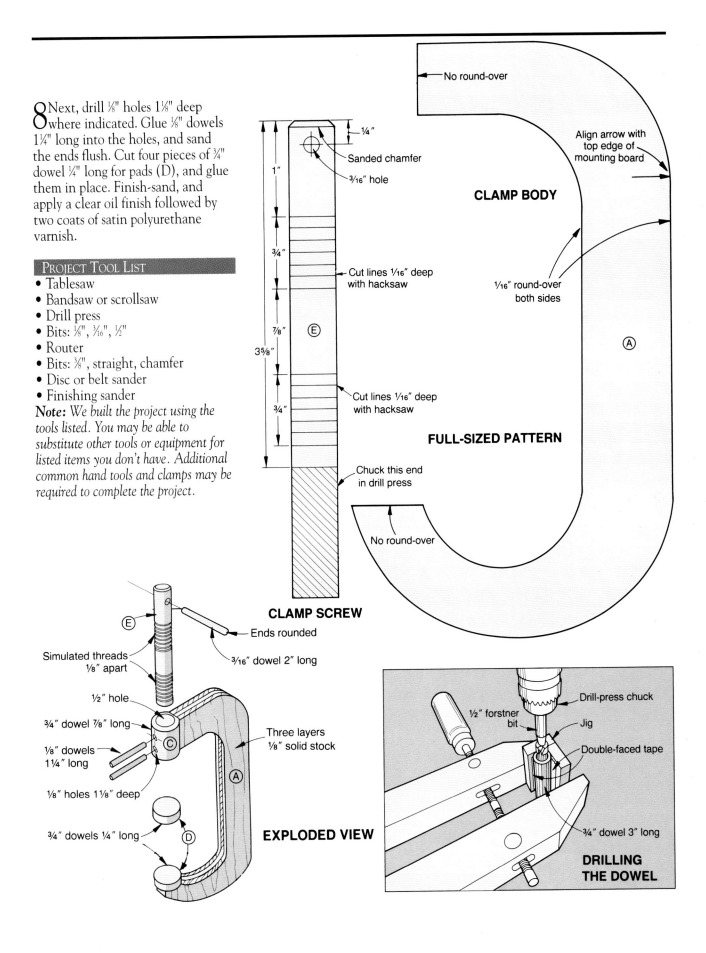

Workshop Clock

Plane and simple

Though a good woodworking project often makes us forget about time, no shop should be without an appropriate clock—for telling when the glue's dry or supper's ready. This tool-topped timepiece, designed by Jim Boelling, begs to be noticed and will serve as a conversation piece among your woodworking friends.

Note: *You'll need 1¹⁄₁₆"-thick stock (also known as five-quarter stock) in cherry, maple, and walnut to build the workshop clock.*

1 From 1¹⁄₁₆"-thick stock, rip three pieces of cherry to 3¹⁄₁₆", and trim each to 12" long. Also rip and crosscut a 3½×12" piece of maple and a 3×8" piece of walnut. Edge-glue the cherry boards together. When the glue dries, cut the panel to 9" square for the clock surround. Sand smooth.

2 Chuck a 3" Forstner bit into your drill press, and bore a centered hole ⅞" deep into the clock surround's back side. Change to a ⅜" bit to drill the shaft hole. Hand-drill an angled ⅛" hanging hole near the top on back.

3 Next, make the plane ornament. Transfer the patterns to your walnut, maple, and cherry stock (use the cutoff from the clock surround for the cherry). Cut the pieces with a bandsaw (we used a ⅛" blade) or a scrollsaw and then sand them to fit together.

4 Tape a copy of the pattern to a scrap piece of plywood, cover it with waxed paper, and then position the maple plane base on the pattern, pinning it in place with 4d finish nails. Next, glue on the walnut knob and handle, followed by the maple frog and iron assembly, and the cherry thumb knob. Once dry, sand both sides, rounding over the edges.

5 Now, glue the plane to the top edge of the surround, offsetting it about ¹⁄₁₆" toward the front. For a uniform offset, lay the clock surround faceup on the plywood, and then place ¼" flat washers under the plane as you glue it on. Clamp the plane to the surround by pinning with 4d finish nails. Sand the

assembled clock, and apply a clear oil finish. Follow with two coats of polyurethane.

6 Carefully center the face and bezel assembly on the front of the surround over the shaft hole. Measure straight up from the bottom of the surround to the 3 o'clock mark and the 9 o'clock mark on the face. Rotate the bezel around the shaft hole until both measurements are the same. Hold it with masking tape. Using a light tack hammer, attach the assembly with the brass brads provided. Install the movement, put on the hands, and insert the battery.

BUYING GUIDE

• **Clock movement, face, bezel, and hands.** Quartz clock movement, face and bezel assembly, mounting hardware, and set of hands.

Product No. 71166. For current prices, contact Klockit, P.O. Box 636, Lake Geneva, WI 53147, or call 800/556-2548 to order.

PROJECT TOOL LIST
• Tablesaw
• Bandsaw or scrollsaw
• Drill press
• Portable drill
• Bits: ⅛", ⅜", 3"
• Finishing sander

Note: *We built the project using the tools listed. You may be able to substitute other tools or equipment for listed items you don't have. Additional common hand tools and clamps may be required to complete the project.*

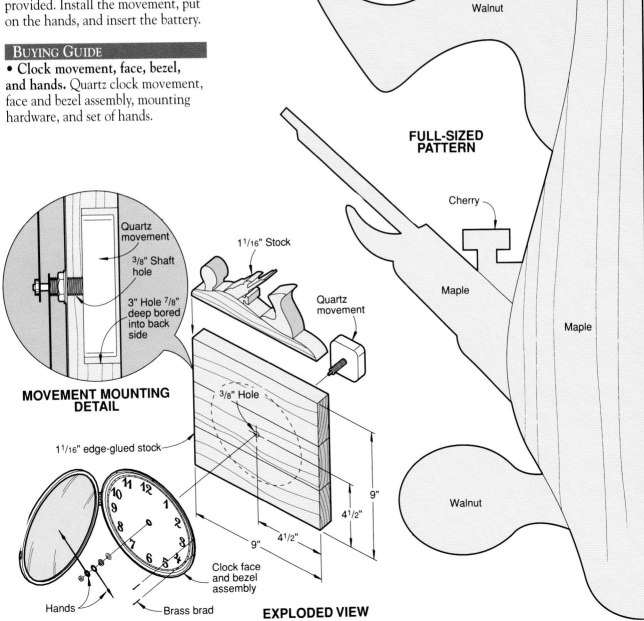

Walnut

FULL-SIZED PATTERN

Cherry

Maple

Maple

Walnut

Quartz movement

⅜" Shaft hole

3" Hole ⅞" deep bored into back side

MOVEMENT MOUNTING DETAIL

1¹/₁₆" Stock

Quartz movement

⅜" Hole

1¹/₁₆" edge-glued stock

9"

4¹/₂"

9"

4¹/₂"

Clock face and bezel assembly

Hands

Brass brad

EXPLODED VIEW

Heirlooms for Home & Hearth

What's the difference between a woodworker and a maker of fine furniture? When you build the showpieces we've collected here, it really doesn't matter because you'll be both. Start with an accent piece like the Charming Cheval Mirror, then work up to the towering Shelving Showcase. Each one makes a lasting statement.

Pedestal-Sized Curio Showcase

If you've been searching for a great-looking cabinet that allows you to show off a prized collection in style, look no further. Our unit has a surprising amount of dust-free storage inside. And the cabinet is just the right height to use as a pedestal for a piece of sculpture, a flower arrangement, or any number of eye-catching decorative accents.

START WITH THE FOUR FRAMES

1 From ¾" cherry, cut the side, back, and door-frame stiles and rails (A, B, C, D, E) to the sizes listed in the Bill of Materials on *page 110*.

2 Dry-clamp each frame as shown on the Side Frames drawing. Make marks for a pair of dowel holes at each glue joint where dimensioned on the Dowel Location drawing. Remove the clamps.

3 With a doweling jig for alignment, drill ⅜" holes ¹³⁄₁₆" deep at each joint where marked. *Note: When working with cherry, or any other wood, for that matter, immediately remove excess glue to prevent light-colored marks from appearing after staining. We wiped off all the glue squeeze-out with a damp cloth after clamping.*

4 Glue, dowel, and clamp the side frames, back frame, and door, checking for square.

5 Mark the center points, and drill the ¼" shelf holes ⁵⁄₁₆" deep where dimensioned on the Side Frames drawing.

NOW, BUILD THE TOP FRAME AND BOTTOM PANEL

1 Cut two pieces of ¾" cherry to 2×60". Using a dado blade and your tablesaw, cut a ¼" rabbet ¼" deep along the top inside edge of each strip.

2 Miter-cut the fronts and backs (F) and sides (G) to the lengths specified in the Bill of Materials from the 2"-wide strips.

3 Using band clamps or a four-corner framing clamp, glue and clamp each frame together, checking for square. Later, remove the clamps, and sand both frames.

4 Measure the rabbeted opening in the bottom panel, and cut the insert panel (H) from ¼" cherry plywood.

5 Glue and clamp the insert in place in the bottom frame.

continued

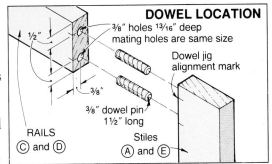

DOWEL LOCATION

½"

⅜"

RAILS
C and D

⅜" holes ¹³⁄₁₆" deep
mating holes are same size

Dowel jig
alignment mark

⅜" dowel pin
1½" long

Stiles
A and E

Pedestal-Sized Curio Showcase

continued

6 Rout ¼" round-overs on the framed panels where noted on the Top and Bottom Panel drawing and the Exploded View drawing.

THE BASE COMES NEXT

1 Miter-cut the base exterior parts (I, J) to size. Now, cut the base cleats (K, L) and glue blocks (M) to size. Drill and countersink screw holes through the cleats.

2 Glue and clamp the exterior parts with a band clamp, checking for square. Then, glue and screw the

cleats into place, flush with the top edge of the exterior base parts. Add the glue blocks, and sand the base smooth.

NEXT, CUT AND INSTALL THE GLASS STOPS

1 Cut four pieces of ¾"-thick cherry to 1½" wide by 36" long. Rout a ¼" round-over along all four edges of each piece.

2 As shown in the two-step drawing *below*, cut four quarter-round cherry stops from each 1½x36" strip. (We used a follow block to prevent kick-back when cutting the long, thin stops.)

3 Miter-cut the glass stops (N, O, P) to length.

4 To drill pilot holes through the glass stops for the brads, start by snipping the head off a 4d finish nail. (Since a ¹⁄₁₆" bit won't chuck securely in many drills and because trying to drive the brads without a pilot hole
continued

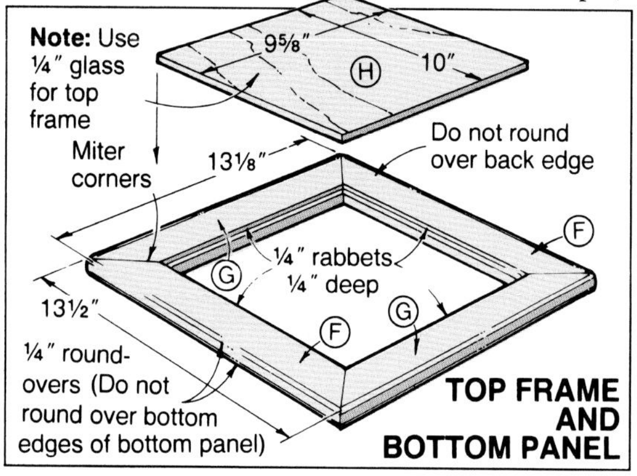

Bill of Materials					
Part	Finished Size			Mat.	Qty.
	T	W	L		
SIDE FRAMES, BACK FRAME, AND DOOR					
A	¾"	1¼"	33⅛"	C	4
B	¾"	2"	33⅛"	C	2
C	¾"	2"	8¾"	C	4
D	¾"	3"	8¾"	C	4
E	¾"	2"	33"	C	2
TOP FRAME AND BOTTOM PANEL					
F*	¾"	2"	13½"	C	4
G*	¾"	2"	13⅛"	C	4
H	¼"	9⅝"	10"	CP	1
BASE					
I	¾"	4"	14"	C	2
J	¾"	4"	13⅜"	C	2
K	¾"	¾"	12½"	C	2
L	¾"	¾"	10⅜"	C	2
M	¾"	¾"	3¼"	C	4
GLASS STOPS AND BACK					
N*	¼"	¼"	28"	C	4
O*	¼"	¼"	8¾"	C	16
P*	¼"	¼"	28⅛"	C	12
TOP RAIL					
Q	¾"	1¾"	11¼"	C	1

*Initially cut parts marked with an * oversized. Then, trim each to finished size according to the how-to instructions.

Material Key: C—cherry, CP—cherry plywood

Supplies: ⅜" dowel pins 1½" long, #8x1¼" flathead wood screws, 3—1⅜x2" brass hinges with 12—#4x½" flathead brass wood screws, #18x½" brads, 1" brass knob, two round magnetic catches and two strikes, ⅛" glass, ¼" glass (for top frame), shelf clips.

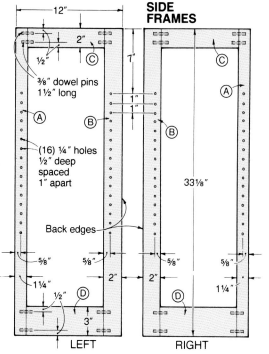

Note: Use ¼" glass for top frame

Miter corners

9⅝" (H) 10"

Do not round over back edge

13⅛"

¼" rabbets ¼" deep

13½"

(F) (G)

¼" round-overs (Do not round over bottom edges of bottom panel)

TOP FRAME AND BOTTOM PANEL

SIDE FRAMES

12"

2"

½" (C)

⅜" dowel pins 1½" long

(A)

(B)

(16) ¼" holes ½" deep spaced 1" apart

Back edges

⅝" ⅝"

2"

1¼"

½" (D)

3"

LEFT

7"

(C)

(A)

1" 1"

(B)

33⅛"

⅝" ⅝"

2"

(D)

1¼"

RIGHT

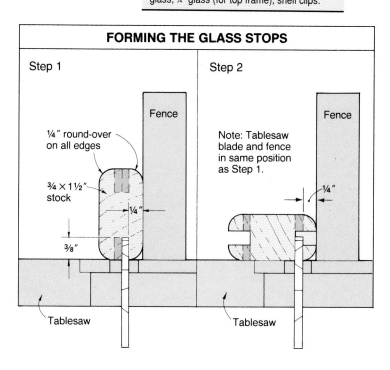

FORMING THE GLASS STOPS

Step 1

Fence

¼" round-over on all edges

¾ × 1½" stock

¼"

⅜"

Tablesaw

Step 2

Fence

Note: Tablesaw blade and fence in same position as Step 1.

¼"

Tablesaw

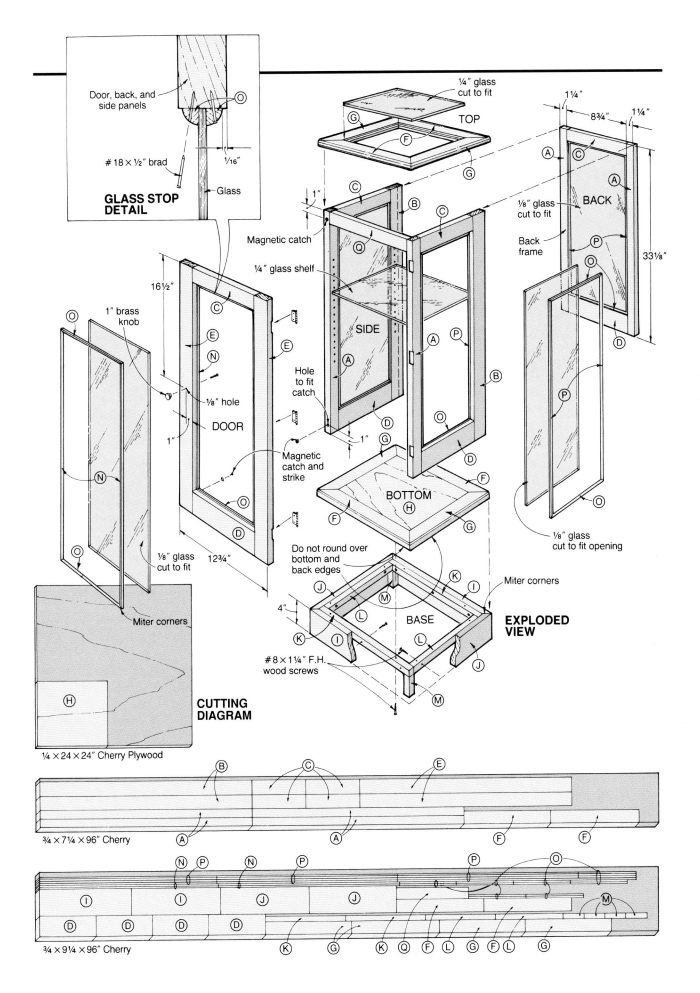

GLASS STOP DETAIL

Door, back, and side panels

#18 × ½" brad

1/16"

Glass

¼" glass cut to fit

TOP

1¼"   8¾"   1¼"

BACK

⅛" glass cut to fit

Back frame

33⅛"

Magnetic catch

1"

SIDE

¼" glass shelf

Hole to fit catch

1"

1" brass knob

16½"

1"

⅛" hole

DOOR

Magnetic catch and strike

⅛" glass cut to fit

Miter corners

12¾"

⅛" glass cut to fit opening

BOTTOM

Do not round over bottom and back edges

4"

BASE

Miter corners

EXPLODED VIEW

#8 × 1¼" F.H. wood screws

CUTTING DIAGRAM

¼ × 24 × 24" Cherry Plywood

¾ × 7¼ × 96" Cherry

¾ × 9¼ × 96" Cherry

Pedestal-Sized Curio Showcase

continued

may cause splitting, we made our own pilot bit.)

5 Chuck the headless nail into your portable drill. Turn the drill on, and hold the rotating nail against a drum sander or disc sander and decrease the diameter of the nail to the same diameter as the brad where shown on the drawing *opposite top*. Then, sharpen the point. Use the drill and "pilot bit" to drill the angled holes through the glass stops. Space the holes about 7" apart.

6 Construct the positioning jig shown *opposite*. Use the jig to position the stops as shown in Photo A. Tap brads into place in the holes just drilled. Fasten the *outside* stops on each side frame and the front stops on both the door and back frames. Set the brads and putty the holes. (You'll use the remaining stops later when installing the glass.)

LET THE ASSEMBLY BEGIN

1 Cut the top front rail (Q) to size. Then, cut a piece of scrap stock to the same length.

2 Glue the back frame and top rail (Q) between the side frames. Insert the scrap spacer between the bottom front corners of the side frames to prevent distortion. *Check that the top and bottom edges of all the pieces are flush and the inside corners are square.*

3 With the back edges flush and centered from side to side, glue and clamp the top frame and the bottom panel to the side and back frame assembly. Wipe off excess glue with a damp cloth.

4 Clamp the base to the bottom panel, centered from side to side and with the back edges flush.

HERE'S HOW TO CUT THE HINGE MORTISES

1 Mark the hinge locations on the right-hand side frame where shown on the Hinge and Mortise drawing. (The middle hinge is centered from top to bottom.)

2 Position the hinges on the marked outlines, mark the screw hole center-points, and drill the pilot holes.

3 Screw the three brass hinges to the side frame, and score their outlines into the frame stile (A) where shown in Photo B. Remove the hinges.

4 Chuck a ¼" or ⅜" straight bit into your router. Clamp a piece of scrap stock to the inside edge to the side frame, making sure to keep the top edges of the scrap stock and frame flush. The scrap stock helps support and level the router when routing the hinges mortise. Next, rout three ¹⁄₁₆"-deep mortises just inside the scribed lines as shown in Photo C. Use a sharp chisel to finish cutting to the scribed outlines.

5 Clamp the door in position in the cabinet-front opening with an equal gap (¹⁄₁₆") at the top and bottom of the door. Transfer the hinge locations to the door. Remove the door from the cabinet, and finish marking the hinge outlines. Using the routing and chiseling method just described, rout ¹⁄₁₆"-deep mortises on the back side of the door frame stile (E).

FINISHING UP YOUR CABINET

1 Carefully measure the openings in the side and back frames and door. Then, install the shelf clips, and measure the distance between the clips for the glass shelves. Order glass cut to fit the openings and for

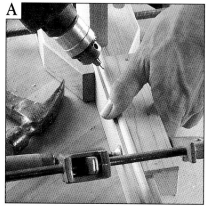

Use the glass stop positioning jig to position the glass stops. Then drill pilot holes and brad the stops into place.

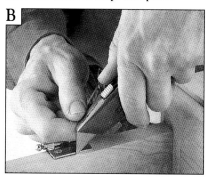

Screw the 2" brass hinges to the cabinet side frame stile. Next, scribe the hinge outlines into the front of the stile.

Clamp a piece of scrap wood to the front of the side frames for additional support for the router base, and rout the hinge mortises.

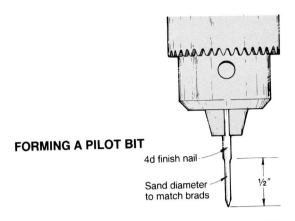

FORMING A PILOT BIT

4d finish nail

Sand diameter
to match brads

½"

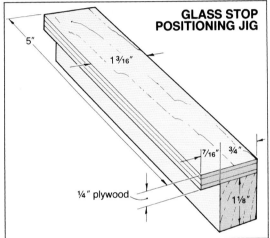

5"

1 3/16"

**GLASS STOP
POSITIONING JIG**

7/16"   ¾"

¼" plywood

1⅛"

5/64" hole
½" deep

9/16"

1⅜ × 2"
brass hinge

1/16"-deep
mortises

**HINGE AND
MORTISE**

9/16"

2"

4 × ½" F.H.
brass wood screw

3"

Side frame

Bottom panel

Door (back side)

2¹⁵/₁₆"

H

A   D

F

N

O

E

I

J

D

the shelves. (We had the glass pieces for the frames cut 1/16" less in length and width to allow for movement of the wood.)

2 Locate and drill the doorknob holes where shown on the Exploded View drawing.

3 Remove the hardware from the cabinet and door. Mask off both sides of the glass. Stain the cabinet and doors if desired (we left ours natural), and apply the finish.

4 Fasten the knob to the door. Attach the door to the cabinet. Then, add the magnetic catches and strike plates to the door and side-frame stile. Set the top piece of glass in the rabbet, and add the glass shelves.

PROJECT TOOL LIST
- Tablesaw
- Dado blade or dado set
- Portable drill
- Doweling jig
- Bits: 5/64", ¼", ⅜"
- Router
- Bits: ¼" round-over, ¼" or ⅜" straight
- Finishing sander

Note: We built the project using the tools listed. You may be able to substitute other tools or equipment for listed items you don't have. Additional common hand tools and clamps may be required to complete the project.

Charming Cheval Mirror

Here's a stand-up mirror that invites a closer look. Its clean lines and wedged mortise-and-tenon construction will certainly reflect your craftsmanship. While building this mirror won't be a problem, deciding who gets it for their room could be.

LET'S START BY FORMING THE FEET

1 To make the feet (A), start by cutting two pieces of ¾" stock and two pieces of 1¹⁄₁₆" (five-quarter) stock to 2½" wide by 21" long each. (We used cherry throughout.) With the edges and ends flush, glue and clamp one piece of ¾" stock to one piece of 1¹⁄₁₆" stock for each foot. (Using these two different thicknesses of wood prevents the joint line from showing on the top surface after you cut the feet to shape.)

2 Scrape the glue from one edge of each foot. Then, plane or joint that edge flat, and rip the opposite edge of each foot on your tablesaw to 2¼" wide. Trim both ends square for a 20" finished length.

3 With the thicker wood on top, and using the dimensions on the Foot drawing for reference, mark a pair of cutlines on one edge of each foot. Next, mark the mortise on the top surface of each foot.

4 Drill holes inside the marked mortises to create rough openings. Next, use a sharp chisel and mallet to clean the mortise sides.

5 Bandsaw the feet to shape, cutting just *outside* the marked lines. Now, sand to the lines to finish shaping the feet. Save the wedge-shaped pieces of scrap—you'll use them later for the tenon wedges.

NOW, MACHINE THE UPRIGHTS

1 To make the tapered uprights (B), cut four pieces of ¾"-thick stock to 2½x43⅜". With the edges and ends

FOOT

Waste · 3" · 8½" · 2¼" · 20" · 1¹⁄₁₆" stock · 1" · ¾" stock · A · 5/8" · Cutlines · 9⅛" · 7/16" · 1¾" · Bottom surface of foot is flat for 3" at center · Cutline ¹³⁄₁₆" from bottom surface

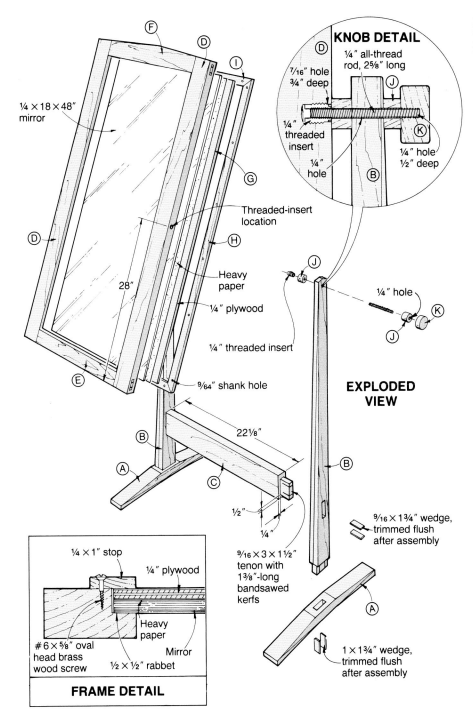

KNOB DETAIL

¼" all-thread rod, 2⅝" long

⁷⁄₁₆" hole
¾" deep

¼" threaded insert

¼" hole

¼" hole
½" deep

¼ × 18 × 48" mirror

Threaded-insert location

Heavy paper

¼" plywood

¼" threaded insert

28"

⁹⁄₆₄" shank hole

22⅛"

½"

¼"

EXPLODED VIEW

⁹⁄₁₆ × 3 × 1½" tenon with 1⅜"-long bandsawed kerfs

⁹⁄₁₆ × 1¾" wedge, trimmed flush after assembly

¼" hole

1 × 1¾" wedge, trimmed flush after assembly

FRAME DETAIL

¼ × 1" stop

¼" plywood

#6 × ⅝" oval head brass wood screw

½ × ½" rabbet

Heavy paper

Mirror

Bill of Materials

Part	Finished Size			Mat.	Qty.
	T	W	L		
A* feet	1¹³⁄₁₆"	2¼"	20"	LC	2
B* uprights	1½"	2¼"	42⅜"	LC	2
C stretcher	1¹⁄₁₆"	4"	25⅛"	C	1
D stiles	1¹⁄₁₆"	2"	51⅝"	C	2
E bottom rail	1¹⁄₁₆"	2"	21⅛"	C	1
F top rail	1¹⁄₁₆"	2½"	21⅛"	C	1
G mirror back	¼"	18"	48"	CP	1
H stops	¼"	1"	49⅛"	C	2
I stops	¼"	1"	19⅛"	C	2
J spacers	½"	¾" dia.		C	4
K knobs	¾"	1½" dia.		C	2

*Initially cut parts marked with an * oversized. Then, trim each to finished size according to the how-to instructions.

Material Key: LC—laminated cherry, C—cherry, CP—cherry plywood
Supplies: two pieces of ¼" all-thread rod 2⅝" long, two ¼" threaded inserts, ¼ × 18 × 48" mirror, #6 × ⅝" oval-head brass wood screws, heavy paper, finish.

flush, glue and clamp two pieces together face-to-face for each upright. Repeat with the other two pieces.

2 Scrape the glue from one edge of each upright lamination. Then, plane that edge flat. Rip the opposite edge for a 2¼" width.

3 Crosscut both ends of each upright lamination for a 42⅜" finished length.

4 Using the Upright drawing and accompanying Taper detail on *page 116* for reference, mark the cutline for taper cut No. 1, the tenon and mortise locations, and a ¼" pivot hole on both uprights. Measure carefully; you want the uprights to be identical. Notice that the uprights taper on the sides and the outside surface. (Do not taper the surface that will be next to the mirror.)

continued

Charming Cheval Mirror

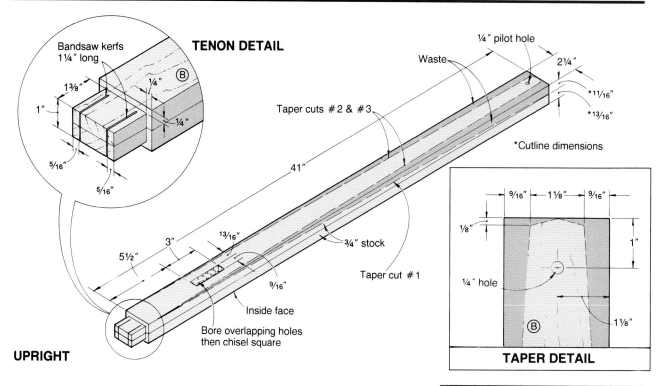

TENON DETAIL

Bandsaw kerfs 1¼" long

1⅜"

1"

⅛"

¼"

¼"

⁵⁄₁₆"

⁵⁄₁₆"

B

¼" pilot hole

Waste

2¼"

*11⁄16"

*13⁄16"

*Cutline dimensions

Taper cuts #2 & #3

41"

¾" stock

Taper cut #1

3"

5½"

13⁄16"

9⁄16"

Inside face

Bore overlapping holes then chisel square

UPRIGHT

TAPER DETAIL

9⁄16"   1⅛"   9⁄16"

⅛"

¼" hole

B

1"

1⅛"

---

5 Measure the mortise opening in the feet, and cut the upright tenons to fit. Be careful not to cut the tenons too small; you want them to fit tight in the mating mortises in the feet.

6 Mark the locations, and cut a pair of kerfs in each tenon where shown on the Tenon detail accompanying the Upright drawing.

7 Drill the ¼" pivot hole in each upright where marked.

8 Drill overlapping holes and chisel the sides clean to form a mortise in each upright.

9 Following the three-cut procedure shown on the Upright drawing, make taper cut No. 1 and sand the cut edge smooth. Mark the lines for taper cuts No. 2 and No. 3, make the cuts, and sand these edges smooth.

10 Mark a vertical centerline on the outside tapered face of each upright. Glue and wedge one upright into each foot. Clamp the two assemblies together with the edges and ends flush as shown in the drawing *above right*. Use a framing square to adjust

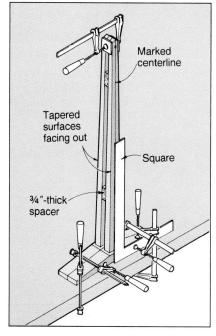

Marked centerline

Tapered surfaces facing out

Square

¾"-thick spacer

the uprights, making them perpendicular to the bottom of the feet.

NEXT, CUT THE STRETCHER, AND JOIN THE UPRIGHTS

1 Cut the stretcher (C) to size. Measure the mortises in the uprights, and cut a tenon on each

Mount a straight screwdriver bit into your drill press, and turn the chuck by hand to drive the threaded inserts.

end of the stretcher where shown on the Exploded View drawing.

2 Cut a pair of kerfs in each tenon. Cut the wedges to size plus ¼" in length.

3 Glue the stretcher between the two upright/feet assemblies. Inject a bit of glue in each tenon kerf, and drive the wedges. Wipe off the excess glue with a damp cloth. Check for square, ensuring that the distance between the uprights is consistent from the top of the uprights to the stretcher. Trim and sand the tenon wedges flush.

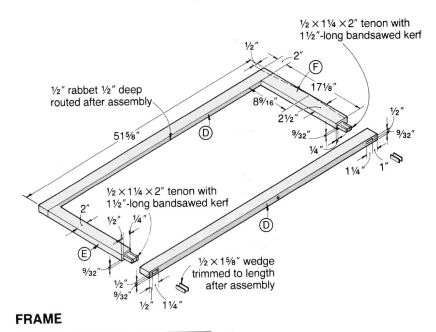

½ × 1¼ × 2″ tenon with
1½″-long bandsawed kerf

½″ rabbet ½″ deep
routed after assembly

51⅝″

½″

2″

(F)

17⅛″

8⁹⁄₁₆″

2½″

⁹⁄₃₂″

¼″

½″

⁹⁄₃₂″

1¼″

1″

(D)

(D)

½ × 1¼ × 2″ tenon with
1½″-long bandsawed kerf

2″

½″ ¼″

(E)

⁹⁄₃₂″

½″

⁹⁄₃₂″

½″ 1¼″

½ × 1⅝″ wedge
trimmed to length
after assembly

FRAME

CUT THE FRAME PARTS, AND ASSEMBLE THEM

1 Cut frame parts (D, E, F) to the sizes stated in the Bill of Materials.

2 Mark the locations and cut mortises in the stiles (D) where located on the Frame drawing.

3 Mark the center points, and drill a ⁷⁄₁₆″ hole ¾″ deep in each stile for the threaded insert. Now, as shown in the photo *opposite*, drive a ¼″ threaded insert into each hole.

4 Form tenons on the ends of the bottom rail (E) and top rail (F) to fit snugly into the mortises. (We attached an auxiliary wood fence to our miter gauge and a dado blade to our tablesaw. Then, we used the wood fence to support the rails while cutting the tenons with the dado blade.)

5 Using the wedge-shaped scrap left from cutting the feet to shape, cut eight tenon wedges.

6 Glue the frame, checking for square. Glue the wedges in place, and trim and sand them flush with the outside of the frame.

7 Rout a ½″ rabbet ½″ deep along the back inside edge of the frame. To minimize splintering, do this in two passes, lowering the bit to ½″ for the second pass.

8 Mark the cutlines across the top rail (F) and top ends of the stiles (D) where shown on the Frame drawing, and cut and sand the frame top to shape.

9 Measure the opening, and cut the backboard (G) to size. (We used ¼″ cherry plywood.)

10 Cut the mirror stops (H, I) to size (we resawed thicker stock), miter-cutting the ends. Drill and countersink mounting holes through the stops for ease in attaching to the mirror frame later.

IT'S TIME TO ADD THE LOCKING KNOBS

1 With a compass, mark four ¾″-diameter circles on a piece of ½″-thick cherry for the spacers (J) and two 1½″-diameter circle knobs (K) on ¾″ stock.

2 Drill a ¼″ hole through each spacer at each center-point used to mark the circles. Drill a ¼″ hole ½″ deep centered in each knob.

3 Bandsaw the spacers and knobs to shape. Sand the cut edges smooth (we used a disc sander).

4 Cut two pieces of ¼″ all-thread rod to 2⅝″ long. Epoxy one end into the hole in each knob.

FINISH IT UP, AND ADD THE MIRROR

1 Finish-sand the stand, frame, backboard, and stops. Stain and finish as desired.

2 Cover your workbench with a blanket, and position the mirror frame facedown on the blanket.

3 Cut paper (we used freezer paper) to the size of the mirror. Place the paper between the mirror and plywood to protect the silvered back of the mirror from abrasion or scratches.

4 Insert the mirror, paper, and backboard into the rabbet in the mirror frame. Tape the stops (H, I) in place. Using the previously drilled shank holes in the stops as guides, drill ³⁄₃₂″ pilot holes ⅜″ deep into the mirror frame. Now, screw the stops in place to secure the mirror and plywood.

5 With a helper, hold the mirror frame in place, slide the threaded knobs through the holes in the uprights and spacers, and screw them into the threaded inserts in the mirror frame. Tighten the knobs slightly to prevent the mirror from swinging too freely.

PROJECT TOOL LIST

- Tablesaw
- Dado blade or dado set
- Bandsaw
- Jointer
- Drill press
- Portable drill
- Bits: ³⁄₃₂″, ⁹⁄₆₄″, ¼″, ⁷⁄₁₆″, ⁹⁄₁₆″, 1″
- Router
- Bits: ½″ Rabbeting bit
- Disc sander
- Finishing sander

Note: *We built the project using the tools listed. You may be able to substitute other tools or equipment for listed items you don't have. Additional common hand tools and clamps may be required to complete the project.*

Shelving Showcase

A natural for traditional interiors

Fluted face-frame stiles and a richly molded top set the style for this full-length bookcase. On the practical side, its capacity may amaze you. As shown here, six shelves (five of which adjust on standards and brackets) measure 13×38⅜" each, leaving more than enough room for three sets of encyclopedias. Once you build the bookcase, you'll find it the perfect accent for a home study, family room, or any other haunt where you enjoy reading.

START WITH THE BASIC CABINET

1 From ¾" plywood (we used walnut), cut the sides (A) and top and bottom (B) to the sizes listed in the Bill of Materials. (To support the thin veneer fibers and minimize splintering when cross-cutting the plywood, we lightly marked the cutlines with a pencil. Next, we placed masking tape next to the cutlines, made the cuts, and then removed the remaining tape.)

2 Referring to the Basic Cabinet drawing *opposite*, mark the rabbet and dado locations across the top inside edge and 5¼" from the bottom edge of the sides (A). Cut or rout the rabbets and dadoes. (We used a router fitted with a straight bit and an edge guide.)

3 Cut a ¼" rabbet ½" deep along the back inside edge of each side piece (A). See the Back Panel detail for reference. Now, cut a pair of ⅝" grooves 3/16" deep on the inside face of each side piece for the shelf standards. (We test-cut the groove in a piece of scrap stock first to verify that our standard would fit snugly into it and remain flush with the surface.)

4 Cut a ⅜" rabbet ⅜" deep along the front outside edge of each side piece to form a tongue.

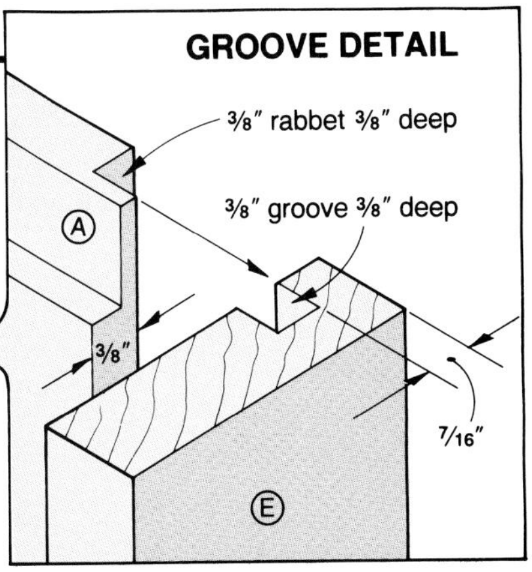
GROOVE DETAIL
3/8" rabbet 3/8" deep
3/8" groove 3/8" deep
A
3/8"
7/16"
E

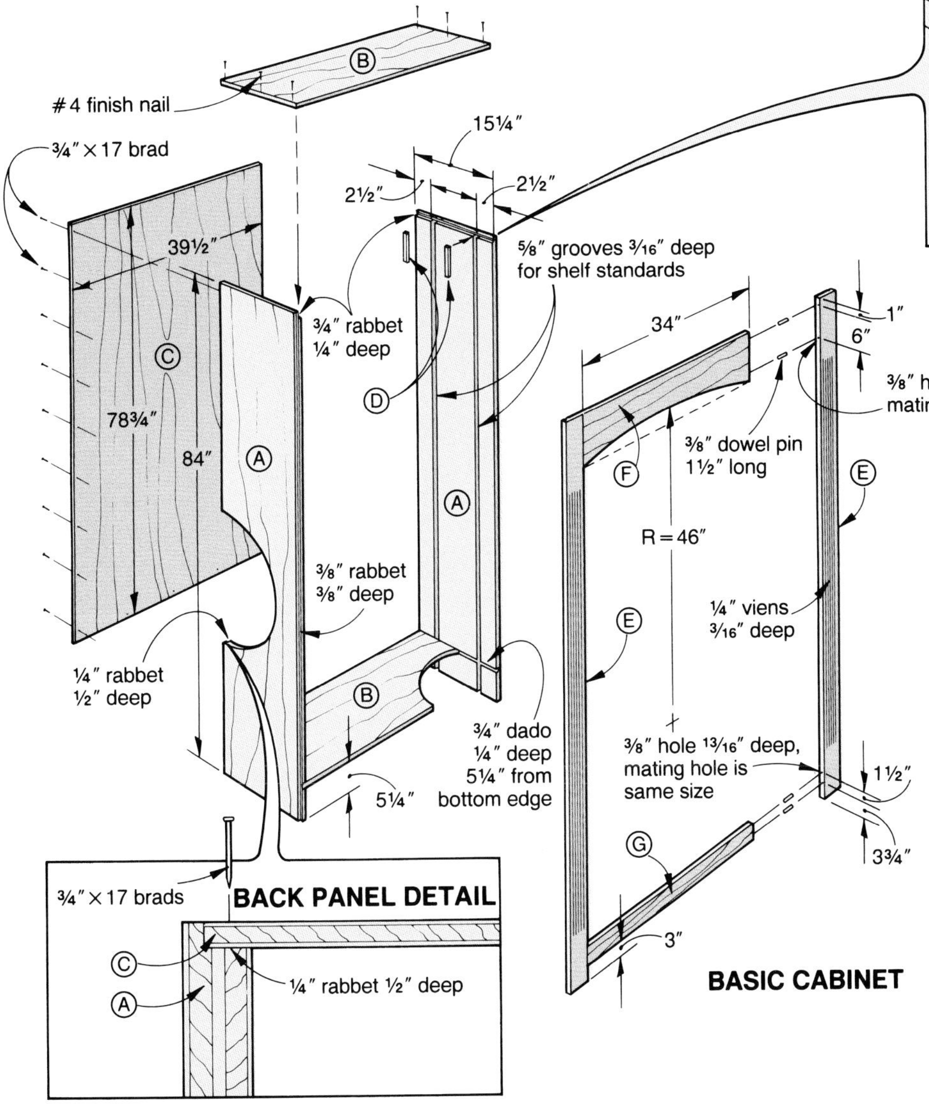
B
#4 finish nail
¾" × 17 brad
15¼"
2½"
2½"
39½"
5/8" grooves 3/16" deep
for shelf standards
¾" rabbet
¼" deep
C
78¾"
84"
A
D
A
34"
1"
6"
3/8" hole 13/16" deep,
mating hole is same size
3/8" dowel pin
1½" long
F
E
R = 46"
3/8" rabbet
3/8" deep
¼" viens
3/16" deep
E
¼" rabbet
½" deep
B
¾" dado
¼" deep
5¼" from
bottom edge
5¼"
3/8" hole 13/16" deep,
mating hole is
same size
1½"
G
3¾"
3"
¾" × 17 brads
BACK PANEL DETAIL
C
A
¼" rabbet ½" deep
BASIC CABINET

5 Dry-clamp the pieces, and check for square. Measure the width of the rabbeted opening in the cabinet back, and cut the back panel (C) to size from ¼" walnut plywood. The plywood back is flush with the top face of the top (B) and flush with the bottom face of the bottom (B).

6 Glue and clamp the basic cabinet; check for square. Glue and nail the back panel in place. Installing the back panel now helps square up the assembly.

7 Temporarily position the shelf standards in the grooves. Measure the grooved opening above each. Then, to match the veneered cabinet interior, cut and resaw four filler blocks (D) from ¾" walnut plywood to fit. Glue the filler blocks in place, and then remove the standards.

LET'S MAKE THE WALNUT FACE FRAME

1 Cut the stiles (E), top rail (F), and bottom rail (G) to the sizes listed in the Bill of Materials.

continued

Bill of Materials

Part	Finished Size T	W	L	Mat.	Qty.
BASIC CABINET					
A	¾"	15¼"	84"	WP	2
B	¾"	14⅝"	39"	WP	2
C	¼"	39½"	78¾"	WP	1
D	3/16"	⅝"	5⅛"	WP	4
E*	¾"	3 1/16"	84"	W	2
F	¾"	9"	34"	W	1
G	¾"	3"	34"	W	1
MOLDING					
H*	1 13/16"	3"	44¼"	LW	1
I*	1 13/16"	3"	17¾"	LW	2
J*	¼"	½"	41"	W	2
K*	¼"	½"	16⅛"	W	4
L*	¾"	⅜"	40¾"	W	1
M*	¾"	⅜"	16"	W	2
N*	⅜"	¼"	3¼"	W	4
O*	⅜"	¼"	15⅞"	W	4
P*	¾"	5"	41½"	W	1
Q*	¾"	5"	16⅜"	W	2
SHELVES					
R*	¾"	13"	38⅜"	WP	5
S*	¾"	1¼"	38⅜"	W	10

*Initially cut parts marked with an * oversized. Then, trim each to finished size according to the how-to instructions.

Material Key: WP—walnut plywood, W—walnut, LW—laminated walnut

Supplies: ⅜" dowel pins 1½" long, #8x1¼" flathead wood screws, #8x1½" flathead wood screws, #4 finish nails, ¾"x#17 brads, ⅝x72" flush-mounted shelf standards (walnut finish) with mounting brads and supports, finish.

Shelving Showcase

continued

2 Cut or rout a ⅜" groove ⅜" deep along the back outside edge of both stiles (E) where shown on the Groove detail accompanying the Basic Cabinet drawing. Note that the stiles (E) extend 1⁄16" past the outside face of the sides (A). This protrusion will be routed flush later.

3 Using double-faced tape, adhere the top rail (F) flush with one end of a sheet of plywood. Using trammel points, swing a 46" arc intersecting the lower corners of the top rail (see the Basic Cabinet drawing for reference) along the bottom edge of the top rail. Bandsaw the arc to shape. Sand the arc to remove the saw marks.

4 Construct a start- and stopblock to the sizes shown on the Stile drawing at *right*. Clamp the longest stopblock to the *top front face* of the stile and the shorter block to the *bottom end* where shown on the Stile drawing.

5 Fit your router with an edge guide and a ¼" core box bit.

6 Now, before routing the veins, position the router against the blocks to check that the router bit will start 8½" from the bottom end of the stile and stop 11½" from the

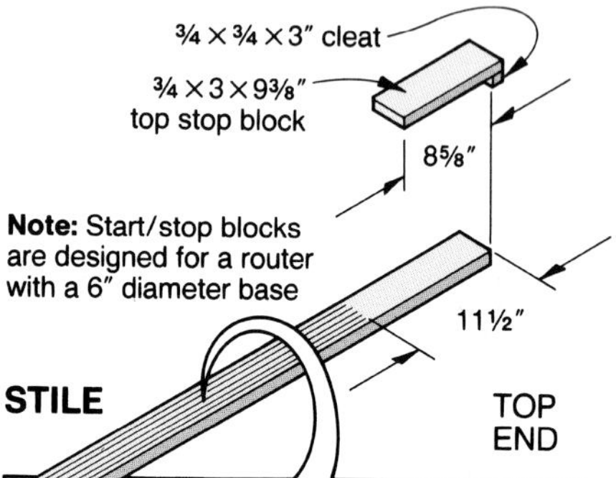
¾ × ¾ × 3" cleat
¾ × 3 × 9⅜" top stop block
8⅝"
Note: Start/stop blocks are designed for a router with a 6" diameter base
11½"
STILE
TOP END

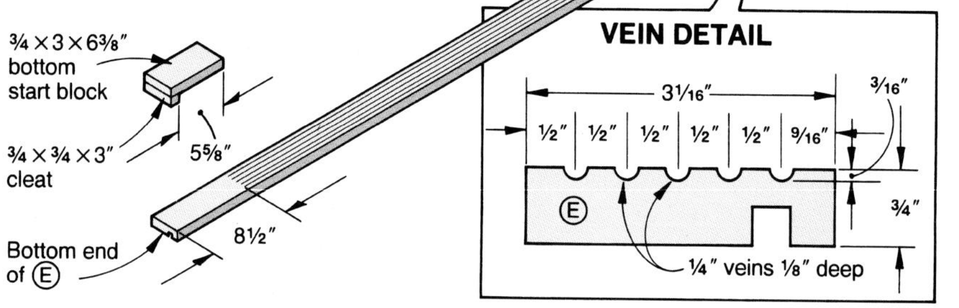
VEIN DETAIL
3 1⁄16"
½" ½" ½" ½" ½" 9⁄16"
3⁄16"
¾"
E
¼" veins ⅛" deep
¾ × 3 × 6⅜" bottom start block
¾ × ¾ × 3" cleat
5⅝"
8½"
Bottom end of E

CUTTING DIAGRAM

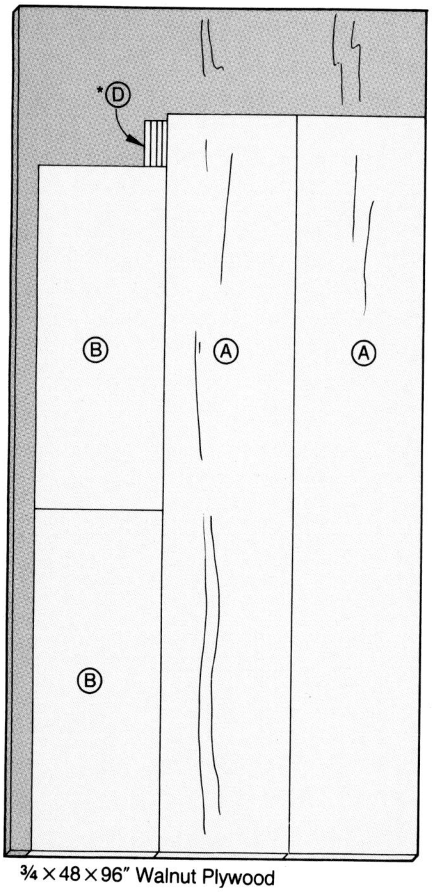
*D
B
A
A
B
¾ × 48 × 96" Walnut Plywood

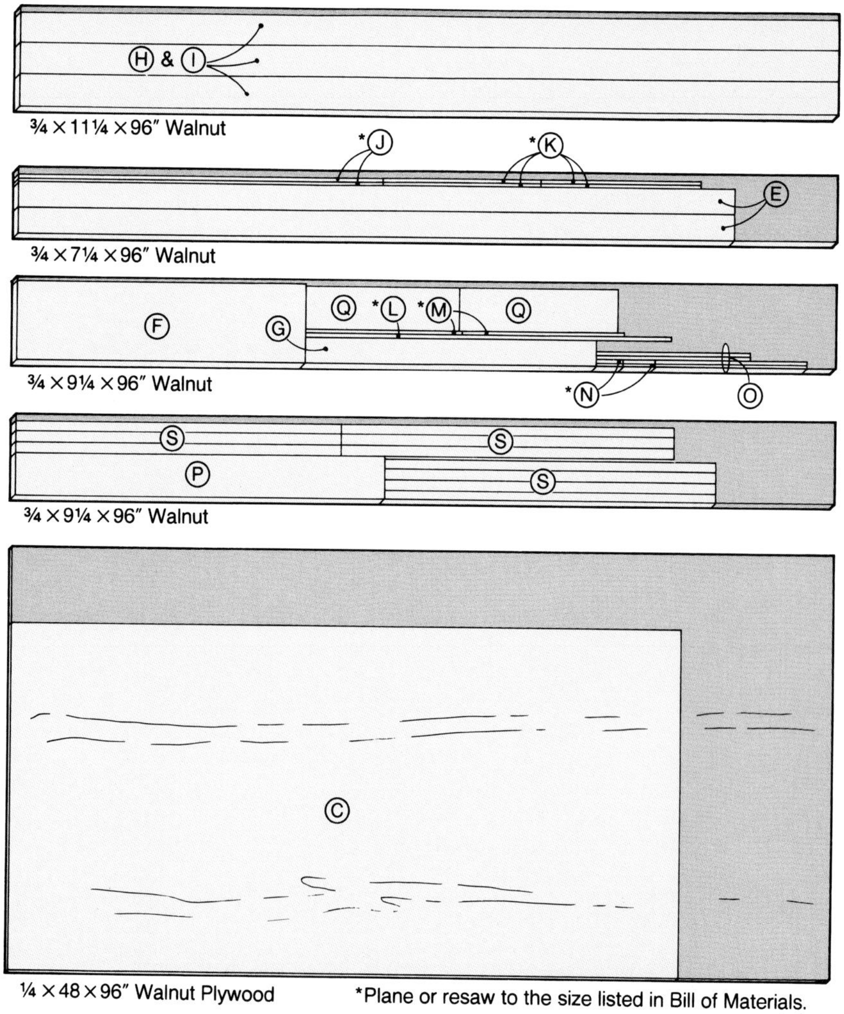
H & I
¾ × 11¼ × 96" Walnut
*J
*K
E
¾ × 7¼ × 96" Walnut
F
G
Q
*L
*M
Q
*N
O
¾ × 9¼ × 96" Walnut
S
S
P
S
¾ × 9¼ × 96" Walnut
C
¼ × 48 × 96" Walnut Plywood

*Plane or resaw to the size listed in Bill of Materials.

Rout ¼" veins ³⁄₁₆" deep using a router fitted with an edge guide and stops clamped to the ends of the stile.

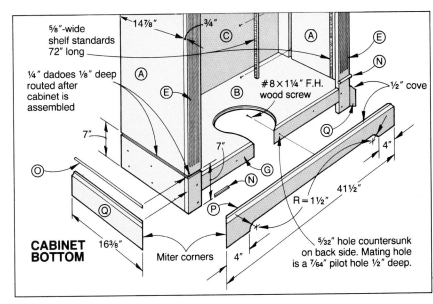

⅝"-wide shelf standards 72" long

¼" dadoes ⅛" deep routed after cabinet is assembled

14⅞"   ¾"

#8 × 1¼" F.H. wood screw

½" cove

7"

7"

R = 1½"

41½"

4"

16⅜"

CABINET BOTTOM   Miter corners   4"

⁵⁄₃₂" hole countersunk on back side. Mating hole is a ⁷⁄₆₄" pilot hole ½" deep.

top; adjust the length of the stops if necessary. *The location of the stops will depend on the size of your router base.*

7 Set the bit to cut ³⁄₁₆" deep, and rout five veins in the front face of both stiles where dimensioned on the Vein detail *opposite.* To minimize sanding later, make a second pass down each vein as shown in the photo *above.*

8 Dry-clamp the face-frame pieces (E, F, G) to the frame, and mark dowel-hole reference lines across the front face of each where dimensioned on the Basic Cabinet drawing. Remove the clamps, and drill mating ⅜" holes ¹³⁄₁₆" deep where marked.

9 Glue and clamp the face frame, checking for square. Later,

remove the clamps, and sand the back surface flush for a tight fit against the cabinet front.

ATTACH THE FACE FRAME, AND ROUT THE MOLDING GROOVE

1 Glue and clamp the face frame to the cabinet. (Before clamping the face frame to the cabinet, we placed masking tape on the walnut plywood next to the joints being glued, so any glue squeeze-out dried on the tape. Later, after the glue dried, we peeled off the tape and excess glue. We've found this process easier then trying to remove the squeeze-out with a

damp cloth or trying to scrape it off after it's dried.)

2 Mount a flush-trimming laminate bit into your router. Rout the ¹⁄₁₆" protruding outside edge of the stiles flush with the outside face of the cabinet sides (A). (We found this more effective than trying to plane the edges flush.)

3 Mount a ¼" straight bit in your router. Clamp a straightedge (we used a piece of plywood) to the cabinet side. Rout a ¼" dado ⅛" deep 10" from the top edge of the cabinet top where shown on the Cabinet Top drawing. Move the straightedge and rout the other side. Now, rout the front face. Using the Cabinet Bottom drawing for reference, rout the dado across the bottom of the cabinet.

NEXT, SHAPE SOME COVE MOLDING FOR THE CABINET TOP

1 To form the thick top cove molding, cut three pieces of ¾"-thick stock to 3½" wide by 8' long. (This will give you enough stock for parts H and I.)

2 Glue and clamp the three pieces of stock face-to-face with the edges and ends flush.

continued

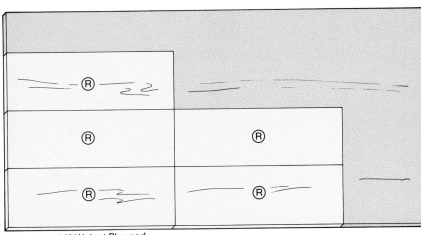

¾ × 48 × 96" Walnut Plywood

Shelving Showcase

continued

3 Scrape the excess glue from one edge, and then joint it flat. Now, rip the opposite edge on your tablesaw for a 3" finished width.

4 Resaw or plane the lamination to 1¹³⁄₁₆" thick.

5 Clamp a piece of straight stock to the top of your 10" tablesaw where shown on the drawing *bottom right*. Raise the blade ⅛" above the saw table surface, and pass the workpiece over the blade. Continue to raise the blade and take light cuts (no more than ⅛" per pass) until you achieve the full ½" depth of the cove. (We found that an 80-tooth, carbide-tipped blade produced the smoothest cuts.)

6 Follow the four-cut sequence *opposite* to trim the edges of the molding to shape.

7 Miter-cut the front cove molding piece (H) and the two side pieces (I) to fit the front and sides of the cabinet.

8 Drill mounting holes through the cabinet for attaching the cove molding pieces (H, I). Glue and screw the pieces in place, flush with the top of the cabinet. (See the Cove Molding detail accompanying the Cabinet Top drawing.)

NOW FOR THE REST OF THE MOLDINGS

1 Cut the remaining molding pieces (J, K, L, M, N, O) to size plus 2" in length. To form the bullnose on the front edge of J and K, rout a pair of ⅛" round-overs along the front edge. See the Bullnose detail accompanying the Cabinet Top drawing.

2 With the back edges flush, glue part L between parts J. Repeat with the side pieces K and M. Miter-cut the ends, and then glue and clamp the trim strips J/L and K/M to the cabinet.

3 Miter-cut the bullnosed strips N and O to length for both the cabinet top and bottom. Glue them

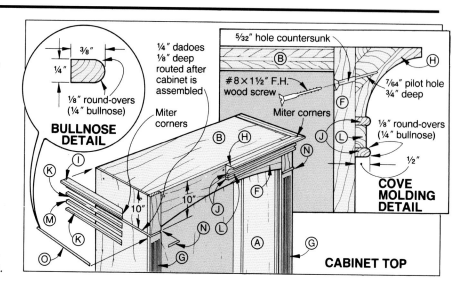

BULLNOSE DETAIL

⅜"
¼"
⅛" round-overs (¼" bullnose)

¼" dadoes ⅛" deep routed after cabinet is assembled

Miter corners

⁵⁄₃₂" hole countersunk

#8 × 1½" F.H. wood screw

Miter corners

⁷⁄₆₄" pilot hole ¾" deep

⅛" round-overs (¼" bullnose)

½"

COVE MOLDING DETAIL

CABINET TOP

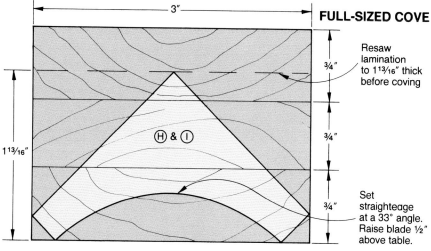

3"

1¹³⁄₁₆"

H & I

FULL-SIZED COVE

Resaw lamination to 1¹³⁄₁₆" thick before coving

¾"

¾"

¾"

Set straightedge at a 33° angle. Raise blade ½" above table.

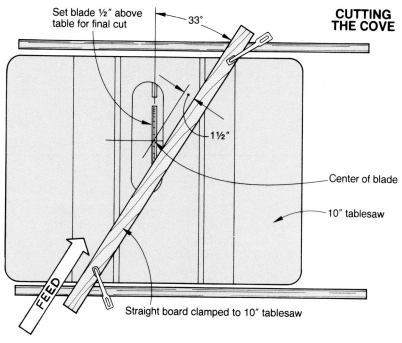

Set blade ½" above table for final cut

33°

1½"

CUTTING THE COVE

Center of blade

10" tablesaw

FEED

Straight board clamped to 10" tablesaw

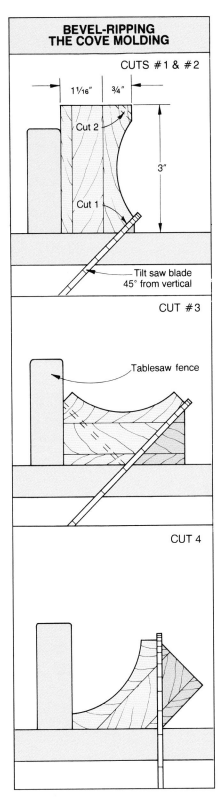

BEVEL-RIPPING THE COVE MOLDING

CUTS #1 & #2

1¹⁄₁₆″   ¾″

Cut 2

3″

Cut 1

Tilt saw blade 45° from vertical

CUT #3

Tablesaw fence

CUT 4

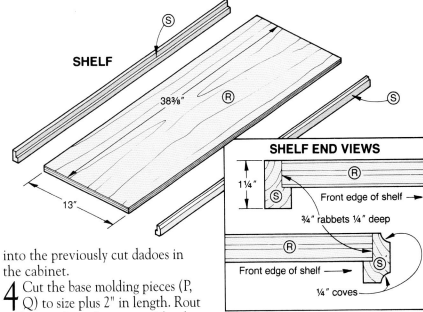

SHELF

38³⁄₈″   Ⓡ

13″   Ⓢ

SHELF END VIEWS

1¼″   Ⓡ
Ⓢ   Front edge of shelf →
¾″ rabbets ¼″ deep

Ⓡ
Front edge of shelf →   Ⓢ
¼″ coves

into the previously cut dadoes in the cabinet.

4 Cut the base molding pieces (P, Q) to size plus 2″ in length. Rout a ½″ cove along the top outside edge of each.

5 Using the Cabinet Bottom drawing for reference, miter-cut the pieces to length, mark the radii on the front piece, and cut it to shape. Drill mounting holes through the cabinet and into the back side of the base molding pieces. Glue and screw the pieces to the cabinet bottom.

CUT AND EDGE THE SHELVES, THEN FINISH YOUR CABINET

1 Cut the walnut plywood shelves (R) and front and back strips (S) to size plus 1″ in length.

2 Cut or rout ¾″ rabbets ¼″ deep in each strip where shown on the Shelf drawing. Next, rout ¼″ coves along the front edge where shown on the End View drawing.

3 Glue the strips to the front and back of the shelf. Later, crosscut both ends to trim the shelves to finished length. Sand smooth (we wrapped sandpaper around a ½″ piece of dowel to sand the coves).

4 Finish the cabinet. (We applied one coat of Watco Dark Walnut Oil Finish, followed by five coats of Watco Natural Oil Finish.)

5 Nail the shelf standards in the grooves, checking that the numbers on the standards are right-side up.

BUYING GUIDE

• **Shelf standards.** 72″ flush-mounted walnut-finished standard, Catalog No. 34058 (four needed). Supports for standard (20 per pack), Catalog No. 33852. For current prices, contact The Woodworkers' Store, 21801 Industrial Blvd., Rogers, MN 55374-9514, or call 612/428-3200 to order.

PROJECT TOOL LIST

• Tablesaw
• Dado blade or dado set
• Router
• Bits: ¼″ straight, ⅜″ straight, ½″ straight, ¼″ rabbeting, ⅜″ rabbeting, ¾″ rabbeting, flush trimming, ¼″ core box, ⅛″ round-over, ¼″ cove, ½″ cove
• Portable drill
• Bits: ⁷⁄₆₄″, ⁷⁄₃₂″, ⅜″
• Finishing sander

Note: We built the project using the tools listed. You may be able to substitute other tools or equipment for listed items you don't have. Additional common hand tools and clamps may be required to complete the project.

Cabriole-Leg Coffee Table

Fit for a Queen

FORMING THE MORTISES

STEP 1. Mark mortise locations on two adjacent surfaces of each leg Ⓐ.

STEP 2. Drill ½" holes ¾" deep at both ends of mortise.

STEP 3. Drill overlapping ⁷⁄₁₆" holes ¾" deep in between the ¾" holes.

STEP 4. Chisel the mortise square.

Marked outline

Inside of leg

Tapering gracefully from its ample knee to its shapely ankle, the double curve of a well-executed pad-foot cabriole leg distinguishes it as the work of a craftsman. We've combined this classic leg with the rich look of solid walnut to create an elegant Queen Anne-style coffee table.

LET'S START WITH THE LEGS

Note: *In keeping with style, you'll need some 3x3" walnut for the legs. You can either purchase furniture squares or laminate thinner stock to size (though this may result in visible joint lines). See the Buying Guide on page 127 for our source of 3"-square stock.*

After laminating the legs and forming the mortises (as described in Steps 1 and 2 above right), refer to the following technique article on cabriole legs for an explanation on how to make these shapely S-curved legs.

1 If you prefer to laminate thinner stock face-to-face to form the 3x3" squares for the legs (A), start by cutting four pieces of ¾"-thick walnut to 3¼" wide by 15½" long for each leg. Then, glue and clamp the pieces together face-to-face, with the edges and ends flush. Next, scrape the excess glue from one edge of each leg, plane or joint that edge smooth, and then rip the opposite edge for a thickness slightly over 3". Joint the cut edge for a 3" finished width. Finally, crosscut the legs to a finished length of 14¾".

2 Following the Mortise detail on the Exploded View drawing on *page 126* and the four steps on the Forming the Mortises drawing *above right*, mark and then make the ½" mortises ¾" deep on two adjacent faces on the inside corner of each leg.

NEXT, FASHION THE APRONS

1 Rip the front and back aprons (B) and side aprons (C) to the sizes listed in the Bill of Materials.

2 Following Step 1 of the four-step drawing *opposite*, cut the tenons on the ends of each apron. See the Tenon detail accompanying the Exploded View drawing for further reference. Without changing the blade height or stop, you'll need to make three cuts on each end to form the tenon. (We test-cut scrap stock first to verify the blade height and stop location to ensure that the tenon fits snugly in the previously formed mortises.)

3 Transfer the full-sized apron patterns to heavy stock. (We used carbon paper to copy the patterns onto poster board.)

4 As shown in Step 2 of the drawing, position the rail-end template flush with the tenon shoulder, and trace its outline onto the outside face of each end of each apron. Center the full-sized center pattern, and trace its outline onto the front and back apron *only*.

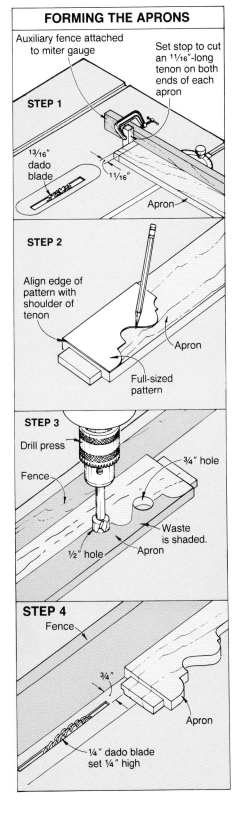

FORMING THE APRONS

Auxiliary fence attached to miter gauge

Set stop to cut an $^{11}/_{16}$"-long tenon on both ends of each apron

STEP 1

$^{13}/_{16}$" dado blade

$^{11}/_{16}$"

Apron

STEP 2

Align edge of pattern with shoulder of tenon

Apron

Full-sized pattern

STEP 3

Drill press

Fence

$^{3}/_{4}$" hole

Waste is shaded.

$^{1}/_{2}$" hole

Apron

STEP 4

Fence

$^{3}/_{4}$"

Apron

$^{1}/_{4}$" dado blade set $^{1}/_{4}$" high

5 For perfect rounded corners along each apron bottom, bore $^{1}/_{2}$" and $^{3}/_{4}$" holes next to the marked outline where shown in Step 3 of the drawing and also where shown on the Aprons drawing at *left*. Next, bandsaw or scrollsaw the aprons to shape.

6 As shown in Step 4 of the drawing, cut a $^{1}/_{4}$" groove $^{1}/_{4}$" deep $^{1}/_{2}$" from the top edge of the front, back, and side aprons.

7 Dry-clamp the four aprons between the legs to check the fit. Then, glue and clamp a side apron (C) between a pair of legs. Repeat with the other side apron and two legs. Now, glue the front and back aprons (B) between the two side assemblies, checking for square. (We measured diagonally to check for square.)

8 Sand the face of the apron flush with the face of the leg shank. Then, following the techniques article, cut the eight knee brackets (D) to $1^{1}/_{4}$x$1^{1}/_{4}$x1", glue them in place, and sand them to shape.

AND NOW, FOR THE TABLETOP

1 Rip and crosscut five pieces of $^{3}/_{4}$" walnut for the tabletop (E), and then joint or plane their edges so each piece has a finished dimension of 4" wide by 39" long.

2 Spread an even coat of glue on the mating edges of the 4x39" tabletop pieces. With the surfaces and ends flush, clamp the tabletop pieces edge to edge.

3 After the glue has dried (we left ours clamped overnight), scrape off the squeeze-out, and crosscut each end square for a finished length of $37^{1}/_{2}$". Next, sand the top and bottom surfaces smooth with progressively finer grits.

4 Mark a $1^{1}/_{2}$" radius on each corner of the tabletop, and cut and sand each corner to shape.

Note: *In an effort to keep your costs down, we try to use standard tools and router bits. But some projects require a special touch. We used a $^{1}/_{2}$"-shank classic table-edge bit (Freud 99-027) for the tabletop to match the high style of the cabriole legs and fancy aprons. See the Buying Guide for our source of bits. You, of course, can use any edge profile you prefer.*

5 In order to use the large-diameter bit featured in the next step, you'll need to make an auxiliary wood base to replace your router's subbase. (To do this, we removed the plastic subbase from our router, and traced the subbase's outline and mounting hole locations onto a piece of $^{1}/_{4}$" plywood. Then, we drilled and countersunk the mounting holes in the plywood subbase, drilled a hole in the center of the subbase big enough for the router bit to pass through, and fastened the subbase to the bottom of the router.)

6 Follow the two-step drawing on *page 127* to rout the top and bottom edges of the tabletop. (When using the large bit, we routed the top edge in two passes to minimize chipping. Lower the bit to the depth shown on the drawing for the second pass.)

ADD THE FINISH, AND FASTEN THE TOP TO THE BASE

1 To form the hold-downs (F), cut a piece of $^{3}/_{4}$" stock to $4^{1}/_{8}$x10". Plane the piece to $^{11}/_{16}$" thick. Using the dimensions on the drawing titled Forming the Hold-Downs on *page 127*, cut a $^{3}/_{8}$" rabbet $^{1}/_{2}$" deep across both ends.

continued

Cabriole-Leg Coffee Table

continued

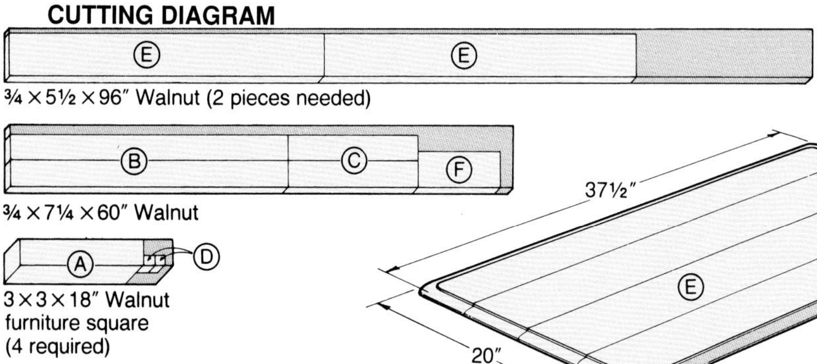
CUTTING DIAGRAM
E
E
¾ × 5½ × 96″ Walnut (2 pieces needed)
B
C
F
¾ × 7¼ × 60″ Walnut
A
D
3 × 3 × 18″ Walnut furniture square (4 required)

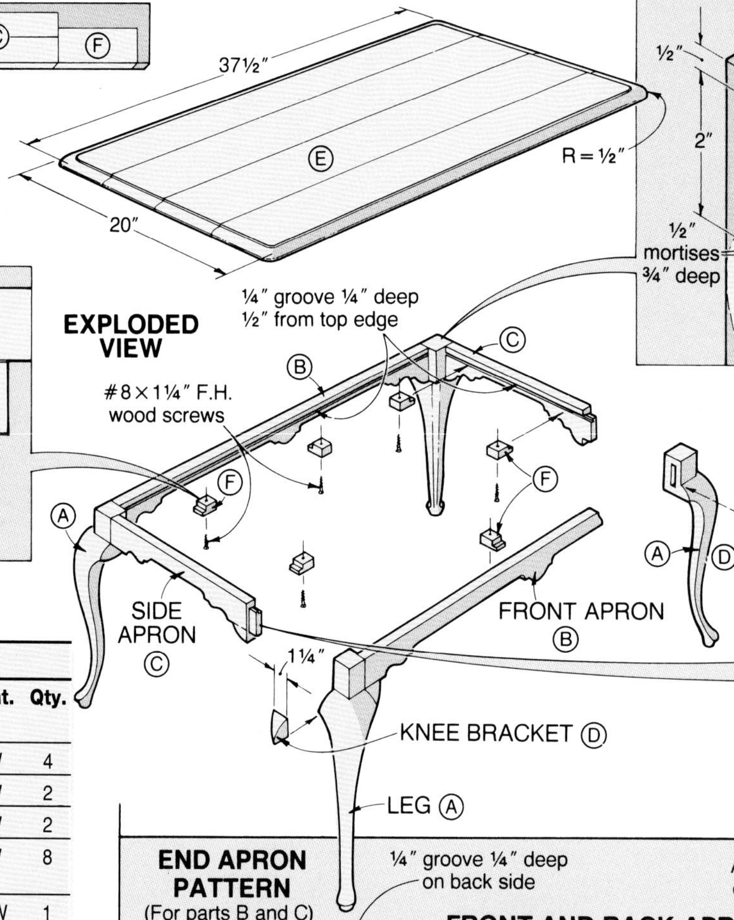
37½″
E
R = ½″
20″
EXPLODED VIEW
¼″ groove ¼″ deep ½″ from top edge
B
C
#8 × 1¼″ F.H. wood screws
F
F
A
SIDE APRON C
FRONT APRON B
A
D
1¼″
KNEE BRACKET D
LEG A

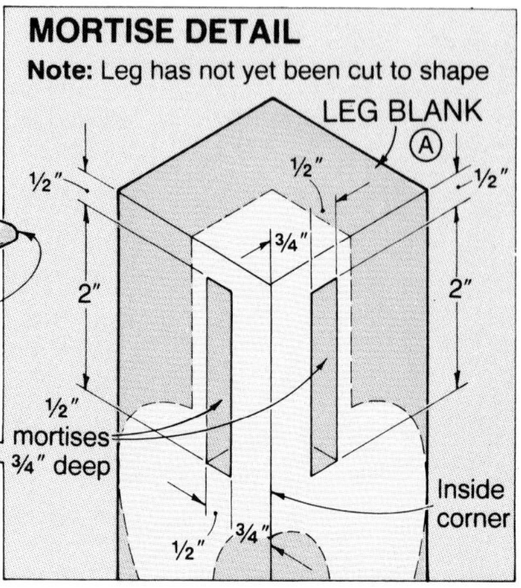
MORTISE DETAIL
Note: Leg has not yet been cut to shape
LEG BLANK A
½″
½″
½″
¾″
2″
2″
½″ mortises ¾″ deep
Inside corner
½″
¾″

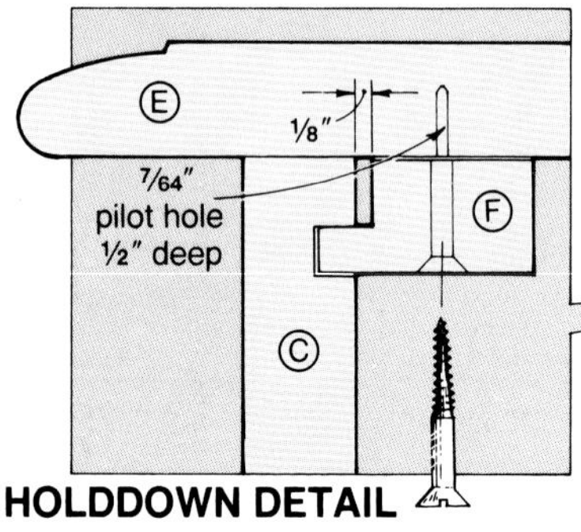
E
⅛″
7/64″ pilot hole ½″ deep
F
C
HOLDDOWN DETAIL

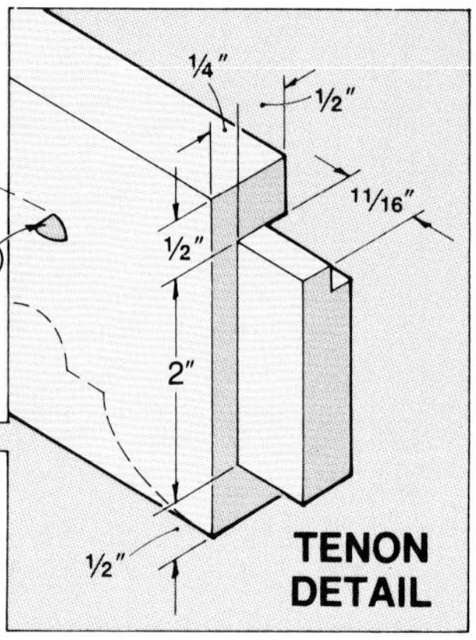
¼″
½″
11/16″
½″
2″
½″
TENON DETAIL

Bill of Materials

Part	Finished Size T	W	L	Mat.	Qty.
A* legs	3"	3"	14¾"	W	4
B aprons	¾"	3"	33"	W	2
C aprons	¾"	3"	15½"	W	2
D* knee brackets	13/16"	1¼"	1"	W	8
E* tabletop	¾"	20"	37½"	EW	1
F* hold-downs	11/16"	1¼"	1½"	W	6

*Initially cut parts marked with an * oversized. Then, trim each to finished size according to the how-to instructions.

Material Key: W—walnut, EW—edge-joined walnut

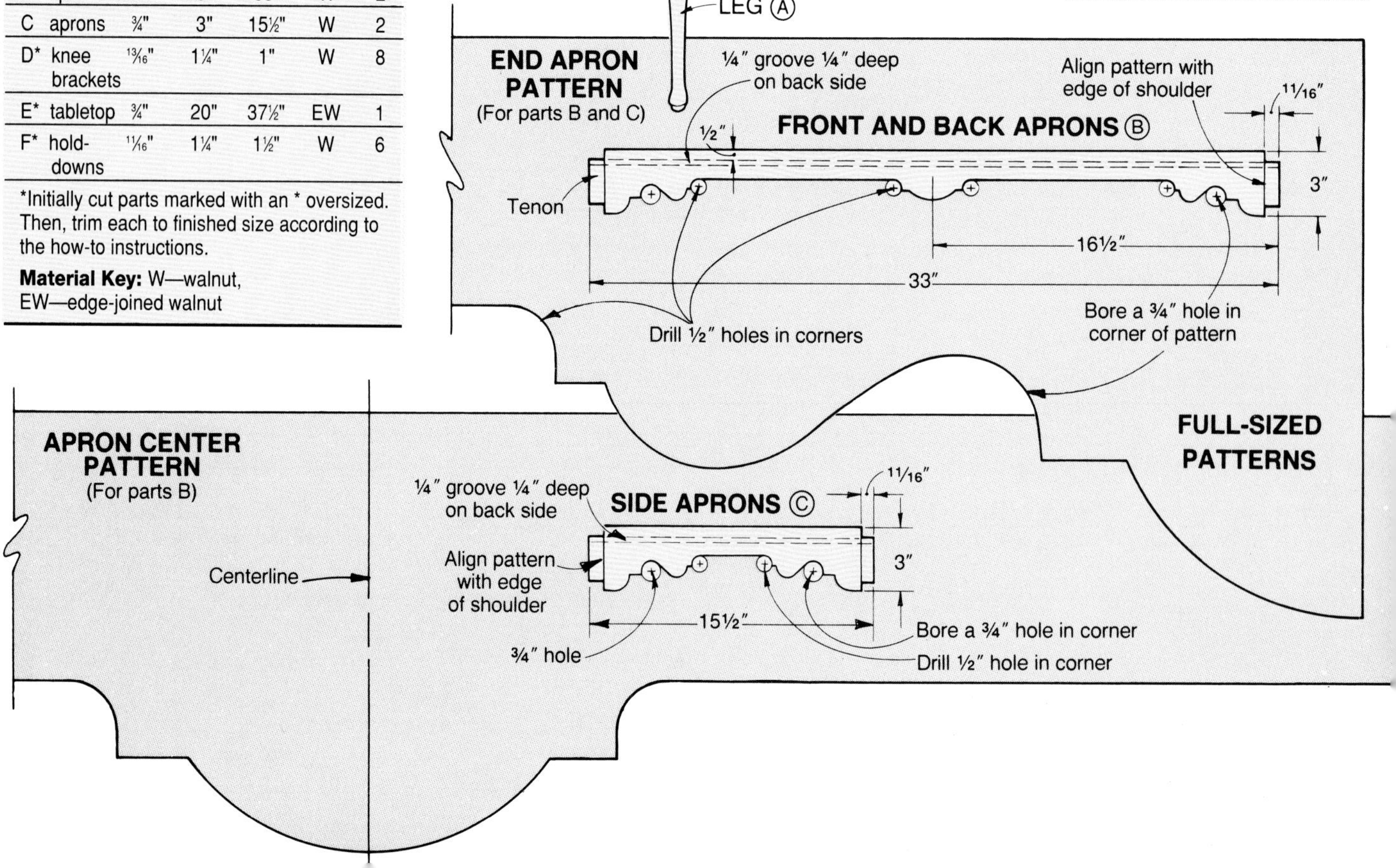
END APRON PATTERN
(For parts B and C)
¼″ groove ¼″ deep on back side
Align pattern with edge of shoulder
11/16″
½″
FRONT AND BACK APRONS B
Tenon
3″
16½″
33″
Drill ½″ holes in corners
Bore a ¾″ hole in corner of pattern
FULL-SIZED PATTERNS
APRON CENTER PATTERN
(For parts B)
Centerline
¼″ groove ¼″ deep on back side
SIDE APRONS C
11/16″
Align pattern with edge of shoulder
3″
15½″
¾″ hole
Bore a ¾″ hole in corner
Drill ½″ hole in corner

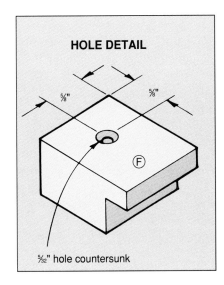

HOLE DETAIL

5/8" 5/8"

(F)

5/32" hole countersunk

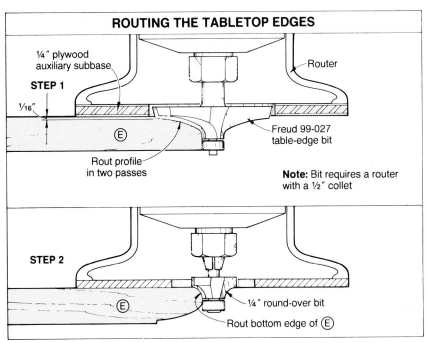

ROUTING THE TABLETOP EDGES

1/4" plywood auxiliary subbase

STEP 1

1/16"

(E)

Rout profile in two passes

Freud 99-027 table-edge bit

Note: Bit requires a router with a 1/2" collet

STEP 2

(E)

1/4" round-over bit

Rout bottom edge of (E)

2 Rip three 1¼"-wide strips from the hold-down blank. Then, using a stop for consistent lengths, crosscut two hold-downs (F) to size from each 10"-long strip.

3 Using the Hole detail drawing *above* for reference, mark the locations, and drill and countersink a 5/32" mounting hole in each hold-down.

4 Finish-sand the base and tabletop. Apply the finish.

5 Lay the tabletop, top side down, on a blanket. Now, place the base top side down on the tabletop. Center and clamp the base to the tabletop, and install the hold-downs to secure the tabletop to the base. Allow a 1/8" gap between the hold-downs and aprons (see the Hold-Down detail accompanying the Exploded View drawing for reference). The hold-downs move in the grooves, allowing the tabletop to expand and contract without splitting the base or top.

BUYING GUIDE
• **Walnut furniture squares.** Four 3x3x18" walnut pieces, rough two sides, Stock No. 11TS51. For current prices, contact Constantine's, 2050 Eastchester Road, Bronx, NY 10461, or call 800/223-8087 or 718/792-1600 to order.

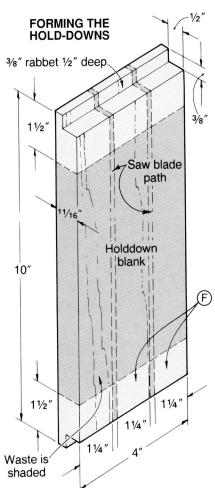

FORMING THE HOLD-DOWNS

1/2"

3/8" rabbet 1/2" deep

1½"

3/8"

Saw blade path

11/16"

Holddown blank

10"

(F)

1½" 1¼"

1¼" 1¼" 4"

Waste is shaded

• **Router bits.** Freud 99-027 carbide-tipped table-edge bit with ½" shank. For current prices, contact Puckett Electric Tools, 841 11th St., Des Moines, IA 50309, or call 800/544-4189 or 515/244-4189 to order.

PROJECT TOOL LIST
• Tablesaw
• Dado blade or dado set
• Bandsaw
• Drill press
• Bits: 7/64", 5/32", 7/16", ½", ¾"
• Drum sander
• Router
• Bits: Table-edge bit, ¼" round-over
• Stationary belt sander
• Disc sander
• Finishing sander

Note: We built the project using the tools listed. You may be able to substitute other tools or equipment for listed items you don't have. Additional common hand tools and clamps may be required to complete the project.

Cabriole Legs

The "you-can't-miss" way to make these classic beauties

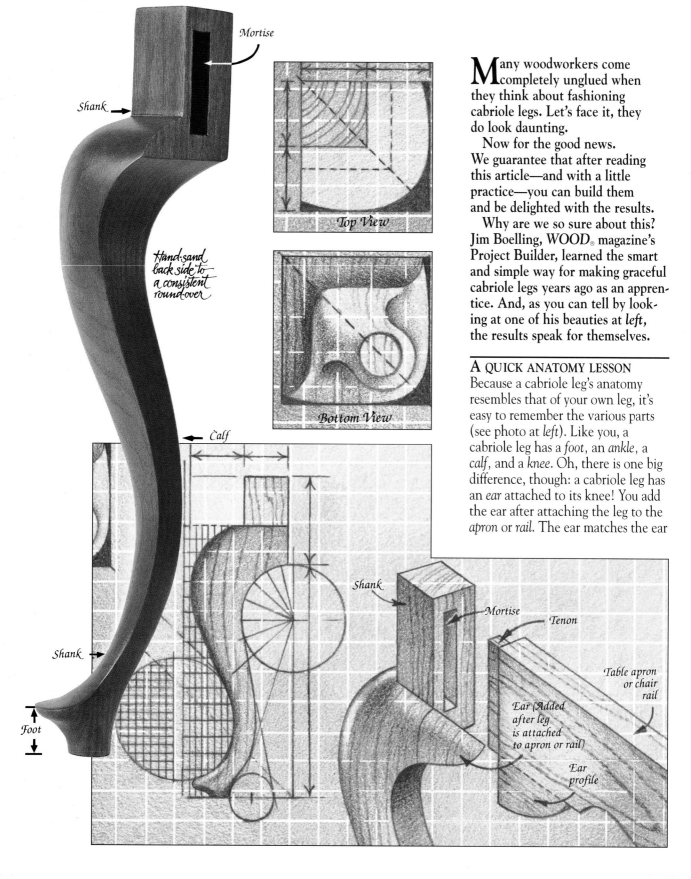

Mortise

Shank

Top View

Bottom View

Hand-sand back side to a consistent round-over

Calf

Shank

Foot

Shank

Mortise

Tenon

Table apron or chair rail

Ear (Added after leg is attached to apron or rail)

Ear profile

Many woodworkers come completely unglued when they think about fashioning cabriole legs. Let's face it, they do look daunting.

Now for the good news. We guarantee that after reading this article—and with a little practice—you can build them and be delighted with the results.

Why are we so sure about this? Jim Boelling, *WOOD*® magazine's Project Builder, learned the smart and simple way for making graceful cabriole legs years ago as an apprentice. And, as you can tell by looking at one of his beauties at *left*, the results speak for themselves.

A QUICK ANATOMY LESSON

Because a cabriole leg's anatomy resembles that of your own leg, it's easy to remember the various parts (see photo at *left*). Like you, a cabriole leg has a *foot*, an *ankle*, a *calf*, and a *knee*. Oh, there is one big difference, though: a cabriole leg has an *ear* attached to its knee! You add the ear after attaching the leg to the *apron* or *rail*. The ear matches the ear profile on the end of the rail. A square *shank* atop the leg has *mortises* for receiving the *tenons* of the adjoining aprons or rails (only one mortise and apron/rail is visible in the view *opposite bottom*).

LAYOUT

After choosing one of the four leg patterns on *pages 134* and *135*, make poster-board templates of the leg and its corresponding ear profile, knee, and foot patterns. The smallest leg (footstool size) doesn't require an ear-profile pattern because of its size.

Next, you'll need a 3x3" square piece of wood for any of the three large legs, and a 2x2" square for the

footstool leg. The length of the stock depends on the length of the leg (wider aprons require longer shanks). We prefer to use furniture squares for their grain uniformity, but you could laminate these workpieces from thinner stock.

Then, square the workpiece so adjoining faces are 90° to one another. Otherwise, you'll bandsaw the leg to a distorted shape in later steps.

As shown in the drawing *below left*, you need to mark the leg pattern on two adjoining faces of the stock. Then, with a try square, extend the lines at the top of the shank onto the end of the stock.

Next, extend the lines at the bottom of the leg onto the other end of the stock as shown in the inset drawing *below left*. With a compass or circle template, draw a circular footprint that just touches all four sides of the square formed by the intersecting lines.

Now, mark the mortises in the necessary locations. As shown in

the drawing *bottom left*, we marked the mortise setback so it's equal to the width of the tenon shoulder. This way, the front faces of the shank and aprons align flush with each other (as shown in the project on *page 124*).

continued

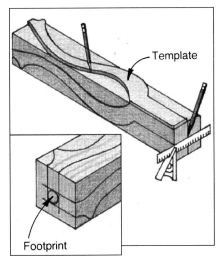

Template

Footprint

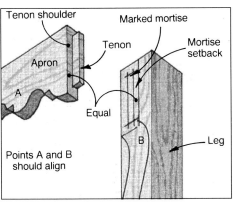

Tenon shoulder

Marked mortise

Tenon

Apron

Mortise setback

A

Equal

B

Leg

Points A and B should align

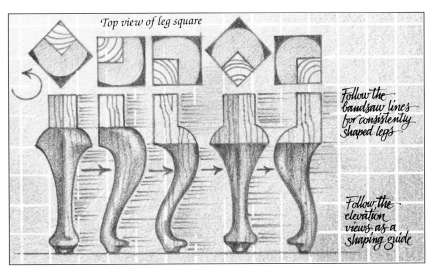

Top view of leg square

Follow the bandsaw lines for consistently shaped legs

Follow the elevation views as a shaping guide

Cabriole Legs

continued

Also, remember that points A and B in the drawing on *page 129, bottom left* should align (for ease in applying the ear later). Keep this in mind when you lay out the apron.
Note: *First cut the mortises, then cut the tenons to fit, and then proceed to the next step.*

THE SHAPING SEQUENCE

So far, all you have is a square length of wood with a few important lines on it—a lifeless form. But watch what happens as you complete each of the steps that follow. You'll be amazed!

BANDSAW THE LEG TO ROUGH FORM

With a ¼" blade (⅛" blade for the footstool-sized leg), bandsaw along the layout lines on either of the marked faces of your workpiece. Be careful to closely follow the layout lines. Then, reattach the scrap pieces with double-

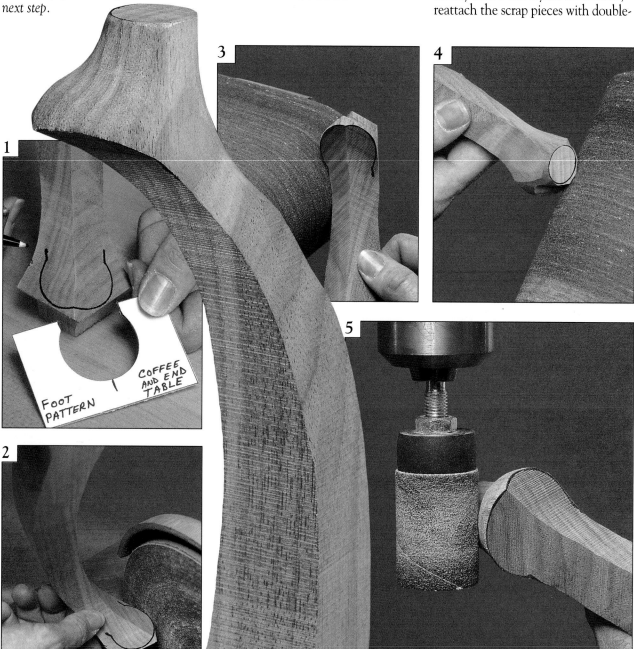

COFFEE AND END TABLE

FOOT PATTERN

faced tape and bandsaw along the layout lines on the adjoining face as shown in the photo on the *previous page*. Save your scrap pieces—you'll need them later.

GET OFF ON THE RIGHT FOOT BY SHAPING IT FIRST

As you go through the following steps, refer often to the photo *below*

of the rough-shaped foot. Use it like a road map and you're sure not to get lost. Each of these steps corresponds to a numbered photo or drawing.

1 Stand the leg upright and center the foot pattern over the foot. Mark along the inside of the pattern as shown.

2 With the leg upright, sand up to the marked foot outline.

3 To sand up to the concave parts of the foot outline, switch to the outboard end of the belt sander.

4 Hold the leg horizontally and sand up to the marked footprint.

continued

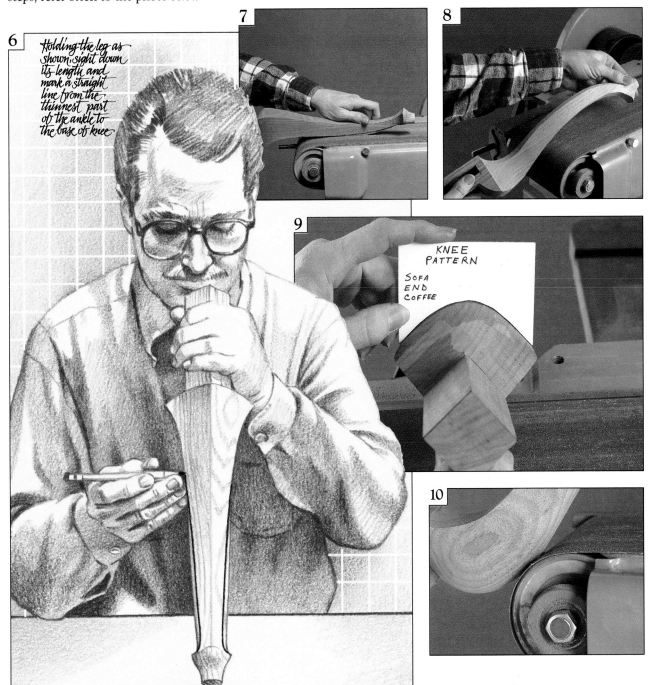

Cabriole Legs

continued

5 With a 1" drum sander, round the stock between the top of the foot and the footprint. (Remember to check the photo of the rough-shaped foot as you work.)

WORK YOUR WAY UP THE CALF

6 Hold the leg as shown and mark a straight line from the thinnest part of the leg just above the foot to just below the knee. For best results, close one eye and sight the line with your other eye.

7 Sand up to the lines you just marked by placing the back faces of the leg onto your belt sander.

8 Sand a ¼"-wide flat along the length of the front and back ridges of the leg as shown. Use this same motion, but rotate the leg side to side to gently round-over the flats.

AND NOW, FOR A SHAPELY KNEE

9 Hold the knee pattern up to the knee (about 1" below the shank). You'll notice that the knee requires

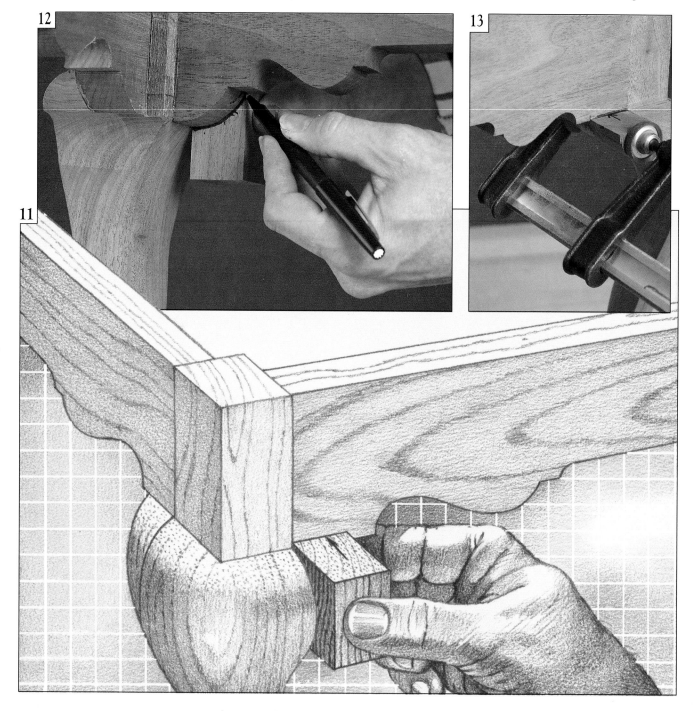

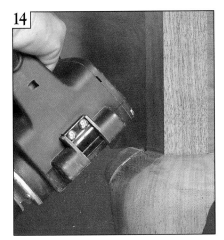

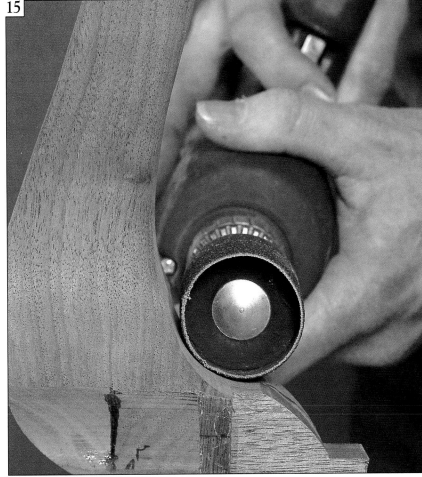

additional rounding over. When the knee matches the pattern as shown, stop sanding. (Be careful not to accidentally sand the shank.)

10 The previous step will create a hump below the knee, so blend together the knee and the front surface of the calf as shown. Sand as far as the ankle.

THE SMART WAY TO GET THEM ALL TOGETHER

To simplify the entire process, we prefer attaching the ears after joining the legs to the aprons, rather than before. Besides making things easier, this also assures you of tight-fitting joints between the ears and the table aprons.

ATTACH AND SHAPE THE EARS

11 After joining the legs to the aprons, choose scrap pieces that are wide enough for an ear. (For the best color and grain matching, choose a scrap piece that came from the same piece of stock as the leg.) For best appearance, position the scrap for each ear so its grain runs in the same direction as the leg's grain. If necessary, square the corner of the scrap that adjoins the leg and apron. Mark an arrow on the scrap to remind you of its position.

12 While holding the scrap in place, trace the outline of the

ear profile on the back side of the scrap. Bandsaw along this line.

13 Glue and clamp the ears in place as shown.

14 After the glue dries, round over each ear with a portable belt sander. To avoid gouges in adjoining pieces, switch to a sanding block as you approach the finished shape.

15 Now, turn the table over and blend the ear into the leg with a 1½" drum sander chucked into your portable drill.

THE FINAL TOUCH

No matter how carefully you have sanded, the legs probably will have some flat spots that need smoothing. Take care of these by sanding the entire leg with 80-grit sandpaper

wrapped around a hardwood block. Then, smooth the legs and other surfaces of your project with a succession of 100-, 150-, and 220-grit abrasives and a soft or padded block.

THE TOOLS AND SUPPLIES YOU'LL NEED TO DO THE JOB

To rough-shape cabriole legs, you'll need a bandsaw. For finish-shaping, we use a stationary belt/disc sander and 1" and 1½" drum sanders, but you can substitute other sanding tools such as a portable belt sander mounted in a stand. Use 50- or 60-grit abrasives, and protect yourself by collecting as much dust as possible and wearing a respirator and goggles.

continued

Cabriole Legs

continued

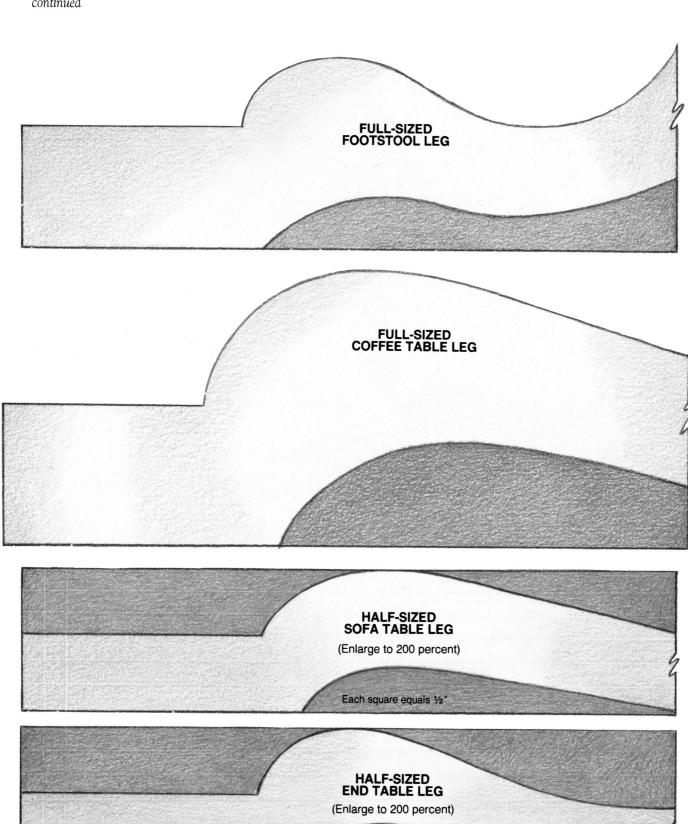

**FULL-SIZED
FOOTSTOOL LEG**

**FULL-SIZED
COFFEE TABLE LEG**

**HALF-SIZED
SOFA TABLE LEG**

(Enlarge to 200 percent)

Each square equals ½″

**HALF-SIZED
END TABLE LEG**

(Enlarge to 200 percent)

Each square equals ½″

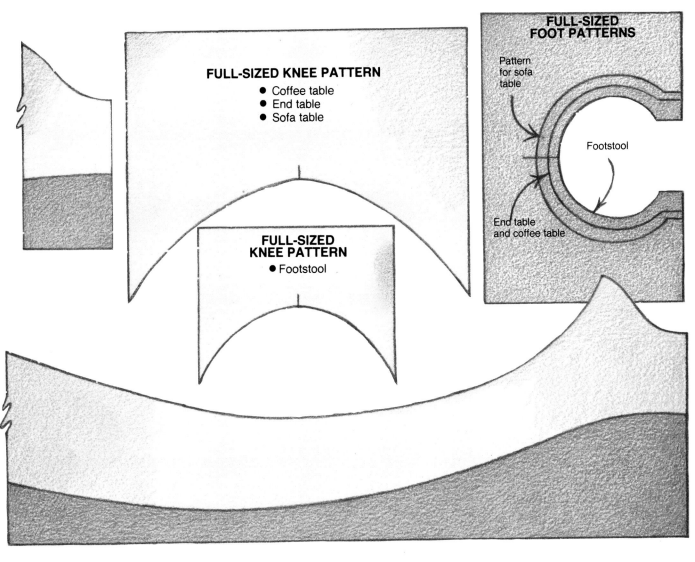

FULL-SIZED KNEE PATTERN

- Coffee table
- End table
- Sofa table

FULL-SIZED KNEE PATTERN

- Footstool

FULL-SIZED FOOT PATTERNS

Pattern for sofa table

Footstool

End table and coffee table

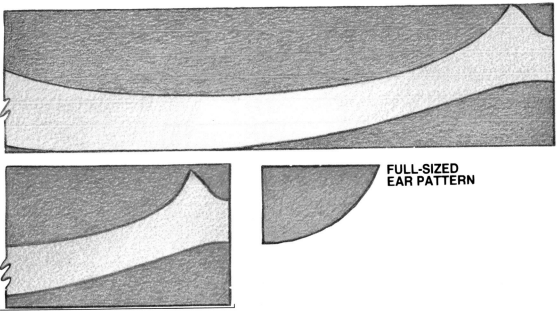

FULL-SIZED EAR PATTERN

Seasonal Trimmings & Trinkets

'Tis the season…to remind everyone on your gift list that you're a woodworker! This treasury of trimmings and trinkets has something for everyone. For a surprising stocking-stuffer, turn out our festive Candy-Striped Rolling Pins. Or for that someone special, turn to our Masterpiece Music Box. When you make these projects, you'll be reminded that it really is more fun to give than to receive!

Masterpiece Music Box

One sweet-sounding turning

This lathe-turned music box will strike a responsive chord with anybody who appreciates beautiful wooden objects—we guarantee it! And even with the rich-looking veneer inlays that accent its traditional lines, you'll waltz right through this project, completing it in just a few enjoyable hours.

1 Trace or draw the full-sized bottom pattern on *page 138* onto a ¼x4x12" piece of walnut. Back the workpiece with scrap wood, and bore a ³⁄₁₆"-deep counterbore where shown with a 1⅛" Forstner bit or spade bit chucked into a drill press. Change to a ⅜" brad-point bit, and drill through the center of the counterbore.

2 With a ¼" brad-point bit in the drill press, drill the center hole and six ⅛"-deep counterbores where shown. Then, drill ⅛" holes through the six counterbores.

3 Cut out the bottom with a bandsaw or scrollsaw. Sand, and apply a clear oil finish to both sides. Mount the musical movement on

continued

Masterpiece Music Box

continued

the flat side with the winding stem protruding through the ⅜" hole, and then set the bottom aside.

START TURNING ON THE INSIDE

1 Glue a piece of scrap wood 1½×4½×4½" to the face of the turning blank that will be the top of your music box. This will become your auxiliary faceplate. Clamp until dry, and then draw diagonal lines on the scrap wood faceplate.

2 Using the junction of the lines as a center, scribe one circle 4½" in diameter and another one the same diameter as your 3–4" lathe faceplate. Bandsaw around the outside line. Then, place your lathe faceplate inside the smaller circle, and screw it to the auxiliary faceplate.

3 True the side of the blank with your gouge. Then, place the tool rest parallel to the face, true the face, and locate the center on it. To do this, move a pencil point across the

rotating workpiece until it marks a point, not a circle.

4 From the center point, mark two circles, one 2⅜" in diameter (1³⁄₁₆" radius) and one 3¼" (1⅝" radius). With your ⅜" gouge, turn a 1½"-deep hole inside the smaller circle (see Turning the Opening drawing, *opposite*). You don't need to sand this recess. Since the music-box movement fits into it, it won't be visible.

5 Inside the larger circle, cut a recess ⅝" deep with your gouge. Test-fit the bottom with the music box mounted on it, adjusting the size of the two openings, if necessary. The wall of the larger hole will show after assembly, so sand it with 100-, 150-, 220-, 320-, and 400-grit sandpaper.

6 Next, transfer the full-sized template to a piece of stiff cardboard, and turn the side profile. With your parting tool, cut the ⅜"-wide groove for the inlay ⅛" deep. Check the width against the inlay as you work.

FORM A TENON TO TURN THE TOP

1 Part off the body at the glue joint. Then, form a tenon on the auxiliary faceplate to fit the large recess in the turning (see Turning the Top drawing, *opposite*). With the body mounted snugly on the tenon, turn the face down to achieve an overall body height of 1¾".

2 Locate the center on the top face, and then mark a 3"-diameter circle on it for the inlay relief. (Measure your round veneer insert to make sure of the size.) Cut the relief ⁵⁄₃₂" deep. The wood in the middle will be less than ⅛" thick as you reach that depth, so make your cuts carefully. Sand the body, except for the inlay areas, with progressively finer sandpaper from 100- to 400-grit.

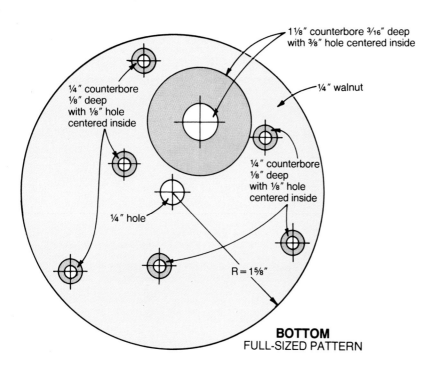

1⅛" counterbore ³⁄₁₆" deep
with ⅜" hole centered inside

¼" counterbore ⅛" deep with ⅛" hole centered inside

¼" walnut

¼" counterbore ⅛" deep with ⅛" hole centered inside

¼" hole

R = 1⅝"

BOTTOM
FULL-SIZED PATTERN

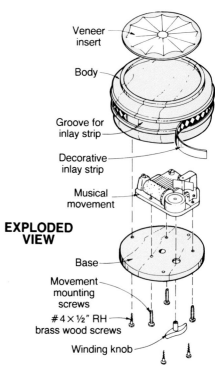

Veneer insert

Body

Groove for inlay strip

Decorative inlay strip

Musical movement

EXPLODED VIEW

Base

Movement mounting screws

#4 × ½" RH brass wood screws

Winding knob

DRESS IT UP WITH VENEERS

1 Apply a thin layer of glue to the back of the inlay strip. Then, starting from one end, press it into the groove. Cut off the overlapping end with an X-acto knife. Secure the inlay with a heavy rubber band, and then wipe away excess glue.

2 Carefully remove the circular inlay from the carrier by cutting the paper tape with an X-acto knife. Apply glue to the wood side of the inlay, position it, and clamp by pressing a scrap wood circle against it with your lathe's tailstock.

3 When the glue is dry, remove the body from the lathe.

Carefully remove the paper tape by moistening a small area with a damp rag and scraping the tape away. Do not wet the inlay excessively. Hand-sand the veneer inlays, and then apply a clear oil finish to the music box, inside and outside. Using the bottom piece as a template, drill ¹⁄₁₆" pilot holes into the music-box body. Finally, attach the bottom with three #4×½" round-head brass wood screws.

BUYING GUIDE

• **Inlays, movement.** Inlay strip for side, round inlay for top, and Swiss musical movement (Brahms' "Lullaby"). Item No. WD892. For current prices, contact

Constantine's, 2050 Eastchester Road, Bronx, NY 10461, or call 800/223-8087 to order.

PROJECT TOOL LIST

• Stock
Walnut bowl-turning blank, 2×4½×4½"
Walnut stock, ¼×4×12"
• Lathe tools
3–4" faceplate with a 4½"-diameter auxiliary faceplate of scrap wood
⅜" gouge, ⅛" parting tool
• Lathe speeds
Roughing: 600–900 rpm
Finishing and sanding: 1,200–1,500 rpm

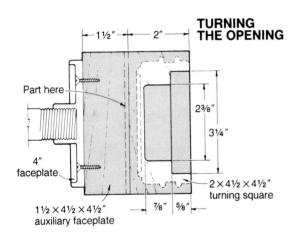

TURNING THE OPENING

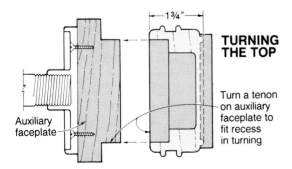

TURNING THE TOP

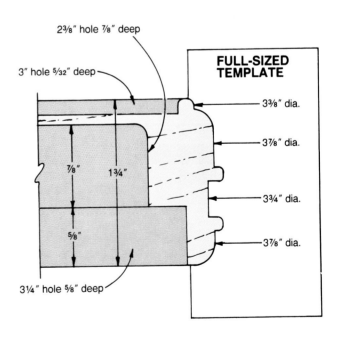

FULL-SIZED TEMPLATE

Hand-Carved Cookie Molds

Give your cookies and your kitchen some hand-carved character

When you're ready for milk and cookies after doing this carving, you won't have to wonder where to get the cookies. Simply make them in your hand-carved molds using our *Better Homes and Gardens®* Test Kitchen recipe *opposite*. Then, hang the molds on your kitchen wall for an old-time accent.

COOKIES FROM WOODCARVINGS

Woodcarvers and bakers first teamed up to turn out fancy cookies more than 400 years ago. From the mid-1600s until well into the 19th century, vendors at European fairs and markets hawked gingerbread portrayals of saints, royalty, and other popular figures.

Bakers accumulated a jumble of molds as they added new patterns. To cut down kitchen clutter, they would have several patterns carved on one board, sometimes on both sides.

Colonists brought the tradition to the New World, carving wooden molds with American themes. Machine-carved wooden molds became common during the 19th century. Later, metal and plastic cookie molds replaced them. Today, collectors treasure those old wooden cookie molds.

NOW, LET'S GET COOKIN'

1 Start with a ¾×3½×27" piece of beech for a functional four-mold board, or select your favorite carving wood for a decorative version.

2 Mark the center point for the decorative rounded top where shown on the Cookie Board drawing, *opposite*. Adjust your compass to 1½" to lay out the circle, and then draw a straight line across the top where shown to form the shoulders. Cut the top profile with your bandsaw or scrollsaw. If you plan to use your cookie molds often, carve them on a 24" board and omit the round top. Why? Leaving

straight ends on the board makes it easier to slap it against a countertop to pop the cookies loose.

3 Draw a line across the board 1¼" above the bottom edge. Now, select four of the patterns on *pages 142–43* and photocopy them. With scissors or an X-acto knife, cut out each pattern, leaving a straight line across the bottom.

4 Pick the pattern you want for the bottom, and then lay it on the board with a piece of graphite transfer paper underneath. Align the bottom pattern edge with the line on the board, and center it from side to side.

5 Secure with masking tape, and trace the red outline onto the stock. A French curve and a straight-edge will help you trace more accurately.

6 Next, draw a line 1¼" above the top of the pattern. Align the next pattern on that line. Repeat for a total of four designs on the board. After tracing the patterns, set them aside; you'll need them again later.

CARVE OUT SOME RELIEFS

1 Treat each mold as a small relief carving. First, remove wood to a depth of about ¾6" within the pattern outline to create the relief area, a process called *grounding*.

2 Start grounding with a vertical knife cut along the pattern outline. This cut, a *stop cut*, enables you to clean out wood with your gouge right up to the edge of the relief area without chipping out wood beyond it.

3 You also can stop-cut with the V-tool, but be sure to keep the cutting edge vertical. You'll need to stop-cut several times as you carve down to the final relief depth with your gouges.

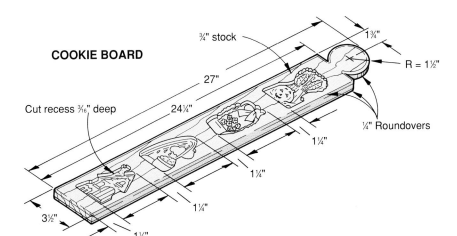

COOKIE BOARD

¾" stock

1¾"

27"

R = 1½"

Cut recess ³⁄₁₆" deep

24¼"

¼" Roundovers

1¼"

1¼"

3½"

1¼"

1¼"

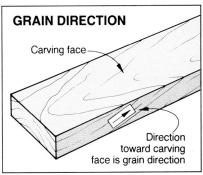

GRAIN DIRECTION

Carving face

Direction
toward carving
face is grain direction

4 You'll accomplish most of the grounding with ⅛" and ⁵⁄₁₆" No. 5 gouges. Although a ⁵⁄₁₆" No. 3 or 5 spoon gouge and a ⅛" No. 12 bent V-tool will come in handy, they aren't essential. Work down to depth in stages of stop-cutting and gouging out wood.

5 Work with the grain when cutting lengthwise. Our beech boards chipped out readily when we turned against the grain. To determine the grain direction, look at the edge of the board. Then, starting at about the middle of the edge, trace with your finger along one of the grain lines. The direction you move your finger along the grain line to reach your carving face is the grain direction. (See illustration, *above right*.)

6 Keep the sides of your reliefs vertical or slightly flared. Be sure not to undercut them. (If you do, the dough won't come out of the mold in one piece.) Carve a crisp junction between the side of the relief area and the bottom.

7 Maintain uniform relief depth within each mold. Be sure to carve all molds to the same depth, too. The cookie-dough shapes will bake better if they pop out of the molds at the same thickness.

WOODCARVER'S COOKIES

¾ cup butter
3 cups all-purpose flour
1 cup sugar
1 egg yolk
¼ cup milk
¼ teaspoon baking powder
¼ teaspoon ground cloves
1 teaspoon ground cinnamon
1 teaspoon ground cardamom

In a bowl beat butter with an electric mixer on medium to high speed about 30 seconds or till softened. Add 1 cup of the flour to the sugar, egg yolk, milk, baking powder, cloves, cinnamon, and cardamom. Beat until thoroughly combined, scraping the sides of the bowl occasionally. Then, stir in remaining flour.

Oil the wooden cookie mold. Press dough firmly into mold and level it. Then, unmold dough onto a greased cookie sheet by rapping the end of the mold firmly on a countertop. Repeat with the remaining dough, placing the cookies about 2 inches apart on the cookie sheet.

In an oven preheated to 375° F. bake for 10 to 14 minutes or till edges are lightly browned. Cool on cookie sheet for 1 minute. Then, remove cookies and cool on a wire rack. Recipe makes about 15 cookies.

8 For quicker grounding, rout the pattern outlines with a ⅛" straight bit in a plunge router. Work down to final depth in several passes. Change to a larger bit to clear the middle of the recess.

9 For the smoothest project flow, ground all four molds on the board first. Then, carve the detail lines for each design, completing one mold before moving to the next one.

ADD DETAIL TO YOUR MOLDS

1 With the grounding done, cut out the paper patterns along the *red* outlines. Trim each one to fit into its carved recess. Then, with a same-sized piece of transfer paper, trace the *black* lines for carving.

2 Cut the design with your ³⁄₆₄" or ⅛" No. 11 U-veiner, as appropriate. The veiner leaves a
continued

Hand-Carved Cookie Molds

continued

round-bottomed groove, which we think looks better than a V-shape for this job. Go at least ⅛" deep; deeper cuts, we found, make better-looking cookies.

3 Switch to gouges to carve the crescent shapes (duck feathers, for example). Select a gouge of the correct sweep and width for each. (Don't worry
if you don't have a lot of gouges; a few will provide enough variety. A ⅛" and a ⁵⁄₁₆" No. 5 and a ¼" No. 7 did the trick for us.)

CUT CRESCENTS THE EASY WAY

1 Carve each one in two steps. (See photos, *below* and *opposite*.) First, lean the gouge away from you at a slight angle so that the bevel on the back of the blade is perpendicular to the work-piece and facing you. Then, force it into the wood (*below*).

2 Next, with the gouge in the carving position, place a corner of the blade at one

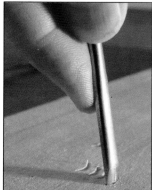

Begin the crescent with the gouge's bevel perpendicular to the carving surface.

FULL-SIZED PATTERNS

Roll the gouge from one side of the arc to the other to complete the cut.

end of the curved incision and at a small angle in front of it. Now, roll the gouge around until the other blade corner meets with the opposite end of the arc (*above*).

FINISHING UP

1 With the carving completed, rout a ¼" round-over along all edges and a hanging slot in the top center of the back side. Turn your ⁵⁄₁₆" No. 5 gouge over to complete the round-overs in the corners between the circle and the board.

2 Sand the board, rounding over the outer edge of each pattern recess. Finish with salad oil.

PROJECT TOOL LIST

- Carving stock. Carve the cookie molds on beech or other carving wood ¾x3½x27".
- Gouges
  ⅛" No. 5, ¼" No. 7, ⁵⁄₁₆" No. 5, ⁵⁄₁₆" spoon gouge, No. 3 or 5 (optional)
- V-tools
  ⅛" No. 12,
  ⅛" No. 12 bent (optional)
- U-veiners
  ³⁄₆₄" No. 11,
  ⅛" No. 11
- Knife
  Bench-type carving knife

Candy-Striped Rolling Pins

To achieve the striking results shown, we turned our rolling pins from Colorwood, a plywood built with dyed laminations. See the Buying Guide to order Colorwood by mail. Of course, you could also laminate your own blank or turn the pins from solid stock.

FIRST, MAKE IT ROUND

1 Draw diagonal lines to locate the center on each end of a 2¼ × 2¼ × 20" turning square. Mount the square between a spur-type drive center at the headstock and a revolving (live) center at the tailstock.

2 With your roughing gouge, round the square to 2" diameter. True the cylinder with your skew chisel. Now, decide which of the three rolling pins—straight, straight with ball handles, or tapered—to make first. We suggest starting with the straight one.

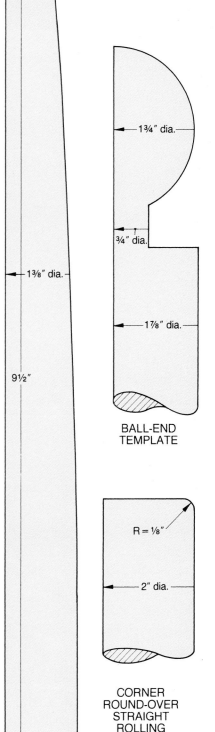

TAPERED
ROLLING
PIN

7/8" dia.

1 3/8" dia.

9 1/2"

1 1/2" dia.

1 3/4" dia.

3/4" dia.

1 7/8" dia.

BALL-END
TEMPLATE

R = 1/8"

2" dia.

CORNER
ROUND-OVER
STRAIGHT
ROLLING
PIN

ALMOST DONE WITH ONE!

1 If you start with the straight French-style rolling pin, you don't have much work left to do. Gauge the turning at several points with calipers to ensure a constant diameter, and lay a straightedge along its axis to check for waviness. A true cylinder makes the best rolling pin.

2 With your parting tool, cut in 3/4" deep 1" from each end of your turning, leaving 18" between the cuts. Turn supporting tenons on the waste ends, and then round over the corner on each end of the rolling pin with your skew. (See the pattern at *right.*)

3 Sand with progressively finer sandpaper, from 100- to 400-grit, using a sanding block to avoid making waves in the surface. Apply clear polyurethane finish.

4 After the finish dries to the touch, remove the rolling pin from the lathe. When it's ready to handle, saw off the supporting tenons. Sand and finish the ends.

NOW, TURN THE TAPERED TYPE

1 For the tapered French rolling pin, mount a turning square on your lathe as above, and then round it down to 1 5/8". Establish the 7/8" diameter at each end where shown by cutting in with your parting tool 3/8" deep 1/2" from each end of the turning.

2 Midway between those marks, cut in 1/16" to set the center diameter 1 1/2". Now, using a 1" or 1 1/4" skew, form a smooth taper toward each end. Avoid bringing the rolling pin to an abrupt peak in the center. Rather, turn a straight-sided cylinder at the center, and then begin the gentle taper down to each end.

3 Sand, finish, and part the rolling pin from the lathe as above.

TRY THE ONE WITH HANDLES

1 A straight pin with ball handles completes the set. Start this one by rounding your square down to 1 7/8" with your roughing gouge and skew chisel.

2 Next, lay out the segments for the handles. With the lathe running at a slow speed, make pencil marks 1/2", 1 3/8", 2 1/4", and 2 3/8" from each end of the turning. Between the two innermost marks on each end, cut in 9/16" to define the 3/4"-diameter handle tenon. At the next mark, cut in 1/16" to establish handle diameter of 1 3/4". On the outside of each outer mark, turn to about 1/2" diameter with a skew or gouge.

3 Turn the handles and tenons to the profile shown. Then, sand, finish, and part off as before.

BUYING GUIDE

• **Colorwood turning square.** Multicolored turning square 2 1/4 x 2 1/4 x 20". For current prices, contact Craft Supplies USA, 1287 East 1120 South, Provo, UT 84605-0300. No telephone orders, please.

PROJECT TOOL LIST

• Stock: 2 1/4 x 2 1/4 x 20" turning square for each rolling pin. (For Colorwood, as shown *opposite*, see Buying Guide, *above*.)
• Lathe tools:
  Spur-type drive center
  Tail center
  1—1 1/4" skew chisel
  3/8—1/2" gouge
  3/4—1 1/4" roughing gouge
  1/8" parting tool
• Lathe speeds
  Rough turning: 600–900 rpm
  Finish turning: 1,200–1,500 rpm
  Sanding: 1,200–1,500 rpm
  (Speeds near these will work.)

Pewter-Topped Potpourri Bowl

A turning that's heaven-scent

Here's a project that makes scents. Turn this stylish bowl and fill it with potpourri—a fragrant mixture of flowers, herbs, and spices. Then, top it off with a rich-looking pewter lid. It's a project that not only looks great, it freshens the air, too.

1 Attach an auxiliary faceplate of ¾"-thick scrap wood to a 3" faceplate. Draw diagonal lines to locate the center on the back of a 3x6x6" bowl blank. Then, scribe a 3"-diameter circle (or one the size of your faceplate) and a 6"-diameter circle around the center. Bandsaw around the larger circle. Then, glue the faceplate to the workpiece inside the smaller circle, and mount it on your lathe.

2 Transfer the template *below* to cardboard, and cut it out. With your ⅜" gouge, turn the blank to 5¼" diameter, and then to the profile. Square the edges of the raised band. To form the grooves, lay the parting tool flat on the rest, and then gently touch the turning with the point. Cut just deep enough to leave a shallow groove—about ¹⁄₁₆".

3 Now, burn in the grooves. Firmly tie each end of a 12" length of wire, such as single-strand picture-hanging wire, to a piece of dowel. With the lathe running, press the stretched wire into each groove.

4 Next, hollow out the bowl with your gouge. Before cutting the rabbet in the top, measure the lid. "They're all hand-cast lids. They can vary, and sometimes they aren't perfectly round," explains Darryl Nish of Craft Supplies USA.

"Turners need to make the hole fit the lid they have."

5 Sand with progressively finer sandpaper, from 100- to 320-grit. Spray on three or four coats of lacquer, rubbing with 000 steel wool between coats. Part from the lathe, and finish the bottom. Apply paste wax and buff.

BUYING GUIDE

• **Pewter humming-bird-design lid.** For current prices, contact Craft Supplies USA, 1287 E. 1120 S., Provo, UT 84601, or call 801/373-0917 to order.

PROJECT TOOL LIST

• Stock
  Walnut bowl-turning blank, 3x6x6"
• Lathe tools
  3" faceplate with scrap wood auxiliary faceplate
  ⅜" gouge
  ¼" roundnose
  ⅛" parting tool
• Lathe speeds
  Roughing: 600–900 rpm
  Finishing and sanding: 1,200–1,500 rpm

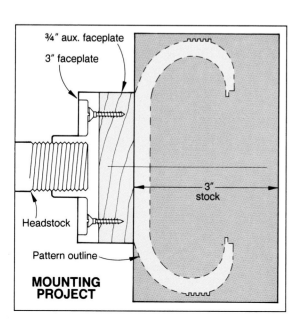

¾" aux. faceplate

3" faceplate

Headstock

3" stock

Pattern outline

MOUNTING PROJECT

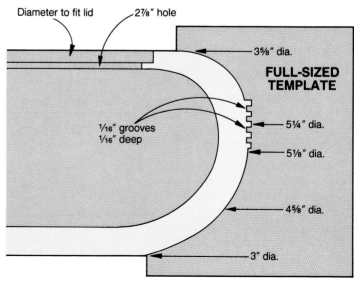

Diameter to fit lid

2⅞" hole

3⅝" dia.

FULL-SIZED TEMPLATE

¹⁄₁₆" grooves ¹⁄₁₆" deep

5¼" dia.

5⅛" dia.

4⅝" dia.

3" dia.

Winter Wonderland

A 3-D scrollsaw spectacular

In addition to the three R's, youngsters in colder climes study the three S's—sleddin', skatin', and snowman-buildin'. These hearty children show their skills on a winter's eve; you can show yours with your scrollsaw.

Note: *Re-create our winter scene with two ¼×5½×12" pieces of walnut, an 8×10" piece of ⅛" Baltic birch plywood, and a 2½×7" mirror ⅛" thick. The small inside cuts require plain-end scrollsaw blades.*

1 Attach a photocopy of the full-sized Base pattern, on *page 148*, to one piece of walnut with rubber cement or spray adhesive. Tilt your scrollsaw table to 30°.

2 Drill a ½" hole inside the pond outline, and thread the blade through it. (We used a #5 blade, .038×.016", with 12.5 teeth per inch.) Cut out the inside of the pond, keeping it on the low side of the scrollsaw table. Next, set the saw table to 90°.

3 Drill ¹⁄₁₆" blade start holes for the four slots in the upper base part. Cut the slots to match the thickness of your plywood.

4 Stack the piece you just cut on the other piece of walnut, and trace around the inside of the pond *continued*

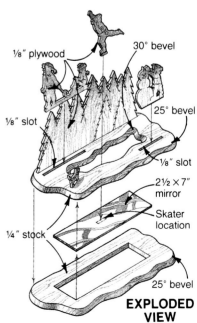

EXPLODED VIEW

FULL-SIZED PATTERNS

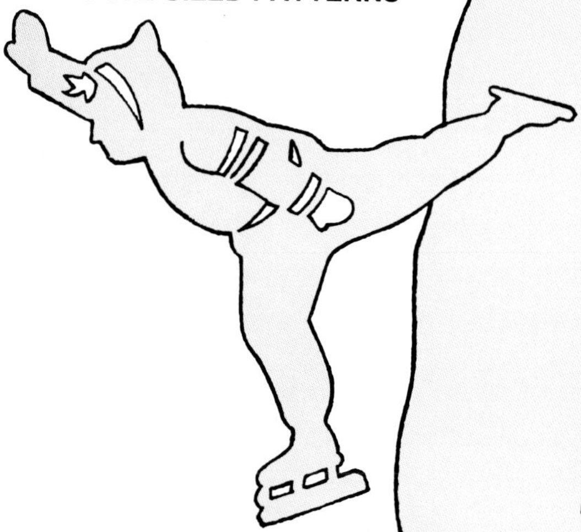

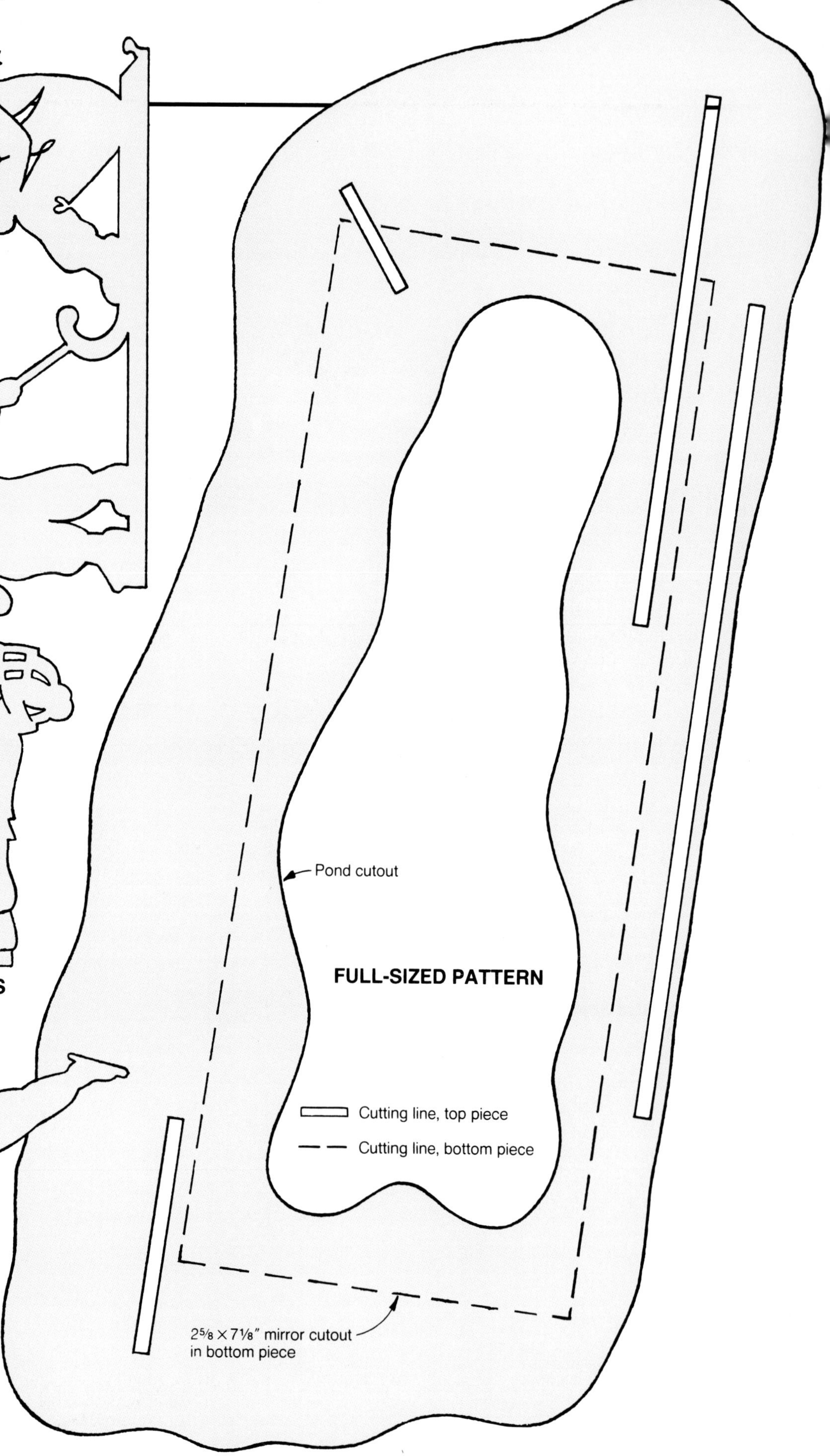

FULL-SIZED PATTERN

Pond cutout

Cutting line, top piece

Cutting line, bottom piece

$2\frac{5}{8} \times 7\frac{1}{8}''$ mirror cutout in bottom piece with a pencil. Then, lay out a 2⅝×7⅛" rectangle on the bottom layer to encompass the pond outline you just drew. Drill a blade start hole, thread the blade, and cut out the opening.

5 Glue the two walnut pieces together, with the pattern on top. Tilt your scrollsaw table to 25°, and then cut around the pattern outline. Keep the patterned piece on the high side of the saw table as you cut.

6 Transfer the full-sized patterns for the figures and trees (*opposite* and at *right*) to your plywood. Drill ¹⁄₁₆" blade start holes, return the saw table to 90°, and cut, starting with the small inside areas. Test-fit the cutouts in the base slots, and then glue them into place. Apply a clear spray finish such as Deft Wood Finish to the assembled scene and the skater.

7 From the bottom, fasten the 2½×7" mirror in place with a bead of hot-melt glue. Then, glue the skater into place.

PROJECT TOOL LIST
- Tablesaw
- Scrollsaw
- Portable drill or drill press
- Bits : ¹⁄₁₆", ½"

Note: *We built the project using the tools listed. You may be able to substitute other tools or equipment for listed items you don't have. Additional common hand tools and clamps may be required to complete the project.*

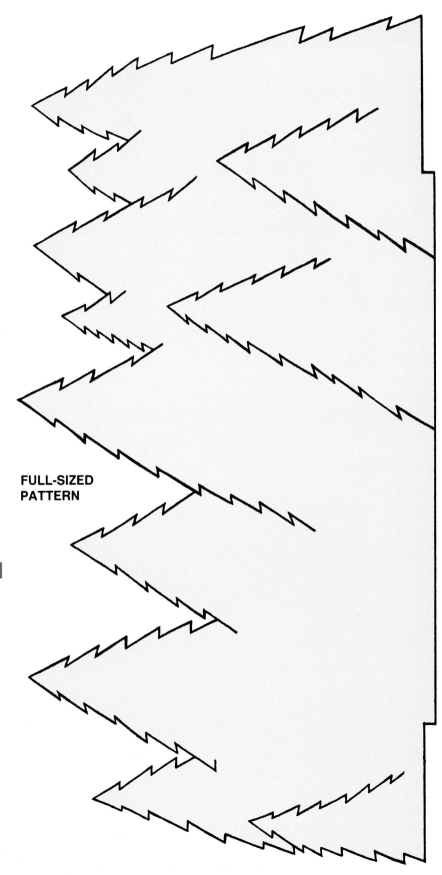

FULL-SIZED PATTERN

Tabletop Tom

A Thanksgiving centerpiece

fan on the ¼" stock, trace around the half-pattern, flop the pattern over, align, and trace the other half of the pattern onto the plywood. See the Exploded View drawing for the shape of the finished tail fan.

3 Cut the tail fan and body pieces to shape (we used a scrollsaw and a #7 blade—.043×.016"—with 12 teeth per inch). You also could use a band-saw equipped with a ⅛" blade for the outline and a coping saw for the hole in front of the neck. (We found it easiest to cut the arcs of the two pieces to shape, and then cut each V-shaped indentation.)

When cutting the notches in the two parts, *remember that the notch width needs to be the same as the thickness of the stock you're using.* (Since we used ¼" material for our project, we show ¼" notches on our full-sized patterns; adjust if necessary.)

4 Fill any voids along the edges with wood putty. Sand the faces and edges of both pieces with 150- and then 220-grit sandpaper. Apply a clear finish.

BUYING GUIDE

• **Void-free ¼" birch plywood.** ¼x9x9". Stock No. W1192T, in series of two pieces (enough for one turkey), four pieces (two turkeys), or ten pieces (five turkeys). For current prices, contact Heritage Building Specialties, 205 North Cascade, Fergus Falls, MN 56537, or call 800/524-4184 to order.

PROJECT TOOL LIST

• Scrollsaw or bandsaw
• Finishing sander
• Portable drill
• ⅛" bit

Note: *We built the project using the tools listed. You may be able to substitute other tools or equipment for listed items you don't have. Additional common hand tools and clamps may be required to complete the project.*

A dd a festive decoration to this year's Thanksgiving table with our super-simple two-part cutout. Using your scrollsaw or bandsaw, you're just minutes away from a completed project, leaving you plenty of time to carve the real turkey (and maybe do a little nibbling just to make sure it's done).

1 Using carbon paper, transfer paper, or two photocopies of the pattern and spray adhesive (we used 3M Super 77 spray adhesive), transfer the two turkey patterns (the entire body and the tail fan) to poster board. Cut the patterns to shape to form the two templates. (Since we planned on making several turkeys, we made poster-board templates; for just one turkey, transfer the two patterns directly to your wood.)

2 Use the templates to transfer the patterns to ¼" stock. (See the Buying Guide for our source of void-free birch plywood.) To form the tail

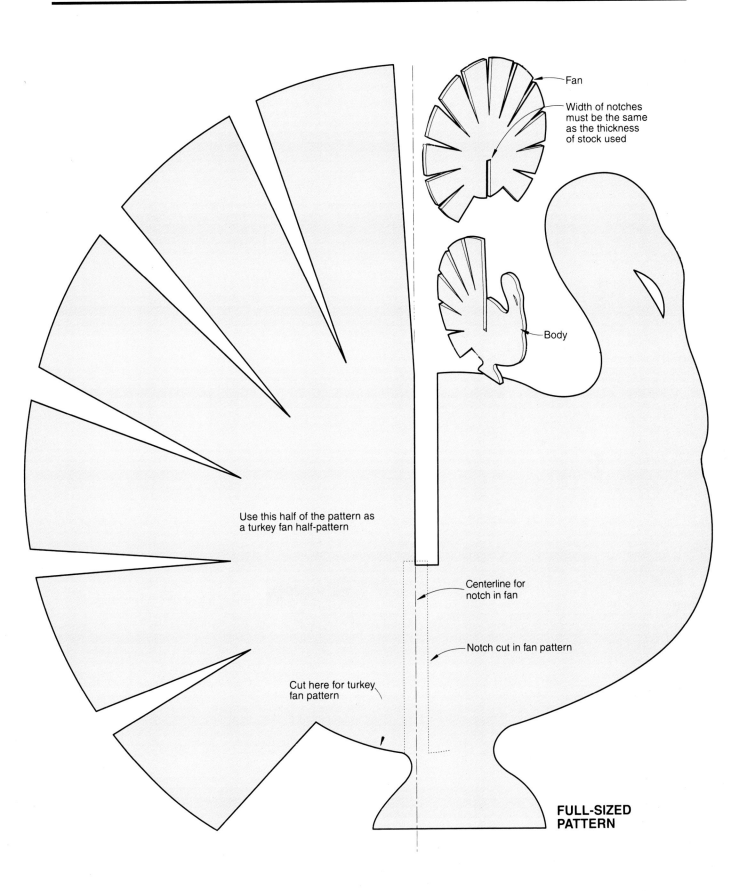

Fan

Width of notches must be the same as the thickness of stock used

Body

Use this half of the pattern as a turkey fan half-pattern

Centerline for notch in fan

Notch cut in fan pattern

Cut here for turkey fan pattern

FULL-SIZED PATTERN

Alpine Santa

This year, why not turn some wood scraps into a Santa that the whole family will enjoy. With bits of household twine, a fabric scrap, and a twig from your backyard, Santa's set for the slopes.

Note: *You'll need an 8x15" piece of ¾" pine for Santa's body, arms, back leg, and skis. Plane or resaw ¾"-thick stock to ⅜" for the banner and to ⅛" for the doll's arms.*

1 Copy the full-sized patterns with tracing paper. Now, photocopy the pattern. Turn over the tracing-paper patterns, and make another photocopy of everything except the skis. Doing this allows you to copy the detail lines onto the back side of your project. Using carbon paper, transfer the outlines of the patterns to the wood. Cut out the pieces with a scrollsaw, using a #5 blade. Then, drill ¹⁄₁₆" and ¼" holes where shown on the patterns.

2 Next, sand all pieces with a succession of 100- and 150-grit sandpapers. Using carbon paper, copy the detail lines onto the parts.

3 Paint Santa, his skis, and banner with a ¼"-wide flat brush. Use the paint color key and the color codes on the patterns. For easier application, thin the acrylic paints with water (5 parts paint to 1 part water). Paint the front, back, and edges of each piece, leaving an unpainted area the size of a quarter where pieces will attach.

4 To make Santa's pipe, first cut a 1" length from a round toothpick. Then, cut a ½" piece of ¼"-diameter dowel. Drill a ³⁄₃₂"-diameter hole ⅛" deep in the side of the dowel. Dab a drop of epoxy on the cut end of the toothpick and insert it into the hole in the dowel. Paint the pipe black.

5 Dip the handle end of a small artist's brush in black paint and make a dot for each eye. Dot the doll's cheeks red. Dip the end of a toothpick into off-white paint, and make a highlight dot in the doll's eyes at the 1 o'clock position, and in Santa's eyes at the 10 o'clock position. Use a toothpick to paint Santa's eyebrows off-white and the doll's mouth red. Wipe a small amount of red on a cotton swab and blush Santa's cheeks and the tip of his nose. Letter the banner with a fine-tipped brush (we used a No. 4 round brush). To remove fuzz raised by acrylic paints, sand with a piece of a paper grocery bag.

6 For a hand-carved look, follow the "Key to Pattern Lines" on the pattern *opposite*. You can use an X-acto knife or crafts knife in place of the V-parting tool.

7 Sand the cut edges down to bare wood with 150-grit sandpaper. Assemble the pieces with quick-setting epoxy. Wire the front arm to the body, twisting the ends in a loop with needle-nosed pliers to secure.

8 Place a dot of epoxy on one end of a 12" length of 16-gauge wire, and insert the end into the banner. After the epoxy sets, push the wire through Santa's hand. Twist the wire as shown in the photo, *above right*.

9 Using a small drop of epoxy, attach cotton "smoke" to the top of the pipe bowl, and the pipe into Santa's mouth. Place a drop of epoxy in the drilled hole in Santa's left hand. Insert the twig ski pole.

10 Attach the arms to the doll's body with 24-gauge wire. Place a drop of epoxy into each of the holes in the top of the doll's head. Insert 1¼" lengths of twine into the holes for hair. Allow the epoxy to set. Tie a fabric-scrap bow around one piece of twine. Spray the front, back, and edges with one coat of clear finish. (Sprayed on after assembly, the finish works like hairspray. It keeps the twine from unraveling too much, and keeps the cotton smoke standing up in the pipe.)

PROJECT TOOL LIST
- Scrollsaw
- Portable drill
- Bits: ¹⁄₁₆", ³⁄₃₂", ¼"

Note: *We built the project using the tools listed. You may be able to substitute other tools or equipment for listed items you don't have. Additional common hand tools and clamps may be required to complete the project.*

¹⁄₁₆" hole ½" deep

BL

AG

PEACE ON EARTH

BANNER FULL-SIZED PATTERN

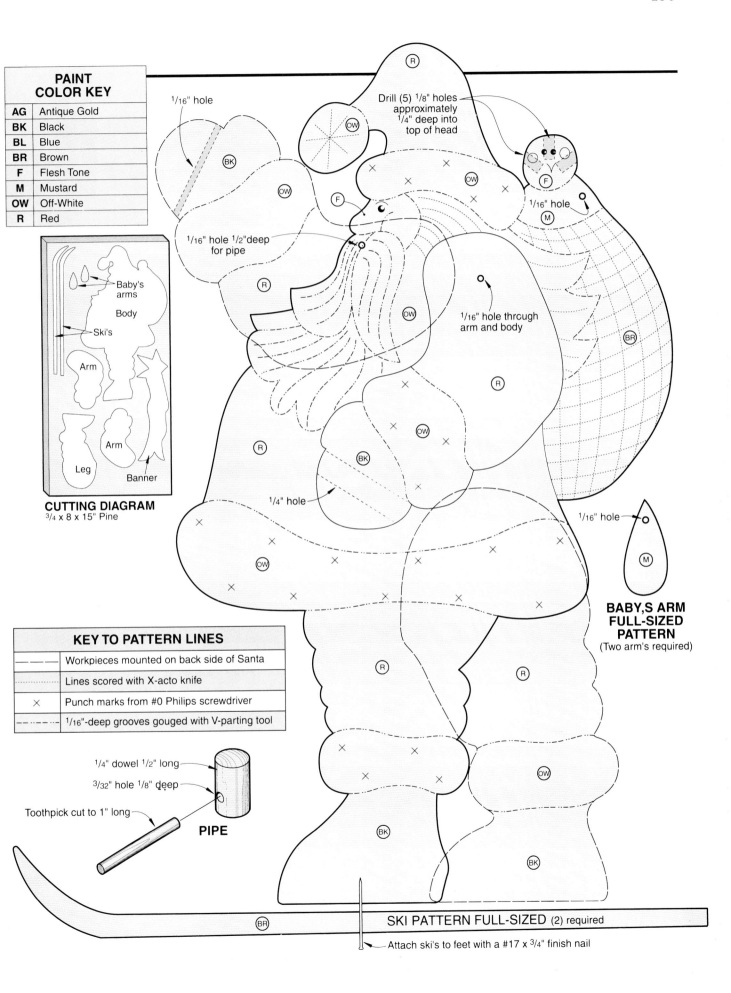

PAINT COLOR KEY

AG	Antique Gold
BK	Black
BL	Blue
BR	Brown
F	Flesh Tone
M	Mustard
OW	Off-White
R	Red

CUTTING DIAGRAM
3/4 x 8 x 15" Pine

Baby's arms
Body
Ski's
Arm
Arm
Leg
Banner

KEY TO PATTERN LINES

— — —	Workpieces mounted on back side of Santa
....	Lines scored with X-acto knife
×	Punch marks from #0 Philips screwdriver
— · — · —	1/16"-deep grooves gouged with V-parting tool

1/4" dowel 1/2" long
3/32" hole 1/8" deep
Toothpick cut to 1" long
PIPE

1/16" hole

Drill (5) 1/8" holes approximately 1/4" deep into top of head

1/16" hole

1/16" hole 1/2"deep for pipe

1/16" hole through arm and body

1/4" hole

BABY,S ARM FULL-SIZED PATTERN
(Two arm's required)

1/16" hole

SKI PATTERN FULL-SIZED (2) required

Attach ski's to feet with a #17 x 3/4" finish nail

Top-Drawer Desk Set

With that pin-striped executive look

Customize your office or home desktop in style with this handsome trio of helpful accessories. We sandwiched thin layers of maple between pieces of walnut to create the snappy business look seen on all three projects.

Note: *You'll need thin stock for this project. You can either resaw or plane thicker stock to the thicknesses listed in the Bill of Materials on pages 156 and 159. Or, see our source of preplaned stock in the Buying Guide on page 159.*

FOR STARTERS, FORM THE MAPLE AND WALNUT LAMINATION

1 Cut two pieces of ½"-thick walnut and one piece of ½"-thick maple to 3⅛" wide by 48" long.

2 Apply a thin, even coat of woodworker's glue to the mating surfaces. With the edges and ends flush, glue and clamp the pieces face-to-face in the configuration shown in Step 1 of the five-step drawing *opposite*.

3 Remove the clamps from the lamination, scrape the glue from one edge, and joint or plane that edge flat. Now, rip the opposite edge for a 3¾" finished width.

4 Referring to Step 2 of the five-step drawing, center the blade on the lamination, and make two cuts where shown to resaw the lamination in two. (We used a thin-kerfed carbide-tipped blade.)

5 Joint or plane the ripped surface of the maple shown in Step 3 of the drawing. Decrease the thickness to 1⁄16". If doing this on a jointer, use a push block for uniform pressure and to keep your fingers safely away from the cutters. Repeat for the second

piece of laminated walnut and maple.

6 Crosscut the two 48"-long laminated pieces in half. Then, cut a piece of ½" walnut to 3¾×24". Glue and clamp the five pieces face-to-face with the edges and ends flush in the configuration shown in Step 4 of the drawing.

7 Scrape the glue from one edge. Then, joint or plane the scraped edge flat.

8 Using the dimensions in Step 5 of the drawing, place the planed edge against the tablesaw fence, and rip one 9⁄16"-thick piece and five 7⁄16"-thick pieces from the laminated block.

9 Lightly plane or sand both surfaces of each laminated strip to remove the saw marks and reduce the thickness of the 7⁄16" strips to ⅜" and the 9⁄16" strip to ½".

continued

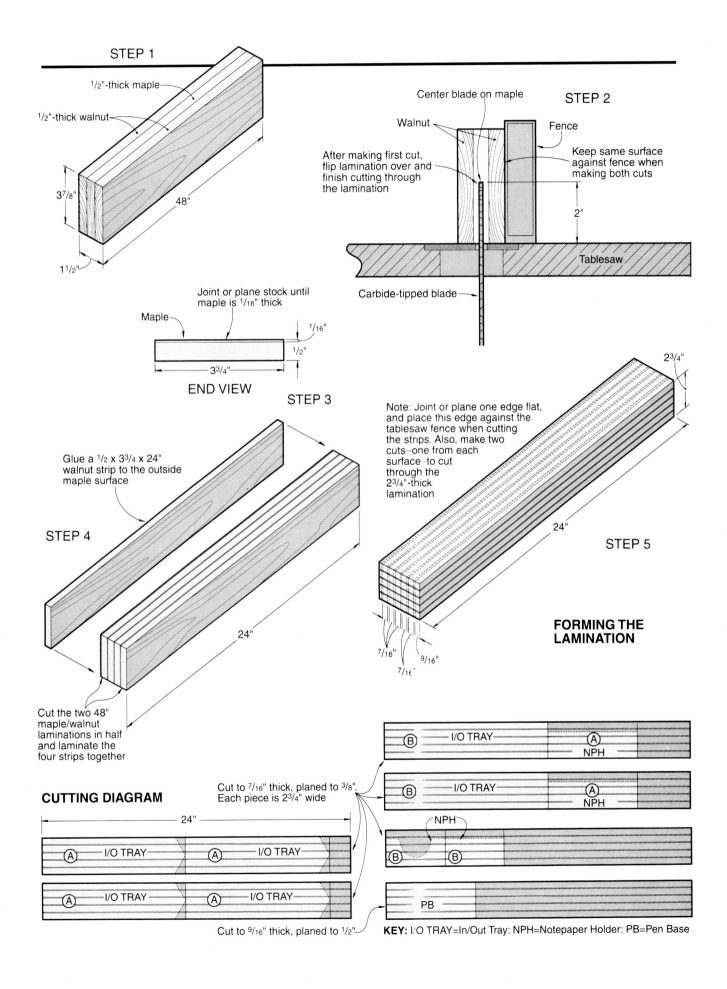

STEP 1

1/2"-thick maple

1/2"-thick walnut

3^7/$_8$"

48"

1^1/$_2$"

STEP 2

Center blade on maple

Walnut

Fence

After making first cut, flip lamination over and finish cutting through the lamination

Keep same surface against fence when making both cuts

2"

Tablesaw

Carbide-tipped blade

Joint or plane stock until maple is 1/16" thick

Maple

1/16"

1/2"

3^3/$_4$"

END VIEW

STEP 3

Glue a 1/2 x 3^3/$_4$ x 24" walnut strip to the outside maple surface

STEP 4

24"

Cut the two 48" maple/walnut laminations in half and laminate the four strips together

Note: Joint or plane one edge flat, and place this edge against the tablesaw fence when cutting the strips. Also, make two cuts—one from each surface—to cut through the 2^3/$_4$"-thick lamination

2^3/$_4$"

24"

STEP 5

FORMING THE LAMINATION

7/16"

7/16"

9/16"

CUTTING DIAGRAM

Cut to 7/16" thick, planed to 3/8". Each piece is 2^3/$_4$" wide

24"

(A) I/O TRAY (A) I/O TRAY

(A) I/O TRAY (A) I/O TRAY

Cut to 9/16" thick, planed to 1/2"

(B) I/O TRAY (A) NPH

(B) I/O TRAY (A) NPH

NPH

(B) (B)

PB

KEY: I/O TRAY=In/Out Tray: NPH=Notepaper Holder: PB=Pen Base

Top-Drawer Desk Set

continued

Part	Finished Size			Mat.	Qty.
	T	W	L		
NOTEPAPER HOLDER					
A sides	⅜"	2³⁄₁₆"	7"	WM	2
B front & back	⅜"	2³⁄₁₆"	4⅝"	WM	2
C bottom	¼"	4½"	6½"	WP	1

Bill of Materials

Material Key: WM—laminated walnut and maple, WP—walnut plywood
Supplies: clear finish.

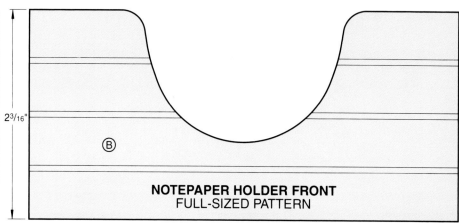

NOTEPAPER HOLDER FRONT
FULL-SIZED PATTERN

2³⁄₁₆"

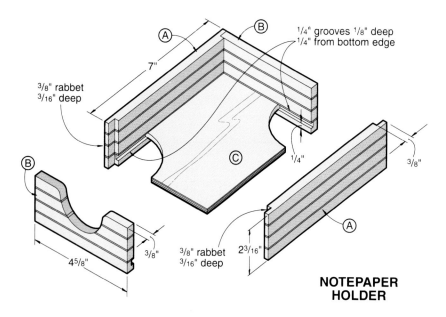

¼" grooves ⅛" deep
¼" from bottom edge

7"

⅜" rabbet
³⁄₁₆" deep

⅛"

4⅝"

⅜"

⅜"

⅜" rabbet
³⁄₁₆" deep

2³⁄₁₆"

⅜"

NOTEPAPER HOLDER

CUT AND ASSEMBLE THE NOTEPAPER HOLDER

Note: *Our holder is designed to house 4x6" notepaper, available at most stationery stores.*

1 Cut the notepaper holder sides (A) and front and back (B) to the sizes listed in the Bill of Materials.

2 Cut a ⅜" rabbet ³⁄₁₆" deep across both ends of the side pieces where shown on the Notepaper Holder drawing. Then, cut a ¼" groove ⅛" deep, ¼" from the bottom inside edge of all four pieces.

3 Transfer the full-sized front view pattern to the front piece (B).

Bandsaw the piece to shape, and then sand the cut edge smooth to remove the saw marks.

4 From ¼" plywood, cut the bottom (C) to size. (We used walnut plywood; you also could choose a less-expensive plywood and stain the top exposed face with a walnut stain.)

5 Dry-clamp (no glue) the pieces to check the fit; trim if necessary. Sand the pieces smooth. Glue and clamp the notepaper holder together, checking for square.

6 Sand a slight round-over on all edges with 150-grit sandpaper.

NEXT, CONSTRUCT THE IN/OUT TRAYS

Note: *The instructions are for two trays and a pair of connectors.*

1 Crosscut four side pieces (A) and two back pieces (B) from the laminated stock to the sizes listed in the Bill of Materials.

2 Cut a ¼" groove ⅛" deep and ¼" from the bottom edge in each side and back piece where shown on the In/Out Tray drawing.

3 Using the drawing titled Cutting the Miters *opposite* for reference, miter-cut the front end of each side piece.

4 Switch to a dado blade, and readjust the stopblock location on your miter-gauge auxiliary fence. Then, using the drawing titled Cutting the Rabbets for reference, cut a rabbet along the bottom front edge of each side piece as shown in the photo *opposite*.

5 Adjust the miter gauge square to the blade, reposition the stop-block, and cut a ⅜" rabbet ³⁄₁₆" deep along the back inside edge of each side piece.

6 From ⅜" walnut (solid stock), cut the tray fronts (C) to size. Transfer the full-sized Tray Front half-pattern to the inside face of the tray fronts. You'll need to do this twice on each front to transfer the entire pattern.

continued

CUTTING THE MITERS

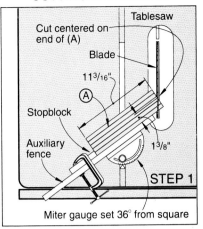

Tablesaw
Cut centered on end of (A)
Blade
11³/₁₆"
(A)
Stopblock
1³/₈"
Auxiliary fence
STEP 1
Miter gauge set 36° from square

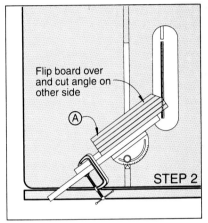

Flip board over and cut angle on other side
(A)
STEP 2

IN / OUT TRAY

8"
1³/₄"
(E)

³/₈" grooves ¹/₈" deep

(A)
(B)
(E)

¹/₄" groove ¹/₈" deep
¹/₄" from bottom edge

³/₈" rabbet ³/₁₆" deep

³/₈" rabbets ³/₁₆" deep

(D)
¹/₄"
2³/₄"
(A)

(C)

18° bevel

12⁷/₈"
36°
Bevel front edge to a 36° angle
36° bevel

CONNECTOR DETAIL

¹/₁₆"   ¹/₁₆"
³/₈"
¹/₈"
(E)
¹/₈"
¹/₂"

CUTTING THE RABBETS

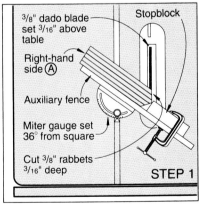

³/₈" dado blade set ³/₁₆" above table
Stopblock
Right-hand side (A)
Auxiliary fence
Miter gauge set 36° from square
Cut ³/₈" rabbets ³/₁₆" deep
STEP 1

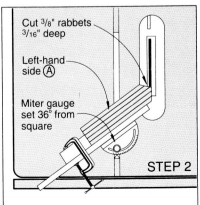

Cut ³/₈" rabbets ³/₁₆" deep
Left-hand side (A)
Miter gauge set 36° from square
STEP 2

Using a miter gauge and a dado blade mounted to your tablesaw, cut a rabbet along the bottom front edge of each tray side piece.

Top-Drawer Desk Set

continued

7 Bevel-rip the top and bottom edges of the front pieces (C) to the angles stated on the Tray Front End View pattern *opposite*.

8 Bandsaw, and then sand the opening in each walnut tray front (C) to shape.

9 Cut the plywood tray bottom (D) to size, bevel-ripping the front edge where shown on the In/Out Tray drawing on *page 157*.

10 Dry-clamp each tray to check the fit, and trim if necessary. Sand the pieces smooth. Glue and clamp each tray together, checking for square.

ADD A PAIR OF CONNECTORS

1 To make the trays stackable, cut two connectors (E) to size from ½"-thick walnut.

2 Using the dimensions on the Connector detail accompanying the In/Out Tray drawing on the previous page, cut a ⅜" groove ⅛" deep centered along both edges of each connector.

3 Check the fit of the connectors on the mating pieces of the tray sides (A). The fit should be snug to prevent wobble. Sand the connectors smooth.

MAKE A SIMPLE PEN HOLDER

1 Crosscut the laminated pen holder base to 7" long from the ½"-thick lamination.

2 There are numerous pen sets on the market. (We selected a set where the funnels come with self-adhesive bottoms; other available funnels screw to the wood base.) See the Buying Guide for our source, or select your own. Sand the pen base.

ADD THE FINISH, AND ATTACH THE PEN FUNNELS

1 Finish-sand the notepaper holder, in/out trays, connectors, and the pen base. (Using a sanding block, we started with 100-grit, and proceeded to 150-grit, and finally 220-grit sandpaper.) Sand a slight round-over along all edges, especially along the curved front opening of the in/out tray and notepaper holder.

2 Adhere the funnels to the base where shown on the drawing *opposite*. (We found that the funnels stick better if you apply them before applying the finish. See the Buying Guide for our source of the pen, pencil, and funnels.)

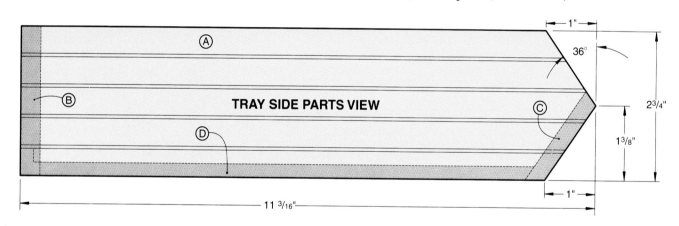

TRAY SIDE PARTS VIEW

36° 1" 2³⁄₄" 1³⁄₈" 1" 11 ³⁄₁₆"

FRONT VIEW (FULL-SIZED PATTERN)

Join pattern here

2¹⁄₈"

3 Mask the pen funnels, and apply the finish to all the parts. (We applied several coats of Deft spray lacquer finish, rubbing lightly with 0000 steel wool. Since off-the-shelf steel wool is often protected from rust with a light coat of oil, we rinsed our steel wool beforehand with lacquer thinner to remove any oil. The oil from uncleaned steel wool can transfer to the wood and contaminate the finish. Also, rub lightly to prevent buffing through the finish to the bare wood.)

4 Apply self-adhesive rubber, cork, or felt pads to the bottom of the

pen holder. Remove the masking from the pen funnels.

BUYING GUIDE

• **Executive pen and pencil set.** Gold-colored pen, pencil, two funnels, and two self-adhesive bases. Kit No. WM1292-B. For current prices, contact Cherry Tree Toys, P.O. Box 369, Belmont, OH 43718, or call 800/848-4363 to order.

• **Hardwood kit.** Five pieces ½×3¾×24" walnut, four pieces of ¹⁄₁₆×3¾×24" maple, plus stock cut slightly oversize for notepad holder part C and tray parts C, D, and E. All-sanded surfaces (no knife

marks). Stock No. W1292. For current prices, contact Heritage Building Specialties, 205 North Cascade, Fergus Falls, MN 56537, or call 800/524-4184 to order.

PROJECT TOOL LIST
• Tablesaw
• Dado blade or dado set
• Jointer
• Bandsaw
• Finishing sander

Note: We built the project using the tools listed. You may be able to substitute other tools or equipment for listed items you don't have. Additional common hand tools and clamps may be required to complete the project.

Bill of Materials

Part	Finished Size			Mat.	Qty.
	T	W	L		
IN / OUT TRAYS (2 TRAYS)					
A sides	⅜"	2¾"	11³⁄₁₆"	WM	4
B backs	⅜"	2¾"	12⅞"	WM	2
C fronts	⅜"	2⅛"	12⅞"	W	2
D bottoms	¼"	9¹³⁄₁₆"	12¾"	WP	2
E connectors ½"		1¾"	8"	W	2

Material Key: WM—laminated walnut and maple, W—walnut, WP—walnut plywood
Supplies: clear finish, rubber or felt self-adhesive feet.

END VIEW

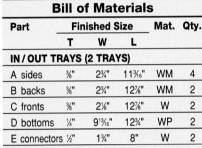

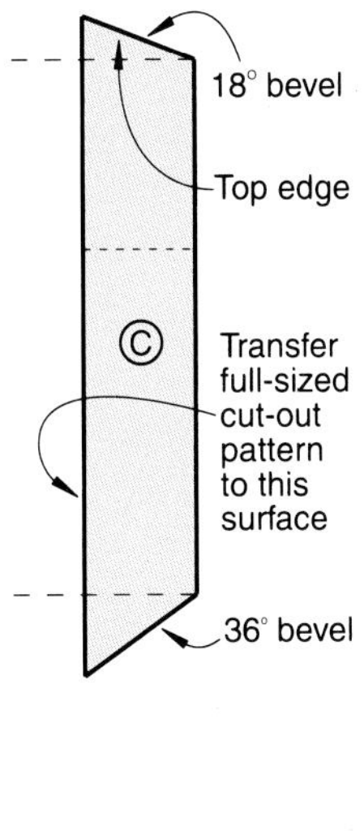

18° bevel
Top edge
Transfer full-sized cut-out pattern to this surface
36° bevel

TRAY FRONT

PEN HOLDER

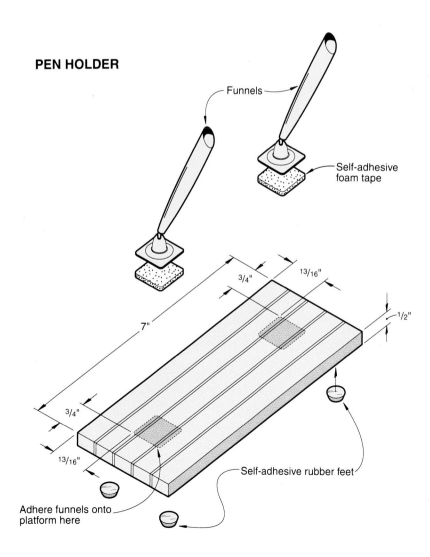

Funnels
Self-adhesive foam tape
3/4"
13/16"
1/2"
7"
3/4"
13/16"
Self-adhesive rubber feet
Adhere funnels onto platform here

Acknowledgments

WRITERS

Bill Krier with Jim Boelling—Tin Punching, 25–29; Making and Installing Dovetailed Drawers, pages 36–41

Bill Krier with James R. Downing—Bandsawed Through-Dovetail Joints, pages 12–17

PROJECT DESIGNERS

Nancy Armstrong—Top-Drawer Desk Set, pages 154-159

David Ashe—Country-Colors Quilt Stand, pages 23–24; Sit-a-Spell Shop Stool, pages 100–103

Jim Boelling—Universal Wall-Cabinet System, pages 79–84; Forstner-Bit Holders, page 85, Collector's-Edition Angle Bevel, pages 86–88, Workshop Clock, pages 106–107; Cabriole-Leg Coffee Table, pages 124–127

Pam Coffman—Alpine Santa, pages 152–153

Scott B. Darragh—Wagons, Ho!, pages 51–55

James R. Downing—Simply Stated Shaker Wall Clock, pages 7–11; Tilting-Table Dovetail Jig, pages 18–20; Knitter's Companion, pages 21–22; Shaker-Style Tall Chest, pages 42–49; Rough 'N' Ready Wrecker, pages 56–59; Sneak-a-Peek Periscope, pages 76–77; Universal Wall-Cabinet System, pages 79–84; Sanding-Supplies Organizer, pages 89–93; A Workhorse of a Workbench, pages 94–99; C-Clamp Coatrack, pages 104–105; Pedestal-Sized Curio Showcase, pages 109–113; Charming Cheval Mirror, pages 114–117; Shelving Showcase, pages 118–123

C.L. Gatzke—Masterpiece Music Box, pages 137–139; Pewter-Topped Potpourri Bowl, page 146

Harlequin Crafts—Standing-Tall Blocks Box, pages 68–69; Winter Wonderland, pages 147–149

George Hans—Tabletop Tom, pages 150–151

Marlen Kemmet—Candy-Striped Rolling Pins, pages 144–145

Bruce Pierce—Happy-Days High Chair, pages 60–67

Jim Stevenson—Hand-Carved Cookie Molds, pages 140–143

Richard J. Zichos—All Aboard the Wood Express, pages 70–75

PHOTOGRAPHERS

John Hetherington
Hopkins Associates
William Hopkins
Scott Little
Perry Struse

ILLUSTRATORS

James R. Downing
Jamie Downing
Kim Downing
Mike Henry
Jim Stevenson
Bill Zaun

Enlarging gridded pattens by hand

Gridded patterns in this book that require enlargement include the statement "Each square = 1"." This means that grid squares in the drawing *must* be enlarged to the size indicated for your full-sized pattern.

To use the hand-enlargement method called transposing, you'll need cross-section graph paper (the kind with heavier lines marking off each square inch), a ruler, an eraser, and a soft-lead pencil. (If graph paper isn't available, make your own by dividing plain paper into the specified-size squares.)

Begin by marking off on your grid paper the same number of squares as indicated on the pattern grid. Next, number each vertical and horizontal grid line in the pattern. Then, number the corresponding grid lines on your graph paper the same way.

Start your pattern enlargement by finding a square on your graph paper that matches the same square on the original gridded pattern. Mark the graph paper grid square with a pencil dot in the same comparative place where a design line intersects a grid line on the original. Work only one square at a time. Continue to neighboring squares, marking each in the same way where a design line intersects a grid line.

To avoid discovering any mistakes too late, mark only part of the design, then stop and join the dots with a pencil line. For more precision, draw all of the straight lines first; then add the curved and angled lines. Once you have transposed part of the design, finish marking the rest of the squares and join those dots in the same way.

Sometimes, you'll only have a *half-pattern* to use. To duplicate a full-sized half-pattern, copy the original with a soft-lead pencil on tracing paper. Next, flip your traced pattern over and place it pencil-lines-down onto one half of the board. After aligning the pattern for position, go over the pattern lines with your pencil to imprint it on the board. Then, flop the pattern onto the second half of the board and again retrace the pattern to imprint it. This method proves faster than copying with carbon paper and doesn't mark up the original pattern.

Using a copier to enlarge a gridded pattern

A photocopier with enlargement capability enlarges a pattern faster than transposing. (Even a copier can be a little inaccurate, so always check your results with a ruler.)

To find out the enlargement percentage you'll need, use a pocket calcuator to divide the scale square size (1") by the actual size of a gridded pattern square (for example, ½"). Your resulting enlargement will need to be 200% of the original.

However, the copier you use may only have an enlargement limit of 150%. If this is the case, make a first enlargement of the original at 150%. Next, divide your desired final enlargement percentage (200) by 150. Your answer will be 133.

Then set the photocopier at 133%, and make a second enlargement of your first copy (which was made at 150%), and you'll end up with a pattern that is 200% larger than the gridded pattern. Check the final copy with a ruler to ensure it is sized correctly. If the final copy isn't exactly correct, adjust the copier up or down a percentage or two until you end up with a pattern that is the correct size.

U.S. Units to Metric Equivalents

To convert from	Multiply by	To get
Inches	25.4	Millimeters (mm)
Inches	2.54	Centimeters (cm)
Feet	30.48	Centimeters (cm)
Feet	0.3048	Meters (m)
Yards	0.9144	Meters (m)

Metric Units to U.S. Equivalents

To convert from	Multiply by	To get
Millimeters	0.0394	Inches
Centimeters	0.3937	Inches
Centimeters	0.0328	Feet
Meters	3.2808	Feet
Meters	1.0936	Yards

If you would like to order any additional copies of our books, call 1-800-678-2803 or check with your local bookstore.